Joseph Stiglitz and the World Bank
The Rebel Within

Selected speeches by Joseph Stiglitz,
former Chief Economist of the World Bank,
with a commentary by Ha-Joon Chang,
University of Cambridge

D0772127

Joseph Stiglitz and the World Bank
The Rebel Within

Selected speeches by Joseph Stiglitz
Commentary by Ha-Joon Chang

ISBN   1 89885 553 6 (paperback)
        1 89885 591 9 (hardback)

Produced in the UK
Cover Design by Andrea Daniel, Partners

Anthem Press

Anthem Press is an imprint of the Wimbledon Publishing Company.
P.O. Box 9779, London SW19 7QA   Fax: +44 (0)20 8944 0825
www.anthempress.com

Joseph E. Stiglitz

Joseph E. Stiglitz is Professor of Economics at Stanford University and Senior Fellow at the Brookings Institution. From 1997 to 1999, he served as the World Bank's Senior Vice President, Development Economics and Chief Economist. From 1993 to 1997, Dr. Stiglitz served as a member and then as the Chairman of the US Council of Economic Advisers. Before teaching at Stanford, he was Professor of Economics at Princeton University from 1979 to 1988. He was first appointed Professor of Economics at Yale University in 1969 at the age of 26, and he has also held the Drummond Chair in Political Economy at All Souls College, Oxford.

Dr Stiglitz earned his B.A. from Amherst College in 1964 and his Ph.D. from the Massachusetts Institute of Technology in 1967, and was a Fulbright Scholar and Tapp Junior Research Fellow at Cambridge University in 1970.

As an academic Dr Stiglitz helped create a new branch of economics – "The Economics of Information" – which has been widely applied throughout the discipline. He has been elected as a fellow to the National Academy of Sciences, the American Academy of Arts and Sciences, the Econometric Society and the American Philosophical Society. International recognition came through his election as a Corresponding Fellow of the British Academy and as the recipient of the Italian Academia Lincei's International Prize, the French UAP's Scientific Prize and the German Recktenwald Prize. He has a reputation as one of the country's leading economic educators, with his textbooks translated into more than a dozen languages.

 Dr Stiglitz was a key member of President Clinton's economic team, where he was involved not only in macroeconomic but also micro-economic and international economic policymaking. In addition, Dr Stiglitz has written extensively on the important but limited role the government should play in the economy. At the World Bank, Dr Stiglitz has played a particularly active role in helping it transform itself into a Knowledge Bank. He has helped rethink strategy toward development, including the role of aid in development, and has played a key role in the formulation of a Comprehensive Development Framework. In the recent global financial crisis, Dr. Stiglitz was active in devising and advocating strategies that would reduce the magnitude of the economic downturn and accelerate its recovery.

Ha-Joon Chang

Ha-Joon Chang, a Korean national, was born in Seoul, Korea on 7 October 1963. He earned his B.A. from the Department of Economics, Seoul National University, Korea, and earned his M.Phil. and Ph.D. from the Faculty of Economics and Politics, University of Cambridge. He has taught Development Economics, Institutional Economics and the Economics of East Asia at the Faculty of Economics and Politics, University of Cambridge, since 1990. He has also served as a member of the editorial board of *Cambridge Journal of Economics* since 1992 and held short-term visiting teaching positions in Korea and Japan.

Apart from his academic activities, Ha-Joon Chang has worked as a consultant for numerous international organisations, including various UN agencies (UNCTAD, WIDER, UNDP, and UNIDO), the World Bank and the Asian Development Bank. He also served as a member of the Advisory Panel for the *Human Development Report*, 1999, of the UNDP during 1998–99.

Ha-Joon Chang has authored *The Political Economy of Industrial Policy* (Macmillan Press, 1994; paperback edition 1996) and edited four books on issues such as the role of the state in economic change, transition economies, the Asian financial crisis, and institutional economics. He has also published numerous articles in journals including *Cambridge Journal of Economics*, *World Development*, *Journal of Development Studies* and *Journal of International Development* on issues such as theories of the state, market, and institutions; industrial policy issues, including privatisation, regulation, technology and transnational corporations; the East Asian economies (their miracle and crises); and the transition economies. His writings have been translated into Spanish, Chinese and Korean.

Contents

List of Figures

List of Tables

Commentary

Ha-Joon Chang
Faculty of Economics and Politics
University of Cambridge

JOSEPH STIGLITZ VS. THE WASHINGTON CONSENSUS

When Joseph Stiglitz was appointed as the Chief Economist and Senior Vice President of the World Bank in February 1997, at first it seemed like an uncontroversial, if somewhat unexpected, choice. He had taught at a number of premier mainstream economics departments in universities such as the Massachusetts Institute of Technology, Princeton, Yale, Oxford and Stanford, and served on the US President's Council of Economic Advisors under President Clinton. To be sure, he was on the "liberal" side of the American political spectrum and had published a number of articles questioning some conventional wisdom in mainstream economics, but no one can claim to have foreseen the controversies that he was to create during his tenure at the World Bank over the next three years.

Initially, Stiglitz kept a relatively low profile, as can be seen from the fact that none of his 30-odd speeches and papers posted on the World Bank website were actually delivered in his first year of office. However, by the end of 1997, he was openly making strident criticisms of the International Monetary Fund's handling of the financial crises in East and Southeast Asia. He was particularly critical of its high interest rate policy, which, according to him, reduced rather than increased confidence in the troubled economies by increasing loan defaults and corporate bankruptcies. Although it was not the first time that the IMF's management of financial crises in developing countries had been subject to criticism, it was a great shock for many people, especially those in the IMF, to find such public chastisement coming from its sister organization's intellectual leader. The IMF reportedly put pressure on the President of the World Bank, James Wolfensohn, to issue the now-infamous "gag order" to Stiglitz in early 1998, but Stiglitz remained undeterred. The speeches and papers that he subsequently produced testify to this.

1

Indeed, Stiglitz's criticism of the IMF was soon extended beyond the IMF to the whole of the development policy-making establishment, including the World Bank itself. Starting with the now-famous World Institute for Development Economics Research (WIDER) lecture, which constitutes Chapter 1 of this volume, Stiglitz launched an intellectual campaign against the prevailing orthodoxy, commonly known as the Washington consensus. It was a campaign that lasted the whole of his (curtailed) tenure at the World Bank.

THE CONTEXT: THE NEO-LIBERAL GLOBAL ECONOMIC ORDER AND ITS LIMITS

What made Stiglitz's criticism of the Washington consensus especially awkward for its the supporters was its timing. It coincided with rising intellectual criticism and a renewed political resistance from the developing countries towards the neo-liberal world order.

What is meant by the neo-liberal world order is that set of policies and attitudes that began to dominate the world stage after the fall of Keynesianism in the developed countries in the 1970s and the collapse of the state-led industrialization models in developing countries following the debt crisis of the 1980s. By the mid-1990s, this new world order seemed to be on the verge of completion. At that point, the neo-liberal economic "reforms" were well under way in many developing and ex-communist (or "transition") economies, a new liberal global trading order seemed to have been settled with the launch of the World Trade Organization (WTO) in 1995, and the launch of the (eventually abortive) Multilateral Investment Agreement (MIA) that aimed for greater freedom for foreign investors seemed almost certain.

However, a series of events during the last few years of the 1990s raised serious questions about the viability of this new global order. The 1995 financial crisis in Mexico, which had until then been regarded as a "star pupil" in its pursuit of neo-liberal reforms since the mid-1980s, was the first such event. The crisis might have been successfully contained by a massive IMF program (which still remains the second biggest IMF package ever, after the Korean one of 1997), but the country's subsequent economic stagnation and increasing inequality eventually led to the ousting of the ruling Institutional Revolutionary Party (PRI), the longest-ever ruling political party in the world (over 70 years), in the 2000 election. Further financial crises in a number of Asian countries, Russia and Brazil between 1997 and 1999 put those who advocated a highly liberalized global financial order on the defensive for the first time since the 1980s. By the end of the 1990s, the painful experiences in Russia and most other transition economies became difficult to ignore even for the defenders of the reforms, especially given China's success, which was based on a different set of policies often at odds with the Washington consensus.

Prompted by these events, the developing countries were finally beginning to rediscover their collective voice, which they had quite effectively exercised before the debt crisis. Although less radical than in the old days, they essentially revolted against what they perceived as a highly skewed and unjust world order that was more or less unilaterally being imposed on them. The MIA initiative collapsed in the autumn of 1998 due to the refusal of the developing countries to be drawn into the discussion of what they saw as a highly biased agenda. And by the beginning of 2000, the OECD, once the champion of the MIA, was talking about the need to introduce a new "code of conduct" for transnational corporations, something that the developing countries desperately pushed for in the 1970s but with few noticeable effects. The growing discontent with what they viewed as the biased rules and, in particular, practices of the WTO finally resulted in the breakdown in the so-called Millennium Round of the WTO talks in Seattle in November 1999. The unexpected success of the campaign groups advocating the "Jubilee" debt cancellation for the poorest countries (otherwise known as the HIPC – Highly Indebted Poor Country – initiative) was another demonstration that the forces supporting a different global order were becoming difficult to ignore.

It was particularly inconvenient for the supporters of the Washington consensus, now on the defensive, that one of their main strategists, namely the Chief Economist of the World Bank, was firing his shots at them as well. It was therefore not surprising that in November 1999, the Bank announced that Stiglitz was going to leave by the end of the year, a few months before the end of his contract. Rumors of course flew, the most controversial of which (never confirmed) was that Stiglitz's departure was the price demanded by the US Treasury for its support for an extra term for Mr Wolfensohn as the President of the World Bank.

The World Bank subsequently appointed as Stiglitz's successor Nick

Stern, a former academic economist at the London School of Economics (LSE) and the former Chief Economist of the European Bank of Reconstruction and Development (EBRD). He was seen as someone who had a more "mainstream" view than Stiglitz's and would not "rock the boat" in the same way as Stiglitz had.

However, the controversies were far from over. In April 2000, Stiglitz created a further stir with an article in the *New Republic* magazine, accusing the IMF of being full of "third-rate students from first-rate universities" with an inflated sense of self-importance. He was thoughtful enough to spare the World Bank the same criticism, which it also deserved.[1] In May 2000, Professor Ravi Kanbur of Cornell University, a former World Bank employee (the Chief Economist for the African Region), resigned from his post as the director of the year 2000's *World Development Report* in protest against the Bank's top echelon's attempt at intellectual censorship of his attempt to put a much greater emphasis on income redistribution as a solution to poverty than the Bank has done before. These events suggested that Stiglitz's departure was not the end but only the end of the beginning of this intellectual and policy struggle.

ABOUT THE VOLUME

Jeff Madrick, the editor of *Challenge* magazine, first came to me with the idea that I could compile a collection of Stiglitz's major speeches and papers during his time at the World Bank. He also suggested that I write an introductory essay putting the pieces into proper intellectual and policy contexts. Choosing the works for the volume, however, was not as easy as I initially thought. During his tenure as the Chief Economist of the World Bank, Stiglitz produced over 30 speeches, lectures and papers, many of which deserve a careful reading. The key selection criteria for this volume were obviously intellectual content and political importance. But some important essays had to be excluded because of their excessive length and/or their frequent overlap with other important pieces – although even then some inevitable overlaps and repetitions remain.

The resulting collection contains nine essays, which I believe provide a diverse but fairly representative selection of Stiglitz's contribution during his time at the World Bank. The essays roughly fall into three groups. The first group, which comprises the first three chapters, is "theoretical". Here Stiglitz's general vision for development and their theoretical underpinnings are spelt out. The second group, which includes the next two chapters, deal with the two key events during his time at the World Bank. These were the tenth anniversary of the collapse of communism and the Asian financial crisis. These, especially the Asian crisis, were in many ways "defining events" for Stiglitz during his time at the Bank, and therefore it will not be possible to understand his position fully without understanding his views on them. The last group of essays, namely the last four chapters in the collection, discuss in depth some key themes that he developed while at the World Bank. They are knowledge (and learning), participation, transparency and economic democracy. This last group of essays makes particularly interesting reading, I think, as he makes more explicit attempts than in the other essays to bring in insights from certain heterodox traditions in economics and other social sciences in order to confront issues that have been neglected by mainstream economists (including himself) up to now.

THE CHAPTERS

The first chapter, Stiglitz's WIDER annual lecture, "More Instruments and Broader Goals: Moving Toward the Post-Washington Consensus", was delivered in January 1998, and was his opening salvo in his campaign against the Washington consensus.

In this lecture, Stiglitz argues that both the goals of development and policy instruments need to be broadened. He points out that the policies recommended by the Washington consensus, namely "liberalized trade, macroeconomic stability and getting prices right", may be important for economic development but are not sufficient. They can also sometimes even be dysfunctional. He offers sophisticated and convincing criticisms of the consensus view on a range of policy issues, including inflation control, budgetary policy, financial reform, privatization and trade policy. He argues that, in order to "make markets work well", more instruments than the ones found in the tool box of the Washington consensus are needed, including "sound financial regulation, competition policy, and policies to facilitate the transfer of technology, and to encourage transparency". At the same time, he argues that the goals of development set by the Washington consensus are too narrowly defined in terms of economic

5

growth and therefore goals such as environmental sustainability, equity and democracy need to be explicitly incorporated in policy design.

Stiglitz points out that many of these points are in fact parts of a newly-emerging consensus in the development community, or what he calls the "post-Washington consensus". He ends the lecture by calling for a greater emphasis on "ownership" of the new ideas by developing countries themselves and for a greater degree of intellectual humility in advancing the new consensus.

The second chapter is the 1998 Prebisch Lecture that Stiglitz delivered at the United Nations Conference on Trade and Development (UNCTAD) in October 1998, titled "Towards a New Paradigm for Development: Strategies, Policies,and Processes". This is an unusual speech in that the World Bank officials have not previously been in the habit of engaging in a dialogue with the UNCTAD, traditionally a home of counter-orthodoxy in development policy.

If his WIDER lecture concentrated on pointing out the problems of the Washington consensus, this lecture spells out Stiglitz's vision of "a new paradigm for development" that is to replace the Washington consensus. The speech, given its aim and scope, is necessarily not as tightly argued as most of the other pieces in this collection, but it still deserves close attention because it is here that he raises many new themes that he is to elaborate in later speeches (see chapters 6–9).

This lecture in fact would not have displeased Raul Prebisch, the distinguished Argentine economist and the first Secretary-General of UNCTAD, after whom the lecture is named and who was one of the intellectual founders of the "heterodox" development strategy that was advocated by the UNCTAD in the 1960s and the 1970s. One regret is that in this lecture Stiglitz fails explicitly to acknowledge the contributions of Prebisch himself and other early development economists (such as Gunnar Myrdal and Albert Hirschman, among others). However, his discussion resurrects some of the themes that very much occupied Prebisch and other heterodox development economists: the criticism of the narrowly economistic and quantitative notion of development in mainstream thinking; the emphasis on cumulative causation (or what Myrdal called the "backwash effect") in the developmental process; the limits of enclave-style development, which in fact was a central topic in Latin American structuralism one of whose founding fathers was Prebisch. Popular participation and the community development that Stiglitz emphasizes has also been a persistent theme in various schools of alternative development thinking, if not necessarily in Latin American structuralism.

By talking about these intellectual precursors to Stiglitz's ideas in the lecture, I am not trying to suggest that he is merely selling old ideas under new brands. Themes such as financial sector development and knowledge management, which he discusses in some depth in this lecture and to which he has made important contributions, have been relatively neglected by heterodox development economists of Prebisch's vintage. His position on the role of economic openness in development is also a lot more sophisticated and nuanced than what was common among the early heterodox development economists (not to speak of the mainstream economists that he is explicitly criticizing in the lecture).

The third chapter, titled "Redefining the Role of the State – *What* should it do? *How* should it do it? And *how* should these decisions be made?", is the speech that he gave in the meeting celebrating the tenth anniversary of the Japan's MITI (Ministry of International Trade and Industry) Research Institute in March 1998.

The role of the state has always been at the top of Stiglitz's intellectual agenda. He is the author of a famous textbook on the economics of the public sector, and has explored this issue in depth in a number of policy areas, especially financial regulation, industrial policy and technology policy.[2] However, this speech breaks some important new ground. It is less concerned with particular justifications of state intervention ("What should it do?"), which he has dealt with before in many ways, but more concerned with the processes of decision-making ("How should these decisions be made?") as well as policies themselves ("How should it do it?").

After providing a brief but theoretically sophisticated and convincing criticism of the currently popular "government failure" arguments (or what he calls the "Conservative Propositions"), Stiglitz argues that we need to see the government and the private sector as partners rather than as opponents. This has in fact frequently been the case. He then makes five propositions for "a better government". They are: (i) restriction of government intervention in areas with significant influence of special interest groups; (ii) a strong presumption against government actions restricting competition; (iii) a strong presumption in favour of openness in government (a theme that is elaborated in chapter 8); (iv) encouragement of private provision of public goods, including through NGOs (non-governmental organizations); (v) a balance between expertise, on the one hand, and democratic representativeness and accountability, on the other (a theme that is further developed in chapter 7). These are generally sensible proposals and contain some insightful ideas, although his view on "special interest groups" remains I believe somewhat simplistic, given the difficulties involved in actually defining "special interest groups" and the complex relationships between "special interests" and "general interests".[3]

After setting out his general propositions, Stiglitz engages in an evaluation of the role of the state in East Asian development. Here, he argues that we should not deny the positive role of the state in East Asian development simply because of the recent crisis, especially when some of the current problems in East Asia are in fact the results of discontinuing some of the past policies (e.g., the end to Thailand's restriction on real estate lending). In the discussion, he also makes an important but usually ignored point that even in the US, the supposed home of free market, industrial policy (the development of railroads and telegraphy in earlier times, as well as the industrial supports through defence policy more recently) and financial regulation have been crucial in fostering development.

One regret is that in this context he fails to mention that infant industry protection played a crucial role in the early days of US development – the country had deliberately adopted, against the advice of the then dominant free trade doctrine of English classical political economy, a strategy of infant industry protection, maintaining the highest tariff rates in the world for about a century between the mid-nineteenth century and World War II.

Chapter 4 of the volume is the paper presented at the Annual Bank Conference on Development Economics (ABCDE) in April 1999, titled "Whither Reform? – Ten Years of the Transition".

As is well known, Stiglitz has been highly critical of the "shock therapy" strategy of transition, most notably in Russia, recommended by the supporters of the Washington consensus. We have read many of his arguments in his celebrated book, *Whither Socialism?*, published in 1996. However, this paper is a particularly devastating attack on the "transition orthodoxy", which maintains that transition failed not because the policies of the Washington consensus were wrong, but because they were poorly implemented by corrupt and incompetent governments.

In the paper, Stiglitz argues that transition failed because the conventional neoclassical model, on which the shock therapy was based, was fundamentally flawed in that it ignored informational inadequacies, opportunistic behavior and human fallibility. He also argues that the process of institutional reform is not something that can be achieved through utopian social engineering in the manner of shock therapy. Karl Popper and Friedrich Hayek had famously made this argument against the Bolshevik attempt to achieve a transition to socialism through their own version of shock therapy. He argues that a more participatory and gradualist approach is required if a genuine transformation is to be achieved.

The case against shock therapy made in the paper is so eloquent and overwhelming that it will be redundant for me to elaborate on it. What I would like to note in particular, however, is that in this paper Stiglitz explicitly acknowledges the intellectual value of "other traditions" in economics, notably those put forward by Joseph Schumpeter and by Friedrich von Hayek (and the Austrian School). Given his intellectual background as a neoclassical economist, although of a rather unconventional kind, this is a notable act, as these "other traditions" have been largely neglected by mainstream economists. In this essay, he is trying to re-interpret some of the insights of the Schumpeterian and the Austrian Schools with the tools of "information economics", thus pushing the boundary of neoclassical economics. Although his re-formulation of these heterodox traditions cannot fully capture all their nuances, it throws up some interesting new possibilities for intellectual fusion.

The fifth chapter, the address that Stiglitz made in February 1998 to the Chicago Council on Foreign Relations, is somewhat misleadingly titled as "The Role of International Financial Institutions in the Current Global Economy", given that it is more of an analysis of the Asian crisis rather than of the role of the international financial institutions.

As I explained at the beginning of this introductory essay, the recent Asian crisis was the defining event during Stiglitz's tenure at the World Bank, and therefore is discussed in many of his speeches and papers during the time in one way or another. Indeed, some of the essays in this volume also deal with the issue in some depth (notably chapters 1, 2 and 3), but given the importance of this issue for him, it is only fitting that there should be a piece in this collection devoted to the issue.

In the speech, Stiglitz readily accepts that there were certain institutional sources of vulnerability in East Asia, such as poor banking regulation and the lack of transparency.[4] However, he is quick to point out that they alone cannot explain the crisis. For example, he points out, even with better banking regulation, foreign borrowing by non-financial corporations (as in Indonesia) and non-bank financial institutions (as in Korea and Thailand), both of which were made possible by capital account liberalization, would have led to foreign debt accumulation. For another example, commenting on the issue of transparency, he points out that, while transparency did not save the Scandinavian countries from their financial crises in the late 1980s, the lack of it did not lead to any financial crisis in Germany for decades.

Instead, he argues, there were a number of flawed government policies, many of them actively encouraged by the IFIs (international financial institutions), that led to the build up of vulnerability, especially in the form of short-term dollar-denominated debt. These included the exchange rate peg, the sterilization of capital inflows, the liberalization of capital account, and excessively rapid (domestic) financial liberalization. He also highlights the negative part that irrational exuberance and pessimism of the foreign investors (and their advisors) had in generating the crisis – as, for example, can be seen from the fact that the rating agencies did not downgrade the East Asian countries until after the onset of the crisis but started downgrading them with a vengeance once the crisis was underway.

Based on this diagnosis, Stiglitz then moves on to discuss the problems involved in financial crisis management policies, such as interest rate policy, financial sector restructuring and corporate governance reform. In the longer run, he argues, there should be state intervention to bring the private risks into line with the social risks, such as policies aimed to influence the pattern of capital flows (e.g., increasing private capital flows to low-income countries, reducing pro-cyclicality of capital flows) and the composition of capital flows (e.g., encouraging longer-term inflows). He also proposes that there should be an attempt to introduce "orderly workouts" of international debts where the lenders also bear responsibility for their lending decisions, in a manner similar to internal bankruptcy laws.

Chapter 6 is titled, "Scan Globally, Reinvent Locally: Knowledge Infrastructure and the Localization of Knowledge", and was delivered as a keynote address to the first Global Development Network Conference in Bonn in December 1999.

Throughout his career, "knowledge" has been one of Stiglitz's favourite themes. His contributions to the economics of technology and learning are well known, but it may be worth noting that the first *World Development*

Report that he orchestrated as the Chief Economist at the World Bank in 1998 was also on the theme of knowledge. However, in this address, he adopts a framework of analysis which goes much beyond his previous work in the area, once again "pushing the boundary" of neoclassical economics. In the essay, he tries to enrich his analysis by incorporating certain concepts that are alien to neoclassical economics, such as the notion of tacit knowledge and the importance of intellectual autonomy.

In this essay, Stiglitz proposes to analyze knowledge along two dimensions, the general-local dimension and the codified-tacit dimension. First, in talking about the general-local dimension, he argues that general knowledge typically needs local adaptation and therefore that we need to "scan globally and reinvent locally". He emphasizes that this adaptation requires considerable effort and should be done through a process of what the Japanese call *nemawashi* (slowly preparing and wrapping each root of a tree before transplantation), if it is to lead to genuine learning and lasting institutional changes.

Second, following the Austrian and the Schumptererian Schools, he argues that much of our knowledge is "tacit", which can only be transferred through "horizontal" knowledge transfer methods (as opposed to the "vertical" method involved in the transfer of "codified" knowledge) such as apprenticeship, (personnel) secondment, imitation, study tours, cross-training, twinning relations and guided learning-by-doing.

He then goes on to argue that the standard view of knowledge transfer, which puts exclusive emphasis on the transfer of "universal" messages and "best practices" by a central authority (be it the World Bank or a country's central government), impairs the self-confidence, self-esteem and self-efficacy of the "clients" – that is, the developing countries or the local communities. According to him, this creates a vicious circle. The dependence of the clients on these universal knowledge principles makes the central authorities believe that there is no need to involve the clients in discussions, thereby discouraging active learning and thus increasing the clients' dependence. He argues that we need to go beyond the technocratic model of development and see development as a process of "democratic social learning" that is to be achieved through greater dialogue and participation aimed at consensus-building.

The seventh chapter of the volume is the speech "Participation and Development: Perspectives from the Comprehensive Development Paradigm", which Stiglitz made at the International Conference on

11

Democracy, Market Economy and Development, organized by the Korean government in Seoul in February 1999. In this essay and the two essays that respectively appear as the eighth and the ninth chapters of the volume, Stiglitz explores some new territories, not simply in terms of the subject matter (participation, transparency, and enterprise democracy, respectively) but also in terms of disciplinary boundaries – these three essays draw on a range of literature in political science, sociology and social psychology.

His starting point in this chapter is that development should be seen as a process of social transformation, which cannot be "ordered" or forced from the outside but has to come from a society-wide change in mindset, which in turn can be most effectively achieved through a participatory process. He argues that participation should not simply refer to voting but also to "transparency, openness and voice". He also extends the notion of participation to the issue of corporate governance, although in this speech he talks only of participation by minority shareholders and bondholders and ignores the issue of worker participation, an issue that he discusses in depth in the speech that appears as chapter 9 of this volume.

Stiglitz argues that a range of policies and institutional changes are needed in order to enhance participation. These include better education; investment in communications infrastructure; introduction of institutions promoting "good government" and "rule of law"; full employment policy; and more effective competition policy. According to him, greater participation may carry some costs (e.g., delays in decision-making), but these costs are more than made up for by its positive impacts, which include, among other things, the increase in the political sustainability of a policy decision and the greater accumulation of social capital.

In the final part of the speech, Stiglitz extends this argument to the analysis of the role of the IFIs. According to him, the lack of openness and transparency in their management has created the perception, rightly or wrongly, that the adjustment packages of the IFIs are unjust and forcefully imposed on the developing countries (some people see an "echo of colonial bond" in them). He points out that the World Bank was trying to address this problem through its CDF (Comprehensive Development Framework), which is supposed to put the developing countries in the drivers' seat. Unfortunately, the subsequent development of events in the World Bank, including his own expulsion, reveals that he had underestimated the power of the Washington consensus.

Chapter 8 is the 1999 Oxford Amnesty Lecture that Stiglitz delivered in January 1999, titled, "On Liberty, the Right to Know and Public Discourse: The Role of Transparency in Public Life". This speech is a pioneering work on the issue of transparency, which has come to prominence after the Asian crisis but has never properly been theorized about by anyone.

Drawing on the classic arguments of a wide range of political thinkers including Jeremy Bentham, John Stuart Mill, Walter Bagehot, Albert Hirschman and above all James Madison, Stiglitz argues that openness in public life is necessary because meaningful participation in democratic process requires informed participants. He argues that greater openness not only has an instrumental value, such as the reduction of the likelihood of the abuse of power, but also an intrinsic value. It protects "the right to know", which he regards as one of basic human rights.

Despite the benefits of openness, he argues, there are strong incentives for those who are in power to maintain secrecy, which include covering up policy mistakes; promotion of special interests' activities; creation of rents; entrenchment of incumbents; and discouragement of democratic participation (also see chapter 3). In fact, he believes that these incentives are so strong that institutional provisions – such as legal provision for better information disclosure (e.g., the Freedom of Information Act of the USA), disclosure of campaign contributions and a free press (but acknowledging that the press is often a central part of the "conspiracy of secrecy" and therefore needs more public exposure) – are not enough to overcome them. Therefore he argues that it is necessary to create "a culture of openness", as, given the wide scope of discretionary actions, it will be impossible to control the public figures through formal rules alone without a change in their intrinsic motivations.

Stiglitz then examines a number of arguments for secrecy: privacy; confidentiality; national security; the desire not to create panic in a potential crisis situation (not to "cry 'fire' in a crowded theatre"); the need not to undermine authority by "airing dirty linen in public". He finds some justifications for most of these arguments, but holds that the situations where they apply are highly circumscribed and therefore they should be applied with caution. He ends the speech by acknowledging that greater openness does not always guarantee better decisions but emphasizes that it is an essential ingredient for the evolution of democratic processes.

The ninth and last chapter of the volume, titled "Democratic Development as the Fruits of Labor", the keynote address delivered at the Industrial Relations Research Association meeting in Boston in January 2000, is a highly unusual piece of work, even for someone like Stiglitz. First, it explicitly advocates worker participation at enterprise level and economic democracy at the social level, subjects that have been almost taboos for mainstream economists. It is methodologically unusual as well, as he draws on a number of intellectual traditions that have been largely neglected by mainstream economists.

Stiglitz starts the speech by pointing out the severe limitations of neoclassical economics in dealing with labor-related issues. Particularly, he emphasizes that issues like worker motivation, income redistribution and corporate organization, which have been de-emphasized by neoclassical economists, are crucial in understanding the role of labor in the economy. He then provides some insightful discussions of these issues drawing both on (neoclassical) information economics and on other more heterodox traditions in economics and other social sciences.

Based on these theoretical discussions, he distinguishes two systems of industrial relations – the "high road" system, which encourages worker involvement and teamwork (e.g., participation in corporate decision-making, profit-sharing, team-oriented remuneration), on the one hand, and the "low road" system, on the other hand, which minimizes worker participation and relies on arms' length worker disciplinary mechanisms (e.g., high unemployment, highly differentiated wages, low contractual security). He then identifies the benefits of the "high road" system and argues that the developing countries should try to move to it, while taking care to avoid the dangers associated with excessive labor market rigidities and excessively strong unions.

In the concluding parts of the speech, reiterating some of the points about "development as democratic transformation" that he had made in other places (for example, see chapters 1, 2 and 7), Stiglitz argues that economic democracy is an essential part of a genuinely democratic society, and argues for greater worker participation and more emphasis on full employment as the central means to promote economic democracy. He thinks full employment is more important than the welfare system for economic democracy, as the latter can never provide the dignity that comes from work.

CONCLUDING REMARKS: PUSHING THE BOUNDARY

As I hope I have showed in this introductory essay, the pieces collected in the volume are truly on the frontiers of research in many theoretical and policy-oriented areas. This is so not simply in terms of tackling new subject matters – transparency (chapter 8) being the most obvious example. It is also so in terms of methodology. When he is confronted with issues that neoclassical economics is not equipped to deal with – transition (chapter 4), knowledge (chapter 6), and labour (chapter 9) being the best examples – Stiglitz is willing to draw on various heterodox traditions in economics and on other social sciences. In doing so, he has clearly extensively consulted those members of his advisory team with backgrounds in these different intellectual traditions, freely acknowledging the limitations of his own background in neoclassical economics (albeit of a highly unconventional kind). This is a testimony to his unusual intellectual humility and openness.

In this way, Stiglitz has been pushing the boundary of mainstream economics. This, certainly in line with his support for a gradualist approach to policies, he has done without making a really clean break with the neoclassical economics in which he is grounded. However, in some areas he has done it to the extent that it becomes difficult to call him a neoclassical economist any more. Sometimes these attempts at theoretical synthesis are highly successful and sometimes less so. However, what is common to all the pieces collected in the volume is that they provide highly stimulating discussions on many key policy issues of our time.

In the end, this volume is not just a tribute to Stiglitz's intellectual achievements and his political courage (some, of course, call it recklessness). It is also a record of a fascinating intellectual drama surrounding some key policy issues of our time, an understanding of which will help the readers better understand why and how the world economy has evolved in the way that it has, how it is likely to change in the future, and what should be done to make the world a better place.

NOTES

I thank Jeff Madrick for suggesting the project to me in the first place and David Ellerman, a key member of Stiglitz's advisory team, for his highly enlightening discussion and comments.

1. Joseph Stiglitz, "What I Learned at the World Economic Crisis", *The New Republic*, 17 April 2000.
2. See especially his essays, "On the Economic Role of the State" in A. Heertje (ed.), *The Economic Role of the State* (Oxford: Basil Blackwell, 1989) and "Alternative Tactics and Strategies for Economic Development" in A.K. Dutt and K. Jameson (eds.), *New Directions in Development Economics* (Aldershot: Edward Elgar, 1992).
3. Asking the following questions enables us to see some weaknesses in Stiglitz's view on "special interest groups" more clearly. Can there be such things as "policies that do not cater for special interest groups", when all policies benefit some people more than others? What should the state do when catering for certain special interest groups can bring net social benefits in the long run (e.g., protecting infant industries)? How do we reconcile our concern for equitable development with the fact that some of the "special interest groups" receiving state protection are disadvantaged groups (e.g., small farmers, small retailers)?
4. For some more detailed discussions on the relative importance of "institutional" factors as opposed to policy failures and international factors in the making of the Asian crisis, see my paper, H-J. Chang, "The Hazard of Moral Hazard – Untangling the Asian Crisis", *World Development*, vol. 26, no. 4 (2000).

Chapter 1

More Instruments and Broader Goals: Moving Toward the Post-Washington Consensus

The 1998 WIDER Annual Lecture
Helsinki, January 1998

INTRODUCTION

I would like to discuss improvements in our understanding of economic development, in particular the emergence of what is sometimes called the "post-Washington consensus". My remarks elaborate on two themes. The first is that we have come to a better understanding of what makes markets work well. The Washington consensus held that good economic performance required liberalized trade, macroeconomic stability and getting prices right (see Williamson, 1990). Once the government dealt with these issues – essentially, once the government "got out of the way" – private markets would allocate resources efficiently and generate robust growth. To be sure, all of these are important for markets to work well: it is very difficult for investors to make good decisions when inflation is running at 100 per cent a year and highly variable. But the policies advanced by the Washington consensus are not complete, and they are sometimes misguided. Making markets work requires more than just low inflation; it requires sound financial regulation, competition policy, and policies to facilitate the transfer of technology and to encourage transparency, to cite some fundamental issues neglected by the Washington consensus.

Our understanding of the instruments to promote well-functioning markets has also improved, and we have broadened the objectives of development to include other goals, such as sustainable development, egalitarian development and democratic development. An important part of development today is seeking complementary strategies that advance these goals simultaneously. In our search for these policies, however, we should not ignore the inevitable tradeoffs. This is the second theme I will address.

SOME LESSONS OF THE EAST ASIAN
FINANCIAL CRISIS

Before discussing these themes, I would like to address the implications of the current East Asian crisis for our thinking about development. Observation of the successful, some even say miraculous, East Asian development was one of the motivations for moving beyond the Washington consensus. After all, here was a regional cluster of countries that had not closely followed the Washington consensus prescriptions but had somehow managed the most successful development in history. To be sure, many of their policies – such as low inflation and fiscal prudence – were perfectly in line with the Washington consensus. Several aspects of their strategy, such as an emphasis on egalitarian policies, while not at odds with the Washington consensus, were not emphasized by it. Their industrial policy, designed to close the technological gap between them and the more advanced countries, was actually contrary to the spirit of the Washington consensus. These observations were the basis for the World Bank's *East Asian Miracle* study (World Bank, 1993), and it stimulated the recent rethinking of the role of the state in economic development.

Since the financial crisis the East Asian economies have been widely condemned for their misguided economic policies, which are seen as responsible for the mess in which those economies find themselves today. Some ideologues have taken advantage of the current problems in East Asia to suggest that the system of active state intervention is the root of the problem. They point to the government-directed loans and the cozy relations between the government and the large *chaebol* in the Republic of Korea. In doing so, they overlook the successes of the past three decades, to which the government, despite occasional mistakes, has certainly contributed. These achievements, which include not only large increases in per capita GDP but also increases in life expectancy, the extension of education and a dramatic reduction in poverty, are real and will prove more lasting than the current financial turmoil.

Even when the governments directly undertook actions themselves, they had notable achievements. The fact that they created the most efficient steel plants in the world challenges the privatization ideologues who suggested that such successes are at best a fluke, and at worst impossible. Nevertheless, I agree that, in general, government should focus on what it alone can do and leave the production of commodities like steel to the private sector. But the heart of the current problem in most cases is not that government has done too much in every area but that it has done too little in some areas. In Thailand the problem was not that the government directed investments into real estate; it was that government regulators failed to halt it. Similarly, the Republic of Korea suffered from problems including overlending to companies with excessively high leverage and weak corporate governance. The fault is not that the government misdirected credit – the fact the current turmoil was precipitated by loans by so many US, European and Japanese banks suggest that *market* entities also may have seriously misdirected credit. Instead the problem was the government's lack of action, the fact that the government underestimated the importance of financial regulation and corporate governance.[1]

The current crisis in East Asia is not a refutation of the East Asian miracle. The basic facts remain: no other region in the world has ever had incomes rise so dramatically and seen so many people move out of poverty in such a short time. The more dogmatic versions of the Washington consensus fail to provide the right framework for understanding either the success of the East Asian economies or their current troubles. Responses to East Asia's crisis grounded in these views of the world are likely to be, at best, badly flawed and, at worst, counterproductive.

MAKING MARKETS WORK BETTER

The Washington consensus was catalyzed by the experience of Latin American countries in the 1980s. At the time markets in the region were not functioning well, partly the result of dysfunctional public policies. GNP declined for three consecutive years. Budget deficits were very high – some were in the range of five to ten per cent of GDP[2] – and the spending underlying them was being used not so much for productive investments as for subsidies to the huge and inefficient state sector. With strong curbs on imports and relatively little emphasis on exports, firms had insufficient incentives to increase efficiency or maintain international quality standards. At first deficits were financed by borrowing – including very heavy borrowing from abroad. Bankers trying to recycle petro-dollars were quick to lend and low real interest rates made borrowing very attractive, even for low-return investments. After 1980, though, real interest rate increases in the United States restricted continued borrowing and raised the burden of interest payments, forcing many countries to turn to seignorage to finance the gap between the continued high level of public spending (augmented by soaring interest payments) and the shrinking tax base. The result was very high and extremely variable inflation. In this environment money became a much costlier means of exchange, economic behavior was diverted toward protecting value rather than making productive investments, and the relative price variability induced by the high inflation undermined one of the primary functions of the price system: conveying information.

The so-called "Washington consensus" of US economic officials, the International Monetary Fund (IMF) and the World Bank was formed in the midst of these serious problems. Now is a good time to reexamine this consensus. Many countries, such as Argentina and Brazil, have pursued successful stabilizations; the challenges they face are in designing the second generation of reforms. Still other countries have always had relatively good policies or face problems quite different from those of Latin America. East Asian governments, for instance have been running budget surpluses; inflation is low and, before the devaluations, was falling in many countries (see figures 1 and 2). The origins of the current financial crises lie elsewhere and their solutions will not be found in the Washington consensus.

The focus on inflation – the central macroeconomic malady of the Latin American countries, which provided the backdrop for the Washington consensus – has led to macroeconomic policies that may not be the most conducive for long-term economic growth, and it has detracted attention from other major sources of macro-instability, namely, weak financial sectors. In the case of financial markets the focus on freeing up markets may have had the perverse effect of contributing to macroeconomic instability by weakening the financial sector. More broadly, in focusing on trade liberalization, deregulation, and privatization, policymakers ignored other important ingredients, most notably competition, that are required to make an effective market economy and which may be at least as important as

20

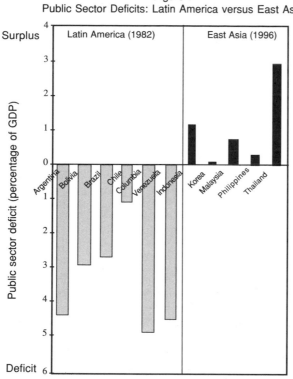

Figure 1
Public Sector Deficits: Latin America versus East Asia

Note: Calculations based on data from IMF International Financial
Statistics Database. Figures for Thailand are from 1995.

the standard economic prescriptions in determining long-term economic
success.[3]

Other essential ingredients were also left out or underemphasized by
the Washington consensus. One – education – has been widely recognized within the development community; others, such as the improvement of technology, may not have received the attention they deserve.

The success of the Washington consensus as an intellectual doctrine
rests on its simplicity: its policy recommendations could be administered
by economists using little more than simple accounting frameworks. A
few economic indicators – inflation, money supply growth, interest rates,
budget and trade deficits – could serve as the basis for a set of policy
recommendations. Indeed, in some cases economists would fly into a

21

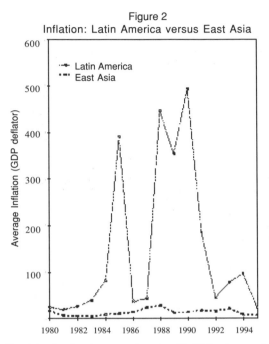

Figure 2
Inflation: Latin America versus East Asia

Note: Unweighted regional averages based on World Development Indicators 1997 data

country, look at and attempt to verify these data, and make macroeconomic recommendations for policy reforms, all in the space of a couple of weeks.[4]

There are important advantages to the Washington consensus approach to policy advice. It focuses on issues of first-order importance, it sets up an easily reproducible framework which can be used by a large organization worried about recommendations depending on particular individuals' viewpoints, and it is frank about limiting itself only to establishing the prerequisites for development. But the Washington consensus does not offer answers to every important question in development.

In contrast, the ideas that I present here are, unfortunately, not so simple. They are not easy to articulate as dogma nor to implement as policy. There are no easy-to-read thermometers of the economy's health, and worse still, there may be trade-offs, in which economists, especially outside economists, should limit their role to describing consequences of alternative policies. The political process may actually have an important say in the choices of economic direction. Economic policy may not be just a matter for technical experts! These conflicts become all the more important when we come to broaden the objectives, in the final part of this talk.

This part of the paper focuses on enhancing the efficiency of the economy. I will discuss macro-stability and liberalization – two sets of issues about which the Washington consensus was concerned – as well as financial sector reform, the government's role as a complement to the private sector, and improving the state's effectiveness – issues that were not included in the consensus. I shall argue that the Washington consensus' messages in the two core areas are at best incomplete and at worse misguided. While macro-stability is important, for example, inflation is not always its most essential component. Trade liberalization and privatization are key parts of sound macro-economic policies, but they are not ends in themselves. They are means to the end of a less distorted, more competitive, more efficient marketplace and must be complemented by effective regulation and competition policies.

ACHIEVING MACROECONOMIC STABILITY

Controlling inflation

Probably the most important policy prescription of the stabilization packages promoted by the Washington consensus was controlling inflation. The argument for aggressive, preemptive strikes against inflation is based on three premises. The most fundamental is that inflation is costly and should therefore be averted or lowered. The second premise is that once inflation starts to rise it has a tendency to accelerate out of control. This belief provides a strong motivation for preemptive strikes against inflation, with the risk of an increase in inflation being weighed far more heavily than the risk of adverse effects on output and unemployment. The third premise is that increases in inflation are very costly to reverse. This line of thought implies that even if maintaining low unemployment were valued more highly than maintaining low inflation, steps would still be taken to keep inflation from increasing today in order to avoid having to induce large recessions to bring the inflation rate down later on. All three of these premises can be tested empirically.

I have discussed this evidence in more detail elsewhere (Stiglitz 1997a). Here I would like to summarize briefly. The evidence has shown only that high inflation is costly. Bruno and Easterly (1996) found that when countries cross the threshold of 40 per cent annual inflation, they fall into a high-inflation/low-growth trap. Below that level, however, *there is little evidence that inflation is costly*. Barro (1997) and Fischer (1993) also confirm that high inflation is, on average, deleterious for growth, but they, too, fail to find any evidence that low levels of inflation are costly. Fischer finds the same results for the variability of inflation.[5] Recent research by Akerlof, Dickens, and Perry (1996) suggests that low levels of inflation may even improve economic performance relative to what it would have been with zero inflation.

The evidence on the accelerationist hypothesis (also known as "letting the genie out of the bottle", the "slippery slope", or the "precipice theory") is unambiguous: there is no indication that the increase in the inflation rate is related to past increases in inflation. Evidence on reversing inflation suggests that the Phillips curve may be concave and that the costs of reducing inflation may thus be smaller than the benefits incurred when inflation is rising.[6]

In my view the conclusion to be drawn from this research is that controlling high and medium-rate inflation should be a fundamental policy priority but that pushing low inflation even lower is not likely to significantly improve the functioning of markets.

In 1995 more than half the countries in the developing world had inflation rates of less than 15 per cent a year (figure 3). For these 71 countries controlling inflation should not be an overarching priority. Controlling inflation is probably an important component of stabilization and reform

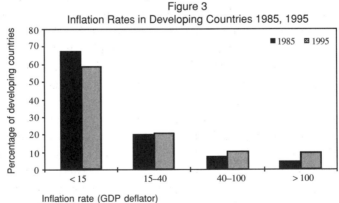

Figure 3
Inflation Rates in Developing Countries 1985, 1995

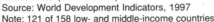

Inflation rate (GDP deflator)
Source: World Development Indicators, 1997
Note: 121 of 158 low- and middle-income countries

24

in the 25 countries, almost all of them in Africa, Eastern Europe and the former Soviet Union, with inflation rates of more than 40 per cent a year. The single-minded focus on inflation may not only distort economic policies – preventing the economy from living up to its full growth and output potentials – but also lead to institutional arrangements that reduce economic flexibility without gaining important growth benefits.[7]

Managing the budget deficit and the current account deficit

A second component of macroeconomic stability has been reducing the size of government, the budget deficit and the current account deficit. I will return to the issue of the optimal size of government later; for now I would like to focus on the twin deficits. Much evidence shows that sustained, large budget deficits are deleterious to economic performance (Fischer, 1993; Easterly, Rodriguez and Schmidt-Hebbel 1994).[8] The three methods of financing deficits all have drawbacks: internal finance raises domestic interest rates, external financing can be unsustainable, and money creation causes inflation.[9]

There is no simple formula for determining the optimum level of the budget deficit. The optimum deficit – or the range of sustainable deficits[10] – depends on circumstances, including the cyclical state of the economy, prospects for future growth, the uses of government spending, the depth of financial markets, and the levels of national savings and national investment. The United States, for example, is currently trying to balance its budget. I have long argued that the low private saving rate and the ageing of the baby boom suggest that the United States should probably be aiming for budget surpluses. In contrast, the case for maintaining budget surpluses in the East Asian countries in the face of an economic downturn, where the rate of private saving is high and the public debt- GDP ratios are relatively low, is far less compelling.

The experience of Ethiopia emphasizes another determinant of optimal deficits, the source of financing. For the last several years Ethiopia has run a deficit of about eight per cent of GDP. Some outside policy advisers would like Ethiopia to lower its deficit. Others have argued that the deficit is financed by a steady and predictable inflow of highly concessional foreign assistance, which is driven not by the necessity of filling a budget gap but by the availability of high returns to investment.

Under these circumstances – and given the high returns to government investment in such crucial areas as primary education and physical infrastructure (especially roads and energy) – it may make sense for the government to treat foreign aid as a legitimate source of revenue, just like taxes, and balance the budget inclusive of foreign aid.

The optimal level of the current account deficit is difficult to determine. Current account deficits occur when a country invests more than it saves. They are neither inherently good nor inherently bad but depend on circumstances and especially on the uses to which the funds are put. In many countries the rate of return on investment far exceeds the cost of international capital. In these circumstances current account deficits are sustainable.[11]

The form of the financing also matters. The advantage of foreign direct investment is not just the capital and knowledge that it supplies, but also the fact that it tends to be very stable. In contrast, Thailand's eight per cent current account deficit in 1996 was not only large but came in the form of short-term, dollar-denominated debt that was used to finance local-currency denominated investment, often in excessive and unproductive uses like real estate. More generally, short-term debt and portfolio flows can bring the costs of high volatility without the benefits of knowledge spillovers.[12]

Stabilizing output and promoting long-run growth

Ironically, macroeconomic stability – as conceived by the Washington consensus – typically downplays stabilizing output or unemployment. Minimizing or avoiding major economic contractions should be one of the most important goals of policy. In the short run large-scale involuntary unemployment is clearly inefficient – in purely economic terms it represents idle resources that could be used more productively. The social and economic costs of these downturns can be devastating: lives and families are disrupted, poverty increases, living standards decline, and, in the worst cases, social and economic costs translate into political and social turmoil.

Moreover, business cycles themselves can have important consequences for long-run growth (see Stiglitz 1994a). The difficulty of borrowing to finance research and development means that firms will need to reduce drastically their research and development expenditures when their cash flow decreases in downturns. The result is slower total factor productivity growth in the future. This effect appears to have been important in the United States; whether or not it matters in countries in which research and development plays a less important role requires further study. Generally, however, variability of output almost certainly contributes to uncertainty and thus discourages investment.[13]

Variability of output is especially pronounced in developing countries (see Pritchett, 1997). The median high-income country has a standard deviation of annual growth of 2.8 per cent (figure 4). For developing countries the standard deviation is five per cent or higher, implying huge deviations in the growth rate. Growth is especially volatile in Europe and Central Asia, the Middle East and North Africa, and Sub-Saharan Africa.

How can macroeconomic stability in the sense of stabilizing output or employment be promoted? The traditional answer is good macroeconomic policy, including countercyclical monetary policy and a fiscal policy that allows automatic stabilizers to operate. These policies are certainly necessary, but a growing literature, both theoretical and empirical, has emphasized the important microeconomic underpinnings of macroeconomic stability. This literature emphasizes the importance of financial markets and explains economic downturns through such mechanisms as credit rationing and banking and firm failures.[14]

In the nineteenth century most of the major economic downturns in industrial countries resulted from financial panics that were sometimes

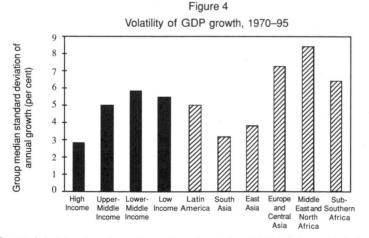

Figure 4
Volatility of GDP growth, 1970–95

Source: Calculations based on real annual growth rates from *World Development Indicators, 1997.*

preceded by and invariably led to precipitous declines in asset prices and widespread banking failures. In some countries improvement in regulation and supervision, the introduction of deposit insurance and the shaping of incentives for financial institutions reduced the incidence and severity of financial panics. But financial crises continue to occur, and there is some evidence that they have become more frequent and more severe in recent years (Caprio and Klingebiel, 1997). Even after adjusting for inflation, the losses from the notorious savings and loan debacle in the United States were several times larger than the losses experienced in the Great Depression. Yet when measured relative to GDP, this debacle would not make the list of the top 25 international banking crises since the early 1980s (table 1).

Table 1

Fiscal costs of banking crises in selected countries (percentage of GDP)	
Country (Date)	**Cost (percentage of GDP)**
Argentina (1980–82)	55.3
Chile (1981–3)	41.2
Uruguay (1981–4)	31.2
Israel (1977–83)	30.0
Cote d'Ivoire (1988–91)	25.0
Senegal (1988–91)	17.0
Spain (1977–85)	16.8
Bulgaria (1990s)	14.0
Mexico (1995)	13.5
Hungary (1991–5)	10.0
Finland (1991–3)	8.0
Sweden (1991)	6.4
Sri Lanka (1989–93)	5.0
Malaysia (1985–8)	4.7
Norway (1987–9)	4.0
United States (1984–91)	3.2

Source: Caprio and Klingebiel 1996.

28

Banking crises have severe macroeconomic consequences, affecting growth over the five following years (figure 5). During the period 1975–94 growth edged up slightly in countries that did not experience banking crises; countries with banking crises saw growth slow by 1.3 percentage points in the five years following a crisis. Clearly, building robust financial systems is a crucial part of promoting macroeconomic stability.

Figure 5
GDP growth before and after banking crises, 1975–94

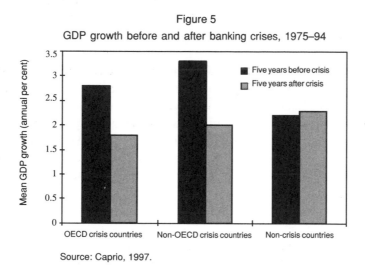

Source: Caprio, 1997.

The process of financial reform

The importance of building robust financial systems goes beyond simply averting economic crises. The financial system can be likened to the "brain" of the economy. It plays an important role in collecting and aggregating savings from agents who have excess resources today. These resources are allocated to others – such as entrepreneurs and home builders – who can make productive use of them. Well-functioning financial systems do a very good job of selecting the most productive recipients for these resources. In contrast, poorly functioning financial systems often allocate capital to low-productivity investments. Selecting projects is only the first stage. The financial system must continue to monitor the use of funds, ensuring that they continue to be used productively. In the process financial markets serve a number of other functions, including reducing risk, increasing liquidity and conveying information. All of these functions are essential to both the growth of capital and the increase in total factor productivity.

Left to themselves financial systems will not do a very good job of performing these functions. Problems of incomplete information, incomplete markets and incomplete contracts are all particularly severe in the financial sector, resulting in an equilibrium that is not even constrained Pareto efficient (Greenwald and Stiglitz, 1986).[15]

The emphasis on "transparency" in recent discussions of East Asia demonstrates our growing recognition of the importance of good information for the effective function of markets. Capital markets, in particular, require auditing standards accompanied by effective legal systems to discourage fraud, provide investors with adequate information about the firms' assets and liabilities, and protect minority shareholders.[16] But transparency by itself is not sufficient, in part because information is inevitably imperfect. A sound legal framework combined with regulation and oversight is necessary to mitigate these informational problems and foster the conditions for efficient financial markets.

Regulation serves four purposes in successful financial markets: maintaining safety and soundness (prudential regulation), promoting competition, protecting consumers, and ensuring that underserved groups have some access to capital. In many cases the pursuit of social objectives – such as ensuring that minorities and poor communities receive funds, as the United States' Community Reinvestment Act does, or ensuring funds for mortgages, the essential mission of the government – created Federal National Mortgage Association – can, if done well, reinforce economic objectives. Similarly, protecting consumers is not only good social policy, it also builds confidence that there is a "level playing field" in economic markets. Without such confidence those markets will remain thin and ineffective.

At times, however, policymakers face tradeoffs among conflicting objectives. The financial restraints adopted by some of the East Asian economies, for example, increased the franchise values of banks, discouraging them from taking unwarranted risks that otherwise might have destabilized the banking sector. Although there were undoubtedly some economic costs associated with these restraints, the gains from greater stability almost surely outweighed those losses. As I comment below, the removal of many of these restraints in recent years may have contributed in no small measure to the current instability that these countries are experiencing.

The World Bank and others have tried to create better banking systems. But changing the system – through institutional development, transformations in credit culture, and creation of regulatory structures which reduce the likelihood of excessive risk-taking[17] – has proved more intractable than finding short-term solutions, such as recapitalizing the banking system. In the worst cases the temporary fixes may even have undermined pressures for further reform. Since the fundamental problems were not addressed, some countries have required assistance again and again.

The Washington consensus developed in the context of highly regulated financial systems, in which many of the regulations were designed to limit competition rather than promote any of the four legitimate objectives of regulation. But all too often the dogma of liberalization became an end in itself, not a means of achieving a better financial system. I do not have space to delve into all of the many facets of liberalization, which include freeing up deposit and lending rates, opening up the market to foreign banks and removing restrictions on capital account transactions and bank lending. But I do want to make a few general points.

First, the key issue should not be liberalization or deregulation but construction of the regulatory framework that ensures an effective financial system. In many countries this will require changing the regulatory framework by eliminating regulations that serve only to restrict competition but accompanying these changes with increased regulations to ensure competition and prudential behavior (and to ensure that banks have appropriate incentives.)

Second, even once the design of the desired financial system is in place, care will have to be exercised in the transition. Attempts to initiate overnight deregulation – sometimes known as the "big bang" – ignore the very sensitive issues of sequencing. Thailand, for instance, used to have restrictions on bank lending to real estate. In the process of liberalization it got rid of these restrictions without establishing a more sophisticated risk-based regulatory regime. The result, together with other factors, was the large-scale misallocation of capital to fuel a real estate bubble, an important factor in the financial crisis.

It is important to recognize how difficult it is to establish a vibrant financial sector. Even economies with sophisticated institutions, high levels of transparency and good corporate governance like the United States and Sweden have faced serious problems with their financial sectors. The challenges facing developing countries are far greater, while the institutional base from which they start is far weaker.

Third, in all countries a primary objective of regulation should be to ensure that participants face the right incentives: government cannot and should not be involved in monitoring every transaction. In the banking system liberalization will not work unless regulations create incentives for bank owners, markets and supervisors to use their information efficiently and act prudentially.

Incentive issues in securities markets also need to be addressed. It must be more profitable for managers to create economic value than to deprive minority shareholders of their assets: rent-seeking can be every bit as much a problem in the private as in the public sector. Without the appropriate legal framework, securities markets can simply fail to perform their vital functions – to the detriment of the country's long-term economic growth. Laws are required to protect the interests of shareholders, especially minority shareholders.

The focus on the microeconomic, particularly the financial, underpinnings of the macroeconomy also has implications for responses to currency turmoil. In particular, where currency turmoil is the consequence of a failing financial sector, the conventional policy response to rising interest rates may be counterproductive.[18] The maturity and structure of bank and corporate assets and liabilities are frequently very different, in part because of the strong incentives for banks to use short-term debt to monitor and influence the firms they lend to and for depositors to use short-term deposits to monitor and influence banks (Rey and Stiglitz,1993). As a result interest rate increases can lead to substantial reductions in bank net worth, further exacerbating the banking crisis.[19] Empirical studies by IMF and World Bank economists have confirmed that interest rate rises tend to increase the probability of banking crises and that currency devaluations have no significant effect (Demirgüç-Kunt and Detragiach,1997).[20]

Advocates of high-interest rate policies have asserted that such policies are necessary to restore confidence in the economy and thus stop the erosion of the currency's value. Halting the erosion of the currency, in turn, is important to both restore the underlying strength of the economy and prevent a burst of inflation from the rise of the price of imported goods.[21] This prescription is based on assumptions about market reactions – i.e., what will restore confidence – and economic fundamentals.

Ultimately confidence and economic fundamentals are inextricably intertwined. Are measures that weaken the economy, especially the financial system, likely to restore confidence? To be sure, if an economy is initially facing high levels of inflation caused by high levels of excess aggregate demand, increases in the interest rate will be seen to strengthen the economic fundamentals by restoring macro-stability. For an economy where there is little initial evidence of macro-imbalances but a predicted large exogenous fall in aggregate demand, high interest rates will lead to an economic slump and the slump will combine with the interest rates themselves to undermine the financial system.

Fostering competition

So far I have argued that macroeconomic policy needs to be expanded beyond a single-minded focus on inflation and budget deficits; the set of policies that underlay the Washington consensus are not sufficient for macroeconomic stability or long-term development. Macroeconomic stability and long-term development require sound financial markets. But the agenda for creating sound financial markets should not confuse means with ends; redesigning the regulatory system, not financial liberalization, should be the issue.

I now want to argue that competition is central to the success of a market economy. Here, too, there has been some confusion between means and ends. Policies that should have been viewed as means to achieve a more competitive marketplace were seen as ends in themselves. As a result, in some instances they failed to attain their objectives.

The fundamental theorems of welfare economics, the results that establish the efficiency of a market economy, assume that both private property and competitive markets exist in the economy. Many countries – especially developing and transition economies – lack both. Until recently, however, emphasis was placed almost exclusively on creating private property and liberalizing trade – trade liberalization being confused with establishing competitive markets. Trade liberalization is

33

important, but we are unlikely to realize the full benefits of liberalizing trade without creating a competitive economy.

Promoting free trade

Trade liberalization, leading eventually to free trade, was a key part of the Washington consensus. The emphasis on trade liberalization was natural: the Latin American countries had stagnated behind protectionist barriers.[22] Import substitution proved a highly ineffective strategy for development. In many countries industries were producing products with negative value added, and innovation was stifled. The usual argument – that protectionism itself stifled innovation – was somewhat confused. Governments could have created competition among domestic firms, which would have provided incentives to import new technology. It was the failure to create competition internally, more than protection from abroad, that was the cause of the stagnation. Of course, competition from abroad would have provided an important source of competition. But it is possible that in the one-sided race, domestic firms would have dropped out of the competition rather than enter the fray. Consumers might have benefited, but the effects on growth may have been more ambiguous.

Trade liberalization may create competition, but it does not do so automatically. If trade liberalization occurs in an economy with a monopoly importer, the rents may simply be transferred from the government to the monopolist, with little decrease in prices. Trade liberalization is thus neither necessary nor sufficient for creating a competitive and innovative economy.

At least as important as creating competition in the previously sheltered import-competing sector of the economy is promoting competition on the export side. The success of the East Asian economies is a powerful example of this point. By allowing each country to take advantage of its comparative advantage, trade increases wages and expands consumption opportunities. For the past 15 years trade has been doing just that – with world trade growing at five per cent a year, nearly twice the rate of world GDP growth.

Interestingly, the process by which trade liberalization leads to enhanced productivity is not fully understood. The standard Hecksher-Ohlin theory predicts that countries will shift intersectorally, moving along their production possibility frontier, producing more of what they are better at and trading for what they are worse at. In reality, the main gains from trade seem to come intertemporally, from an outward shift in the production possibility frontier as a result of increased efficiency, with little sectoral shift. Understanding the causes of this improvement in efficiency requires an understanding of the links between trade, competition and liberalization. This is an area that needs to be pursued further.[23]

Facilitating privatization

State monopolies in certain industries have stifled competition. But the emphasis on privatization over the past decade has stemmed less from concern over lack of competition than from a focus on profit incentives. In a sense, it was natural for the Washington consensus to focus more on privatization than on competition. Not only were state enterprises inefficient, their losses contributed to the government's budget deficit, adding to macroeconomic instability. Privatization would kill two birds with one stone, simultaneously improving economic efficiency and reducing fiscal deficits.[24] The idea was that if property rights could be created, the profit-maximizing behavior of the owners would eliminate waste and inefficiency. At the same time the sale of the enterprises would raise much needed revenue.

Although in retrospect the process of privatization in the transition economies was, in several instances at least, badly flawed, at the time it seemed reasonable to many. Although most people would have preferred a more orderly restructuring and the establishment of an effective legal structure (covering contracts, bankruptcy, corporate governance and competition) prior to or at least simultaneous to promulgations, no one knew how long the reform window would stay open. At the time privatizing quickly and comprehensively – and then fixing the problems later on – seemed a reasonable gamble. From today's vantage point, the advocates of privatization may have overestimated the benefits of privatization and underestimated the costs, particularly the political costs of the process itself and the impediments it has posed to further reform. Taking that same gamble today, with the benefit of seven more years of experience, would be much less justified.

Even at the time many of us warned against hastily privatizing without creating the needed institutional infrastructure, including competitive markets and regulatory bodies. David Sappington and I showed in the fundamental theorem on privatization that the conditions under which privatization can achieve the public objectives of efficiency and equity are very limited and are very similar to the conditions under which competitive markets attain Pareto-efficient outcomes (Sappington and Stiglitz, 1987). If, for instance, competition is lacking, creating a private, unregulated monopoly will likely result in even higher prices for consumers. And there is some evidence that, insulated from competition, private monopolies may suffer from several forms of inefficiency and may not be highly innovative.

Indeed, both large-scale public and private enterprises share many similarities and face many of the same organizational challenges (Stiglitz, 1989). Both involve substantial delegation of responsibility – neither legislatures nor shareholders in large companies directly control the daily activities of an enterprise. In both cases the hierarchy of authority terminates in managers who typically have a great deal of autonomy and discretion. Rent-seeking occurs in private enterprises, just as it does in public enterprises. Shleifer and Vishny (1989) and Edlin and Stiglitz (1995) have shown that there are strong incentives not only for private rent-seeking on the part of management but for taking actions that increase the scope for such rent-seeking. In the Czech Republic the bold experiment with voucher privatization seems to have foundered on these issues, as well as the broader issues of whether, without the appropriate legal and institutional structures, capital markets can provide the necessary discipline to managers as well as allocate scarce capital efficiently.

Public organizations typically do not provide effective incentives and often impose a variety of additional constraints. When these problems are effectively addressed, when state enterprises are embedded in a competitive performance-based environment, performance differences may narrow (Caves and Christenson, 1980).

The differences between public and private enterprises are blurry, and there is a continuum of arrangements in between. Corporatization, for instance, maintains government ownership but moves firms toward hard budget constraints and self-financing; performance-based government organizations use output-oriented performance measures as a basis for incentives. Some evidence suggests that much of the gains from privatization occur before privatization as a result of the process of putting in place effective individual and organizational incentives (Pannier, 1996).

The importance of competition rather than ownership has been most vividly demonstrated by the experience of China and the Russian Federation. China extended the scope of competition without privatizing state-owned enterprises. To be sure, a number of problems remain in the state-owned sector, which may be addressed in the next stage of reform. In contrast, Russia has privatized a large fraction of its economy without doing much to promote competition. The contrast in perform- ance could not be greater, with Russia's output below the level attained almost a decade ago, while China has managed to sustain double-digit growth for almost two decades. Though the differences in performance may be only partially explained by differences in the policies they have pursued, both the Chinese and Russian experiences pose quandaries for traditional economic theories.

In particular, the magnitude and duration of Russia's downturn is itself somewhat of a puzzle: the Soviet economy was widely considered rife with inefficiencies, and a substantial fraction of its output was devoted to military expenditures. The elimination of these inefficiencies should have raised GDP, and the reduction in military expenditures should have increased personal consumption still farther.[25] Yet neither seems to have occurred.

The magnitude and success of China's economy over the past two decades also represents a puzzle for standard theory. Chinese policymakers not only eschewed a strategy of outright privatization, they also failed to incorporate numerous other elements of the Washington consensus. Yet China's recent experience is one of the greatest economic success stories in history. If China's 30 provinces were treated as separate economies – and many of them have populations exceeding those of most other low-income countries – the 20 fastest-growing economies between 1978 and 1995 would all have been Chinese provinces (World Bank, 1997a). Although China's GDP in 1978 represented only about one-quarter of the aggregate GDP of low-income countries and its population represented only 40 per cent of the total, almost two-thirds of aggregate growth in low-income countries between 1978 and 1995 was accounted for by the increase in China's GDP.

While measurement problems make it difficult to make comparisons between Russia and China with any precision, the broad picture remains persuasive: real incomes and consumption have fallen in the former Soviet Union, and real incomes and consumption have risen rapidly in China.

One of the important lessons of the contrast between China and Russia is for the political economy of privatization and competition. It has proved difficult to prevent corruption and other problems in privatizing monopolies. The huge rents created by privatization will encourage entrepreneurs to try to secure privatized enterprises rather than invest in creating their own firms. In contrast, competition policy often undermines rents and creates incentives for wealth creation. The sequencing of privatization and regulation is also very important. Privatizing a monopoly can create a powerful entrenched interest that undermines the possibility of regulation or competition in the future.

The Washington consensus is right – privatization is important. The government needs to devote its scarce resources to areas the private sector does not and is not likely to enter. It makes no sense for the government to be running steel mills. But there are critical issues about both the sequencing and the scope of privatization. Even when privatization increases productive efficiency, it may be difficult to ensure that broader public objectives are attained, even with regulation. Should prisons, social services, or the making of atomic bombs (or the central ingredient of atomic bombs, highly enriched uranium) be privatized, as some in the United States have advocated? Where are the boundaries? More private sector activity can be introduced into public activities (through contracting, for example, and incentive-based mechanisms, such as auctions). How effective are such mechanisms as substitutes for outright privatization? These issues were not addressed by the Washington consensus.

Establishing regulation

Competition is an essential ingredient in a successful market economy. But competition is not viable in some sectors – the so-called natural monopolies. Even there, however, the extent and form of actual and potential competition are constantly changing. New technologies have expanded the scope for competition in many sectors that have historically been highly regulated, such as telecommunications and electric power.

Traditional regulatory perspectives, with their rigid categories of regulation versus deregulation and competition versus monopoly have not been helpful guides to policy in these areas. These new technologies do not call for wholesale deregulation, because not all parts of these industries are adequately competitive. Instead, they call for appropriate changes in regulatory structure to meet the new challenges. Such changes must recognize the existence of hybrid areas of the economy, parts of which are well suited to competition, while other parts are more vulnerable to domination by a few producers. Allowing a firm with market power in one part of a regulated industry to gain a stranglehold over other parts of the industry will severely compromise economic efficiency.

Forging competition policy

Although the scope of viable competition has expanded, competition is often imperfect, especially in developing countries. Competition is suppressed in a variety of ways, including implicit collusion and predatory pricing. Control of the distribution system may effectively limit competition even when there are many producers. Vertical restraints can restrict competition. And new technologies have opened up new opportunities for anticompetitive behavior, as recent cases in the US airline and computer industry have revealed.

The establishment of effective antitrust laws for developing countries has not been examined adequately. The sophisticated and complicated legal structures and institutions in place in the United States may not be appropriate for many developing countries, which may have to rely more on per se rules.

Competition policy also has important implications for trade policy. Currently, most countries have separate rules governing domestic competition and international competition (Australia and New Zealand are exceptions). With little if any justification, rules governing competition in international trade (such as anti-dumping provisions and countervailing duties) are substantially different from domestic antitrust laws (see Stiglitz, 1997b); much of what we consider as healthy price competition domestically would be classified as dumping.[26] These abuses of fair trade were pioneered in the industrial countries but are now spreading to the developing countries – which surpassed industrial countries in the initiation of antidumping actions reported to the General Agreement on Tariffs and Trade (GATT) and the World Trade Organization (WTO) for the first time in 1996 (World Bank, 1997b).

The best way to curtail these abuses would be to integrate fair trade and fair competition laws based on the deep understanding of the nature of competition that antitrust authorities and industrial organization economists have evolved over the course of a century.

Government acting as a complement to markets

For much of this century people have looked to government to spend more and intervene more. Government spending as a share of GDP has grown with these demands (figure 6). The Washington consensus policies were based on a rejection of the state's activist role and the promotion of a minimalist, noninterventionist state. The unspoken premise is that governments are worse than markets. Therefore the smaller the state the better the state.

It is true that states are often involved in too many things, in an unfocused manner. This lack of focus reduces efficiency; trying to get government better focused on the fundamentals – economic policies, basic education, health, roads, law and order, environmental protection – is a vital step. But focusing on the fundamentals is not a recipe for minimalist government. The state has an important role to play in appropriate regulation, social protection and welfare. The choice should

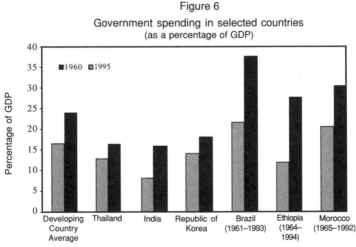

Figure 6
Government spending in selected countries
(as a percentage of GDP)

Note: Data from IMF Government Financial Statistics

40

not be whether the state should be involved but how it gets involved. Thus the central question should not be the size of the government, but the activities and methods of the government. Countries with successful economies have governments that are involved in a wide range of activities.

Over the past several decades, there has been an evolving framework within which the issue of the role of the government can be addressed: the recognition that markets might not always yield efficient outcomes – let alone socially acceptable distributions – led to the market failures approach.[27] There was a well-defined set of market failures, associated with externalities and public goods, that justified government intervention. This list of market failures was subsequently expanded to include imperfect information and incomplete markets, but the market failure approach continued to focus on dividing sectors and activities into those which should be in the government domain and those that fall within the province of the private sector. More recently, there has been a growing recognition that the government and private sector are much more intimately entwined. The government should serve as a complement to markets, undertaking actions that make markets work better and correcting market failures. In some cases the government has proved to be an effective catalyst – its actions have helped solve the problem of undersupply of (social) innovation, for example. But once it has performed its catalytic role, the state needs to withdraw.[28]

I cannot review all of the areas in which government can serve as an important complement to markets. I shall discuss briefly only two, building human capital and transferring technology.

Building human capital

The role of human capital in economic growth has long been appreciated. The returns to an additional year of education in the United States, for instance, have been estimated at five to 15 per cent (Willis, 1986; Kane and Rouse, 1995; Ashenfelter and Krueger, 1994). The rate of return is even higher in developing countries: 24 per cent for primary education in Sub-Saharan Africa, for example, and an average of 23 per cent for primary education in all low-income countries (Psacharopoulos, 1994). Growth accounting also attributes a substantial portion of growth in developing countries to human capital accumulation.[29] The East Asian economies, for instance, emphasized the role of government in providing universal education, which was a necessary part of their transformation from agrarian to rapidly industrializing economies.

Left to itself, the market will tend to underprovide human capital. It is very difficult to borrow against the prospects of future earnings since human capital cannot be collateralized. These difficulties are especially severe for poorer families. The government thus plays an important role in providing public education, making education more affordable and enhancing access to funding.

Transferring technology

Studies of the returns to research and development (R & D) in industrial countries have consistently found individual returns of 20–30 per cent and social returns of 50 per cent or higher – far exceeding the returns to education (Nadiri, 1993). Growth accounting usually attributes the majority of per capita income growth to improvements in total factor productivity – Solow's (1957) pioneering analysis attributed 87.5 per cent of the increase in output per man-hour between 1909 and 1949 to technical change. Based on a standard Cobb-Douglas production function, per capita income in the Republic of Korea in 1990 would have been only $2,041 (in 1985 international dollars) if it had relied solely on capital accumulation, far lower than actual per capita income of $6,665. The difference comes from increasing the amount of output per unit of input, which is partly the result of improvements in technology.[30]

Left to itself, the market underprovides technology. Like investments in education, investments in technology cannot be used as collateral. Investments in R & D are also considerably riskier than other types of investment and there are much larger asymmetries of information that can impede the effective workings of the market.[31] Technology also has enormous positive externalities that the market does not reward. Indeed, in some respects, knowledge is like a classical public good. The benefits to society of increased investment in technology far outweigh the benefits to individual entrepreneurs. As Thomas Jefferson said, ideas are like a candle, you can use them to light other candles without diminishing the original flame. Without government action there will be too little investment in the production and adoption of new technology.

For most countries not at the technological frontier, the returns associated with facilitating the transfer of technology are much higher than the returns from undertaking original research and development. Policies to facilitate the transfer of technology are thus one of the keys to development. One aspect of these policies is investing in human capital, especially in tertiary education. Funding of universities is justified not because it increases the human capital of particular individuals but because of the major externalities that come from enabling the economy to import ideas. Of course, unemployment rates for university graduates are high in many developing countries, and many university graduates hold unproductive civil service jobs. These countries have probably overemphasized liberal arts educations.[32] In contrast, the Republic of Korea and Taiwan (China) have narrowed the productivity gap with the leading industrial countries by training scientists and engineers (figure 7).

Figure 7
Tertiary level students in technical fields
(percentage of population)

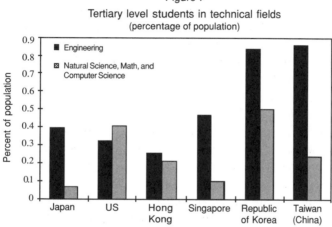

Source: UNESCO, Statistical Yearbook, 1995, Government of Taiwan, Taiwan Statistical Yearbook, 1994, Ministry of Education (Singapore)

Another policy that can promote the transfer of technology is foreign direct investment. Singapore, for example, was able to assimilate rapidly the knowledge that came from its large inflows of foreign direct investment.

Policies adopted by the technological leaders also matter. There can be a tension between the incentives to produce knowledge and the benefits from more dissemination. In recent years concern has been expressed that the balance industrial countries have struck – often under

43

pressure from special interest groups – underemphasizes dissemination. The consequences may slow the overall pace of innovation and adversely affect living standards in both richer and poorer countries.[33]

Making government more effective

How can policies be designed that increase the productivity of the economy? Again, ends must not be confused with means. The elements stressed by the Washington consensus may have been reasonable means for addressing the particular set of problems confronting the Latin American economies in the 1980s, but they may not be the only, or even the central, elements of policies aimed at addressing problems in other circumstances.

Part of the strategy for a more productive economy is ascertaining the appropriate role for government – identifying, for instance, the ways in which government can be a more effective complement to markets. I now want to turn to another essential element of public policy, namely, how we can make government more effective in accomplishing whatever tasks it undertakes.

World Development Report 1997 shows that an effective state is vital for development (World Bank, 1997c). Using data from 94 countries over three decades, the study shows that it is not just economic policies and human capital but the quality of a country's institutions that determine economic outcomes. Those institutions in effect determine the environment within which markets operate. A weak institutional environment allows greater arbitrariness on the part of state agencies and public officials.

Given very different starting points – unique histories, cultures, and societal factors – how can the state become effective? Part of the answer is that the state should match its role to its capability. What the government does, and how it does it, should reflect the capabilities of the government – and those of the private sector. Low-income countries often have weaker markets and weaker government institutions. It is especially important, therefore, that they focus on how they can most effectively complement markets.

But capability is not destiny. States can improve their capabilities by reinvigorating their institutions. This means not only building administrative or technical capacity but instituting rules and norms that provide officials with incentives to act in the collective interest while restraining arbitrary action and corruption. An independent judiciary, institutional checks and balances through the separation of powers, and effective watchdogs can all restrain arbitrary state action and corruption. Competitive wages for civil servants can attract more talented people and increase professionalism and integrity.

Perhaps some of the most promising and least explored ways to improve the function of government is to use markets and market-like mechanisms. There are several ways the government can do this:

i. It can use auctions both for procuring goods and services and for allocating public resources;
ii. It can contract out large portions of government activity;
iii. It can use performance contracting, even in those cases where contracting out does not seem feasible or desirable;
iv. It can design arrangements to make use of market information. For instance, it can rely on market judgments of qualities for its procurement (off-the-shelf procurement policies); it can use information from interest rates paid to, say, subordinated bank debt to ascertain appropriate risk premiums for deposit insurance.

At the same time, governments are more effective when they respond to the needs and interests of their citizens, while at the same time giving them a sense of ownership and stake in the policies. Michael Bruno emphasized the importance of consensus building in ending inflations. The reason for this should be obvious: if workers believe that they are not being fairly treated, they may impose inflationary wage and other demands, making the resolution of the inflationary pressures all but impossible (see Bruno, 1993).

At the microeconomic level, governments aid agencies and non-governmental organizations have been experimenting with ways of providing decentralized support and encouraging community participation in the selection, design, and implementation of projects. Recent research provides preliminary support for this approach: a study by Isham, Narayan and Pritchett (1995) found the success rate for rural water projects that involved participation was substantially higher than the success rate for those that did not. It is not just that localized information.

is brought to bear in a more effective way; but the commitment to the project leads to the long-term support (or "ownership" in the popular vernacular) which is required for sustainability.

BROADENING THE GOALS OF DEVELOPMENT

The Washington consensus advocated use of a small set of instruments (including macroeconomic stability, liberalized trade, and privatization) to achieve a relatively narrow goal (economic growth). The post-Washington consensus recognizes both that a broader set of instruments is necessary and that our goals are also much broader. We seek increases in living standards – including improved health and education – not just increases in measured GDP. We seek sustainable development, which includes preserving natural resources and maintaining a healthy environment. We seek equitable development, which ensures that all groups in society, not just those at the top, enjoy the fruits of development. And we seek democratic development, in which citizens participate in a variety of ways in making the decisions that affect their lives.

Knowledge has not kept pace with this proliferation of goals. We are only beginning to understand the relationship between democratization, inequality, environmental protection and growth. What we do know holds out the promise of developing complementary strategies that can move us toward meeting all of these objectives. But we must recognize that not all policies will contribute to all objectives. Many policies entail tradeoffs. It is important to recognize these tradeoffs and make choices about priorities. Concentrating solely on "win-win" policies can lead policymakers to ignore important decisions about "win-lose" policies.

Achieving multiple goals by improving education

Promoting human capital is one example of a policy that can help promote economic development, equality, participation and democracy. In East Asia universal education created a more egalitarian society, facilitating the political stability that is a precondition for successful long-term economic development. Education – especially education that emphasizes critical, scientific thinking – can also help train citizens to participate more effectively and more intelligently in public decisions.

Achieving multiple goals through joint implementation of environmental policy

To minimize global climate change, the nations of the world need to reduce the production of greenhouse gases, especially carbon dioxide, which is produced primarily by combustion. The reduction of carbon emissions is truly a global problem. Unlike air pollution (associated with sulfur dioxide or nitrogen dioxide), which primarily affects the polluting country, all carbon emissions enter the atmosphere, producing global consequences that affect the planet as a whole.

Joint implementation gives industrial countries (or companies within them) credit for emissions reductions they would not otherwise have undertaken anywhere in the world. It may be a feasible first step toward designing an efficient system of emission reductions because it requires commitments only from industrial countries and therefore does not entail resolving the huge distributional issues involved either in systems of tradable permits or the undertaking of obligations by developing countries.

The premise of joint implementation is that the marginal cost of carbon reductions may differ markedly in different countries. Because developing countries are typically less energy efficient than industrial countries, the marginal cost of carbon reduction in developing countries may be substantially lower than in industrial countries. The World Bank has offered to set up a carbon investment fund that would allow countries and companies that need to reduce emissions to invest in carbon-reducing projects in developing countries. For developing countries this plan would offer increased investment flows and pro-environment technology transfers. These projects would also be likely to reduce the collateral environmental damage caused by dirty air. Joint implementation allows industrial countries to reduce carbon emissions at a lower cost. This strategy is designed to benefit the developing countries as it improves the global environment.

Recognizing the tradeoffs involved in investing in technology

One important example of a potential tradeoff is investment in technology. Earlier I discussed the way investments in tertiary technical education promote the transfer of technology and thus economic growth. The direct beneficiaries of these investments, however, are almost inevitably better off than average. The result is thus likely to be increased inequality.

The transfer of technology may also increase inequality. Although some innovations benefit the worst off, much technological progress raises the marginal products of those who are already more productive. Even when it does not, the opportunity cost of public investment in technology might be forgone investment in anti-poverty programs. By increasing output, however, these investments can benefit the entire society. The potential trickle down, however, is not necessarily rapid or comprehensive.

Recognizing the tradeoff between protecting the environment and increasing participation

A second example of a tradeoff is the choice between environmental goals and participation. Participation is essential. It is not, however, a substitute for expertise. Studies have shown, for instance, that popular views on the ranking of various environmental health risks are uncorrelated with the scientific evidence (United States Environmental Protection Agency, 1987; Slovic, Layman and Flynn, 1993). In pursuing environmental policies, do we seek to make people feel better about their environment, or do we seek to reduce real environmental health hazards? There is a delicate balance here, but at the very least, more dissemination of knowledge can result in more effective participation in formulating more effective policies.

CONCLUDING REMARKS

The goal of the Washington consensus was to provide a formula for creating a vibrant private sector and stimulating economic growth. In retrospect the policy recommendations were highly risk-averse – they were based on the desire to avoid the worst disasters. Although the Washington consensus provided some of the foundations for well-functioning markets, it was incomplete and sometimes even misleading.

The World Bank's East Asian miracle project was a significant turning point in the discussion. It showed that the stunning success of the

48

East Asian economies depended on much more than just macroeconomic stability or privatization. Without a robust financial system – which the government plays a huge role in creating and maintaining – it is difficult to mobilize savings or allocate capital efficiently. Unless the economy is competitive, the benefits of free trade and privatization will be dissipated in rent seeking, not directed toward wealth creation. And if public investment in human capital and technology transfers is insufficient, the market will not fill the gap.

Many of these ideas – and more still that I have not had time to discuss – are the basis of what I see as an emerging consensus, a post-Washington consensus consensus. One principle that emerges from these ideas is that whatever the new consensus is, it cannot be based on Washington. If policies are to be sustainable, developing countries must claim ownership of them. It is relatively easier to monitor and set conditions for inflation rates and current account balances. Doing the same for financial sector regulation or competition policy is neither feasible nor desirable.

A second principle of the emerging consensus is that a greater degree of humility is called for, acknowledgment of the fact that we do not have all of the answers. Continued research and discussion, not just between the World Bank and the International Monetary Fund but throughout the world, is essential if we are to better understand how to achieve our many goals.

NOTES

1. There are, to be sure, many other dimensions to the turmoil. Misguided foreign exchange policies and the potential for political instability are a few other significant issues that I discuss at more length in Stiglitz (1998).
2. Argentina, for example, had a deficit of over five per cent of GDP in 1982 and seven per cent in 1983, Colombia's budget deficit was over four per cent from 1982 to 1984, and Brazil's deficit increased from 11 per cent in 1985 to 16 per cent by 1989 (World Bank, 1997d).
3. See Vickers and Yarrow (1988) for a fuller discussion of privatization, competition and incentives.
4. These issues came up in the management of the US economy. Although much research showed that the United States was able to operate at lower levels of unemployment without an acceleration of inflation, reports from some international institutions, using oversimplified models of the US economy, recommended tightening monetary policy. Had this advice been followed, the remarkable economic expansion, and the resulting low unemployment rate, which has brought marginalized groups into the labor force, reduced poverty and contributed

substantially to the reduction of welfare rolls, would all have been thwarted (see Chapter 2 of the *Economic Report of the President* 1997 for some of this analysis).

5. Because the level and variability of inflation are correlated, Fischer reported great difficulty in disentangling their separate effects at any level/variance of inflation. This point holds true generally: any study of the consequences of inflation probably also picks up costs associated with the variability of inflation. The strength of nonlinearity in the relationship between inflation and social welfare is clear from the outcome of research conducted by the US Federal Reserve Bank. Despite the efforts of their first-rate economists – some of them working full time on the costs of inflation – the Fed has still failed to find definitive evidence of costs of inflation in the United States. Should they eventually succeed in finding such results, they will have proven only that data mining works, not that inflation is costly.

6. Stiglitz (1997c) discusses the evidence in the United States. Tentative research at the World Bank discussed in Stiglitz (1997a) extends the results to a number of other countries, including Australia, Canada, France, Germany, Italy, Japan and Brazil. Mexico was the only country with adequate data to run the tests where the Phillips curve appeared convex.

7. Some have argued that central banks should have an exclusive mandate to maintain price stability. This perspective has even been introduced into IMF programs in economies such as Korea with no history of an inflation problem. There is no evidence that such constraints (whether embodied in legislation or formal commitments such as inflation targets) improve real economic performance as measured by growth (see Alesina and Summers, 1993). Such results are consistent with the earlier empirical evidence concerning the real effects of inflation. More importantly, these issues involve fundamental political judgments, values, and trade-offs in addition to technical expertise. For example, I – as well as most other members of the Clinton Administration's economics team – strongly opposed proposals to change the charter of the Federal Reserve Board to make price stability its primary or sole mandate. Such proposals might well have been the center of a major political debate if they had been pushed. See Stiglitz (1997a) for a broader discussion of these issues.

8. The theoretical literature on Ricardian equivalence (Barro, 1974) criticizes the view that the deficit by itself has significant economic effects. The Washington consensus was not based on models that explicitly addressed the issue of Ricardian equivalence.

9. Easterly and Fischer (1990) summarize the simple analytics of the macroeconomic effects of government budget deficits.

10. I use the terms optimum and sustainable loosely. In this context, "sustainable" does not necessarily mean "sustained" at a high level indefinitely. Rather, it refers to situations such as when large deficits are used to stimulate the economy out of an economic downturn expected to be of short duration. "Optimum" has to be defined relative to a clearly articulated objective such as maximizing in an intertemporal social welfare function. There are circumstances and reasonable social welfare functions that give markedly different values for today's optimal level of deficit – one cannot assert that desirable level of deficit without knowing both factors. The same observation applies to the following discussion of the optimal level of the current account deficit.

11. The current account deficit is an endogenous variable. Assessing whether it is too "high" depends on the source of its size. If, for example, misguided foreign exchange policies account for the deficit, it is too high.

50

12. Traditional government macro-policies focus on aggregates such as capital flows and budget deficits and do not deal directly with these issues. If the maturity structure of foreign borrowing leads to significant risks, other capital restraints or interventions may be necessary.

13. There are also other channels through which economic downturns leave a longer term adverse legacy: the attrition of human capital has, for instance, been emphasized in the literature on the hysteresis effect and may be a factor in the sustained high levels of unemployment in Europe (see Blanchard and Summers, 1987). As I discuss in the following section, economic downturns, when severe enough, can undermine the strength of the financial system.

14. In the Great Depression, falling prices combined with fixed interest payments reduced firms' net cash flows, eroding net worth, and decreasing their investment and further weakening the economy. As a result, these models are sometimes called debt-deflation models. See Greenwald and Stiglitz (1988, 1993a, 1993b).

15. The term "constrained Pareto efficient" means that there are (in principle) government interventions which can make some people better off without making anyone else worse off, which respect the imperfections of information and the incompleteness of markets – and more broadly, the costs of offsetting these imperfections.

16. For a fuller discussion of the role of these protections as part of the basic architecture of modern capitalism, see Greenwald and Stiglitz (1992).

17. This is sometimes referred to as the problem of moral hazard.

18. Supporters of these policies, while recognizing these problems, argue that a temporary increase in interest rates is required to restore confidence and that as long as the interest rate measures are very short-term, little damage will be done. Whether increases in interest rates will, or should, restore confidence has been much debated. The evidence from the recent experience is not fully supportive. Thailand and Indonesia have been pursuing high-interest rate policies since summer 1997.

19. Most analyses of the US savings and loan crisis place the ultimate blame on the unexpectedly large increases in interest rates that began in the late 1970s under Fed Chairman Paul Volcker. This increase in interest rates caused the value of their assets to plunge, leaving many with low or negative net worth. Attempts to allow individual savings and loans to try to solve their own problems (part of regulatory forbearance) failed, worsening the eventual debacle.

20. There is another reason that government should perhaps be more sensitive to interest rate changes than to exchange rate changes: while there is an economic logic to maturity mismatches, there is no corresponding justification for exchange rate mismatches. There is a real cost associated with forcing firms to reduce maturity mismatches. Exchange rate mismatches, in contrast, simply represent speculative behavior. In practice, policy cannot rely on these general nostrums but needs to look carefully at the situation within the country in crisis. It is possible that currency mismatches are far larger than maturity mismatches, and while future actions might be directed at correcting such speculation with its systemic effects, current policy must deal with the realities of today.

21. The persistence of the inflationary effects of a devaluation raise subtle questions. Earlier I argued against the "precipice" theory of inflation. One might argue that an increase in the price level associated with a devaluation is even less likely to give rise to inflation inertia than other sources of increases in prices, particularly when there may be a perception that the exchange rate has overshot.

51

22. Advocates of import substitution point out that during certain periods countries that pursued protectionist policies, notably Brazil and Taiwan (China) in the 1950s, did achieve strong economic growth.
23. The adverse effects associated with protectionism may come more from its impact on competition and its inducement to rent-seeking behavior. These forces are so strong that even when there might be seemingly strong arguments for trade interventions in particular cases, most economists view intervention in trade policy with considerable skepticism.
24. Short-term impacts on deficits were, however, often markedly different from the long-term impacts. In those cases where the state enterprises were reasonably well run, the latter could be negligible or even negative while the former could be substantial. In response, some governments disallowed the inclusion of capital transactions in the annual budget – an accounting practice consistent with views that such public sector financial reorganization may have little impact on macro-behavior, or at least far different effects.
25. This can be thought of either as a movement toward the production possibilities curve or as an outward shift of the production possibilities curve (a "technological improvement", where the curve has embedded in it the institutional constraints reflecting how production and distribution is organized).
26. Lester Thurow has noted that, "if the [anti-dumping] law were applied to domestic firms, 18 out of the top 20 firms in Fortune 500 would have been found guilty of dumping in 1982." (Thurow, 1985, p.359.)
27. See Stiglitz (1989) for an extended discussion of the economic role of the state from this perspective.
28. The US government, for example, established a national mortgage system, which lowered borrowing costs and made mortgages available to millions of Americans. Having done so, however, it may be time for this activity to be turned over to the private sector.
29. Mankiw, Romer and Weil (1992).
30. While more recent studies (Young, 1994, for example) have questioned the robustness of these results and some growth accounting exercises for the United States suggest little increase in total factor productivity growth over the past quarter century, the observation that changes in technology have played a major role in improvements in standards of living seems uncontroversial.
31. The innovator will be reluctant to describe his innovation to a provider of capital, lest he steal his idea; but the provider of capital will be reluctant to supply capital without an adequate disclosure. A clear regulatory structure for protecting intellectual property rights is necessary, but not sufficient, to overcome these sorts of problems.
32. There may also be an absence of complementary factors, such as the conditions required for new enterprises to develop to use these skills.
33. Knowledge is a key input into the production of knowledge; an increase in the "price" of knowledge (as a result of stricter intellectual property standards) may thereby reduce the production of knowledge. There is also a concern that an excessive amount of expenditures on research are directed at trying to convert "common knowledge" into a form that can be appropriated. While in principle "novelty" standards are intended to guard against this, in practice the line is never perfectly clear, and stricter intellectual property regimes are more likely to commit "errors" of privatizing public knowledge, thereby creating incentives for misdirecting intellectual energies in that direction.

REFERENCES

Akerlof, George, William Dickens and George Perry. 1996. "The Macroeconomics of Low Inflation." *Brookings Papers on Economic Activity* 1: 1–76.

Alesina, Alberto, and Larry Summers. 1993. "Central Bank Independence and Macroeconomic Performance: Some Comparative Evidence." *Journal of Money Credit and Banking.* 25 (2), May.

Ashenfelter, Orley, and Alan Krueger. 1994. "Estimates of Economic Returns to Schooling from a New Sample of Twins." *American Economic Review* (December).

Barro, Robert. 1974. "Are Government Bonds Net Wealth?" *Journal of Political Economy* 81(6): 1095–1117.

Blanchard, Olivier' and Larry Summers. 1986. "Hysteresis and the European Unemployment Problem." In Stanley Fischer, ed., *NBER Macroeconomics Annual*, vol. 1. Cambridge: MIT Press.

Bruno, Michael. 1993. *Crisis, Stabilization and Economic Reform: Therapy by Consensus.* Oxford: Clarendon Press.

Bruno, Michael' and William Easterly. 1996. "Inflation and Growth: In Search of a Stable Relationship." *Federal Reserve Bank of St Louis Review* 78(3): 139–46.

Caprio, Gerard. 1997. "Safe and Sound Banking in Developing Countries: We're Not in Kansas Anymore." *Research in Financial Services: Private and Public Policy* 9: 79–97.

Caprio, Gerard, and Daniela Klingebiel. 1996. "Bank Insolvencies: Cross-Country Experience." World Bank Policy Research Working Paper 1620. Washington, DC

———. 1997. "Bank Insolvency: Bad Luck, Bad Policy, or Bad Banking?" In Michael Bruno and Boris Pleskovic, eds., *Annual World Bank Conference on Development Economics 1996.* Washington, DC: World Bank.

Caves, Douglas, and Laurits Christensen. 1980. "The Relative Efficiency of Public and Private Firms in a Competitive Environment: The Case of Canadian Railroads." *Journal of Political Economy* 88 (5): 958–76.

Demirgüç-Kunt, Asli, and Enrica Detragiache. 1997. "The Determinants of Banking Crises: Evidence from Industrial and Developing

Countries." World Bank Policy Research Working Paper 1828. Washington, DC

Easterly, William, Carlos Rodriguez and Klaus Schmidt-Hebbel, eds. 1994. *Public Sector Deficits and Macroeconomic Performance*. Washington, D.C.: World Bank.

Easterly, William and Stanley Fischer. 1990. "The Economics of the Government Budget Constraint." *World Bank Research Observer* 5(2): 127–42.

Edlin, Aaron and Joseph E. Stiglitz. 1995. "Discouraging Rivals: Managerial Rent-Seeking and Economic Inefficiencies." *American Economic Review* 85(5): 1301–12.

Feldstein, Martin. 1996. "The Costs and Benefits of Going from Low Inflation to Price Stability." NBER Working Paper 5469. Cambridge, Mass.: National Bureau of Economic Research.

Fischer, Stanley. 1993. "The Role of Macroeconomic Factors in Growth." *Journal of Monetary Economics* 32: 485–512.

Greenwald, Bruce, and Joseph E. Stiglitz. 1986. "Externalities in Markets with Imperfect Information and Incomplete Markets." *Quarterly Journal of Economics* 101(May): 229–64.

——. 1988. "Examining Alternative Macroeconomic Theories." *Brookings Papers on Economic Activity* 1: 207–70.

——. 1992. "Information, Finance and Markets: The Architecture of Allocative Mechanisms." *Industrial and Corporate Change* 1(1): 37–63.

——. 1993a. "Financial Market Imperfections and Business Cycles." *Quarterly Journal of Economics* 108(1): 77–114.

——. 1993b. "New and Old Keynesians." *Journal of Economic Perspectives* 7(1): 23–44.

Isham, Jonathan, Deepa Narayan and Lant Pritchett. 1995. "Does Participation Improve Performance? Establishing Causality with Subjective Data." *World Bank Economic Review* 9(2): 175–200.

Kane, Thomas, and Cecilia Rouse. 1995. "Labor Market Returns to Two- and Four-Year College: Is a Credit a Credit and Do Degrees Matter?" *American Economic Review* 85(3): 600–14.

Mankiw, N. Gregory, David Romer and David N. Weil. 1992. "A Contribution to the Empirics of Economic Growth." *Quarterly Journal of Economics* 107, 2 (May): 407–37.

Nadiri, Ishaq. 1993. "Innovations and Technological Spillovers." NBER

Working Paper 4423. Cambridge, Mass.: National Bureau of Economic Research.

Pannier, Dominique, ed. 1996. *Corporate Governance of Public Enterprises in Transitional Economies*. World Bank Technical Paper 323. Washington, DC.

Pritchett, Lant. 1997. "Patterns of Economic Growth: Hills, Plateaus, Mountains, Cliffs and Plains." World Bank, Policy Research Department. Washington, DC.

Psacharopoulos, George. 1994. "Returns to Investment in Education: A Global Update." *World Development* 22(9): 1325–43.

Rey, Patrick, and Joseph E. Stiglitz. 1993. "Short-term Contracts as a Monitoring Device." NBER Working Paper 4514. Cambridge, Mass.: National Bureau of Economic Research.

Sappington, David, and Joseph E. Stiglitz. 1987. "Privatization, Information and Incentives." *Journal of Policy Analysis and Management* 6(4): 567–82.

Shleifer, Andrei, and Robert Vishny. 1989. "Management Entrenchment: The Case of Manager-Specific Investments." *Journal of Financial Economics* 25(1): 123–39.

Slovic, Paul, Mark Layman and James Flynn. 1993. "Perceived Risk, Trust and Nuclear Waste: Lessons from Yucca Mountain." In R. Dunlap, M. Kraft and E. Rosa, eds., *Public Reactions to Nuclear Waste*. Durham, N.C.: Duke University Press.

Solow, Robert. 1957. "Technical Change and the Aggregate Production Function." *Review of Economics and Statistics* (August).

Stiglitz, Joseph E. 1989. "The Economic Role of the State: Efficiency and Effectiveness." In A. Heertje, ed., *The Economic Role of the State*. London: Basil Blackwell and Bank Insinger de Beaufort NV.

———. 1993. "The Role of the State in Financial Markets." In *Proceedings of the World Bank Conference on Development Economics 1993*. Washington, D.C.: World Bank.

———. 1994a. "Endogenous Growth and Cycles." In Y. Shionoya and M. Perlman, eds., *Innovation in Technology, Industries and Institution*. Ann Arbor, Mich.: University of Michigan Press.

———. 1994b. *Whither Socialism?* Cambridge, Mass.: MIT Press.

———. 1996. "Some Lessons of the East Asian Miracle." *World Bank Research Observer* 11(2): 151–77.

——. 1997a. "Central Banking in a Democratic Society." The Tinbergen Lecture.

——. 1997b. "Dumping on Free Trade: The US Import Trade Laws." *Southern Economic Journal* 64(2), 402–24.

——. 1997c. "Reflections on the Natural Rate Hypothesis." *Journal of Economic Perspectives* 11(1): 3–10.

——. 1998. "The Role of International Institutions in the Current Global Economy." Speech to the Council on Foreign Relations in Chicago, 27 February 1998.

Thurow, Lester. 1985. *The Zero-Sum Solution: Building a World-Class American Economy.* New York: Simon and Schuster.

United States Council of Economic Advisers. 1997. *Economic Report of the President 1997.* Washington, DC: Government Printing Office.

United States Environmental Protection Agency. 1987. *Unfinished Business: A Comparative Assessment of Environmental Problems.* Washington, DC: GPO.

Vickers, John, and George Yarrow. 1988. *Privatization: An Economic Analysis.* Cambridge: MIT Press.

Williamson, John. 1990. "What Washington Means by Policy Reform." In John Williamson, ed., *Latin American Adjustment: How Much Has Happened?* Washington, DC: Institute for International Economics.

Willis, Robert. 1986. "Wage Determinants: A Survey and Reinterpretation of Human Capital Earnings Functions." In Orley Ashenfelter and Richard Layard, eds., *Handbook of Labor Economics Volume I.* Amsterdam: Elsevier Science Publishers/North-Holland.

World Bank. 1993. *The East Asian Miracle.* New York: Oxford University Press.

——. 1997a. *China 2020.* Washington, DC.

——. 1997b. *Global Economic Prospects and the Developing Countries.* Washington, DC.

——. 1997c. *World Development Report 1997: The State in a Changing World.* New York: Oxford University Press.

——. 1997d. *World Development Indicators 1997.* Washington DC

Young, Alwyn. 1994. "The Tyranny of Numbers: Confronting the Statistical Realities of the East Asian Growth Experience." *Quarterly Journal of Economics* 110 (August): 641–80.

Chapter 2

Towards a New Paradigm for Development: Strategies, Policies and Processes

The 1998 Prebisch Lecture at UNCTAD
Geneva, October 1998

In an address to the World Institute for Development Economics Research (WIDER) in Helsinki at the beginning of this year [Ch.1 of this volume – *Ed*.], I argued that we needed to go beyond the Washington consensus: there were broader objectives to development than were embodied in that consensus, the set of policy recommendations upon which it focused was certainly not sufficient for development, and indeed some of the most successful developers had paid little heed to its dicta. That consensus all too often confused means with ends: it took privatization and trade liberalization as ends in themselves, rather than as means to more sustainable, equitable and democratic growth. I talked there about many of the ways in which the Washington consensus had gone astray. It focused too much on price stability, rather than growth and the stability of output. It failed to recognize that strengthening financial institutions is every bit as important to economic stability as controlling budget deficits and increasing the money supply. It focused on privatization, but paid too little attention to the institutional infrastructure that is required to make markets work, and especially to the importance of competition.

In today's lecture, I want to go beyond these by now well-documented failures of the Washington consensus to begin providing the foundations of an alternative paradigm, especially one relevant to the least developing country. It is based on a broad conception of development, with a concomitantly broader vision of development strategies and a quite different perspective on the role of international assistance and the ways in which it should be delivered. The remainder of this lecture is organized around five parts. First, I shall describe this broader vision. Second, I shall explain why not only the Washington consensus, but earlier development paradigms, failed: they viewed development too narrowly. I shall outline briefly some of the key factors – beyond the most recent events to which I have briefly alluded – that have helped us realize the inadequacies of the old approaches. Third, I shall outline what I refer to as the key principles of the *new development strategy* based on this broader vision of development. Fourth, I shall outline the major components of what I call the new development strategies. And fifth, I shall conclude with some general observations, focusing on the importance of trade and the work of UNCTAD in furthering development based on this new paradigm.

I. DEVELOPMENT AS A TRANSFORMATION OF SOCIETY

Development represents a *transformation* of society, a movement from traditional relations, traditional ways of thinking, traditional ways of dealing with health and education, traditional methods of production, to more "modern" ways. For instance, a characteristic of traditional societies is the acceptance of the world as it is; the modern perspective recognizes change, it recognizes that we, as individuals and societies, can take actions that, for instance, reduce infant mortality, increase lifespans and increase productivity. Key to these changes is the movement to "scientific" ways of thinking, identifying critical variables that affect outcomes, attempting to make inferences based on available data, recognizing what we know and what we do not know.

All societies are a blend. Even in more "advanced" societies there are sectors and regions that remain wedded to traditional modes of operation, and people wedded to traditional ways of thinking. But while in more advanced societies, these constitute a relatively small proportion, in less advanced societies, they may predominate. Indeed, one characteristic of many less developed countries is the failure of the more advanced sectors to penetrate deeply into society, resulting in what many have called "dual" economies in which more advanced production methods may co-exist with very primitive technologies.

Change is not an end in itself, but a means to other objectives. The changes that are associated with development provide individuals and societies more control over their own destiny. Development enriches the lives of individuals by widening their horizons and reducing their sense of isolation. It reduces the afflictions brought on by disease and poverty, not only increasing lifespans, but improving the vitality of life.

Given this definition of development, it is clear that a development strategy must be aimed at facilitating the transformation of society, in identifying the barriers as well as potential catalysts for change. These notes outline some of the ingredients of such a new development strategy. It is organized around three themes. The first outlines the need for a new development strategy, both the failures of past conceptions and the changes in the world which lead to the necessity of a new conception. The second defines the two critical roles of a new development strategy, catalyzing change and transforming *whole* societies. The third outlines some of the key ingredients of the new development strategy, including the role of the aid donors.

II. THE NEED FOR A NEW DEVELOPMENT STRATEGY

The experience of the past 50 years has demonstrated that development is possible, but not inevitable. While a few countries have succeeded in rapid economic growth, narrowing the gap between themselves and the more advanced country, and bring millions of their citizens out of poverty, many more countries have actually seen that gap grow and poverty increase, so that today the number of people living in poverty – even measured by the minimal standard of a dollar a day – is about 1.3 billion. Strategies of the past, even when they have been assiduously followed, have not guaranteed success. Furthermore, many of the most successful countries (representing the largest part of growth within the low income countries) have not actually followed the "recommended" strategies, but have carved out paths of their own.

WHAT DEVELOPMENT IS NOT: A CRITIQUE OF PREVIOUS CONCEPTIONS

Many previous development strategies have focused on pieces of this transformation, but because they have failed to see the broader context, they have failed, and often miserably. Most of these have focused narrowly on *economics*. Economics is important: after all, one of the features which distinguishes more developed from less developed countries is their higher GDP per capita. But the focus on economics has confused not only means with ends, but also cause with effect. It has confused means with ends because higher GDP is not an end in itself, but a means to improved living standards and a better society, with less poverty, better health and improved education. By and large, increases in GDP per capita are accompanied by reductions in poverty. It has confused cause with effect because, to some extent, the changes in society which may be called *modernization* are as much a cause of the increases in GDP as a result.

For instance, the development programming models that were popular in the 1960s saw development as simply solving a complicated dynamic programming problem, which would improve the efficiency of the allocation of resources, plus the accumulation of capital (either through the transfer from abroad or through higher savings rates at home). Except for possible inefficiencies in resource allocations (which would be resolved by the dynamic programming problem) and the lack of capital, less developed countries were portrayed as identical to more developed countries.

The same fallacy pervaded the philosophies of the 1970s and 1980s, even though the new approaches saw the problem of development somewhat differently. The central role that government played in the planning/programming approaches was seen as part of the *problem* of development, rather than as part of the *solution*. Governments claimed for themselves too large a role, even though they were intrinsically unsuited for it. Not only did they lack the capabilities, but incentives in the political process ensured that whatever capabilities they had were often directed not at increasing national production, but at diverting rents to the politically powerful. The solution, in this perspective, was reliance on markets, and in particular the elimination of government-imposed distortions associated with protectionism, government subsidies, and government ownership. In the 1980s, the focus shifted to macroeconomic problems, to "adjustment" to fiscal imbalances and misguided monetary policies. Given the macroeconomic imbalances, it was impossible for markets to function, or at least function well.

Notice that all three of these development strategies saw development as a *technical* problem requiring technical solutions – better planning algorithms, better trade and pricing policies, better macroeconomic frameworks. They did not reach deep down into society, nor did they believe such a participatory approach was necessary. The laws of economics were universal: demand and supply curves and the fundamental theorems of welfare economies applied as well to Africa and Asia as they did to Europe and North America. These scientific laws were not bound by time or space, in their view, which made the technical approach an appropriate one.

The lessons of history

As remarkable as the narrow focus of these approaches was their ahistoric context. They failed to recognize that: (a) successful development efforts in the United States as well as many other countries had involved an active role for government; (b) many societies in the decades before active government involvement – or interference, as these doctrines would put it – failed to develop; indeed, development was the exception around the world, not the rule; and (c) worse still, capitalist economies before the era of greater government involvement were characterized not only by high levels of economic instability, but also by widespread social/ economic problems; large groups, such as the aged and the unskilled, were often left out of any progress and were left destitute in the economic crashes that occurred with such regularity.

Indeed, one of the puzzles that these narrow approaches ignored was the failure of certain regions within seemingly developed countries to develop, such as the south of Italy. No trade barriers separated the north from the south; the overall macroeconomic framework in both regions was the same; and the south even benefited from economic policies specifically designed to encourage it. Yet while the north boomed, the south stagnated. This by itself should have suggested that there was more to development than acknowledge by the technical approaches.

DEFINING EVENTS

Three events of the past quarter-century are beginning to shape views concerning development strategies.

61

Collapse of the socialist/communist economies and the end of the Cold War

The first event is the collapse of the socialist/communist economies and the end of the Cold War. Some have focused on a single lesson that emerges – the inefficacy (and dangers) of a large government role in the economy. From this, some jump to the opposite conclusion: that reliance should be placed on markets. But there are two broader implications of the end of the Cold War: the ideological debates should be over; there should be agreement that while markets are at the center of the economy, governments must play an important role. The issue is one of balance, and *where that balance is may depend on the country, the capacity of its government, the institutional development of its markets.* In other words, development advice should be adapted to the circumstances of the country.

But the failure of the communist system was as much a failure of the political and social order on which it was based as of the economic system itself. The economic models that showed the equivalence between market socialism and capitalist economies were fundamentally misguided, partly because they did not grasp the role of institutions (beyond abstract markets) in the economy, but partly because they did not grasp the importance of the interface between the economy, narrowly defined, and society more generally.

The limitations of the Washington consensus

The second defining event was that many countries followed the dicta of liberalization, stabilization and privatization, the central premises of the so-called Washington consensus, and still did not grow. The technical solutions were evidently not enough. This should not have come as a surprise; as I noted before, history was not encouraging. Moreover, developments in theoretical economics, many of which emphasized the limitations of the market, should have served to provide insights into both the historical as well as these more recent "market failures."

One prominent example of the limitations of the consensus is provided by Russia, the fuse that set off the most recent financial turmoil in world markets. In many ways, the problems there seem of a very different nature from those in East Asia, which I will discuss in a moment: in Russia, we see an economy in transition facing huge government deficits and severe political problems. Yet there are some common threads. In both cases, the Washington consensus failed, and for similar reasons: a failure to understand the subtleties of the market economy, to understand that private property and "getting prices rights" (that is, liberalization) are not sufficient to make a market economy work. An economy needs an institutional infrastructure. While the banks in East Asia lacked adequate supervision, the banks in Russia not only lacked that supervision; they did not even perform their core function of providing capital to new and growing enterprises. We all know that the standard theorems of economics emphasize that an economy needs both private property and competition. The Washington consensus, while occasionally paying lip service to the latter, placed its emphasis on the former, thinking that with private property, at least owners would have an incentive to increase efficiency. Worries about distribution and competition – or even concerns about democratic processes being undermined by excessive concentration of wealth – could be addressed later! Russia did succeed in turning ordinary economic laws on their head, in that it managed to reverse the usual tradeoffs between equity and efficiency. Reforms such as moving from inefficient central planning to decentralized pricing mechanism, from inefficient state ownership to private property and the profit motive, should have increased output, even if perhaps at the price of a slight increase in inequality. Instead, Russia achieved a huge increase in inequality, at the same time that it managed to shrink the economy, by up to a third according to some estimates. Living standards collapsed with GDP statistics, as life spans were shortened and health worsened. All too late, it was recognized that without the right institutional infrastructure, the profit motive – combined with full capital market liberalization – could fail to provide incentives for wealth creation and could instead spark a drive to strip assets and ship wealth abroad.

The East Asian miracle

The third defining event was the East Asian miracle: the rapid growth of the countries of East Asia showed that development was possible, and that successful development could be accompanied by a reduction of poverty, widespread improvements in living standards, and even a process of democratization. But for those advocating the technical solutions, the East Asian miracle countries were deeply disturbing. For these countries did not follow the standard prescriptions. In most cases, government played a large role. They followed some of the standard technical prescriptions, such as (by and large) stable macroeconomic policies, but ignored others. For example, rather than privatizing, government actually started some highly productive steel mills, and more generally pursued industrial policies to promote particular sectors. Governments intervened in trade, though more to promote exports than to inhibit particular imports. And governments regulated financial markets, engaging in mild financial restraint, lowering interest rates and increasing profitability of banks and firms (as opposed to financial repression, which results in negative real interest rates). Many of the policies on which the governments focused were simply areas that had been ignored in the past; these included, for example, the heavy emphasis on education and technology, on closing the knowledge gap between them and the more advanced countries. While the impact of individual policies remains a subject of dispute, the mix of policies clearly worked well. Perhaps had these countries followed all of the dictums of liberalization and privatization, they would have grown even faster, but there is little evidence for that proposition. In some cases, such as financial restraint, there is some evidence – as well as a considerable body of theory – that suggests that these policies did enhance growth.

But perhaps the most important lesson of East Asia was that, to a large extent, they succeeded in a transformation of their societies, a fact that is evident to any visitor to the region. To be sure, the transformation is far from complete: witness the sectors in several of these countries that exhibit rigidities and have failed to adopt modern technologies and modes of business. And the crisis facing East Asia today has raised questions in many circles concerning the East Asia miracle. Yet the fact of the *transformation* remains; and even if these countries face a few years of zero or even negative growth, their per capita GDP as they enter the twenty-first century will be a multiple of what it was a half-century ago, and far higher than those of countries that have pursued alternative development strategies. Equally important, poverty rates will be a fraction of what they were a half century ago, though undoubtedly higher than at the beginning of the decade. Literacy will remain near-universal, and health standards will remain high. A careful reading of the East Asian experience over the last several decades – of what strategies led to those remarkable achievements – will reveal that many of the views reflected here were incorporated in the development strategies of the fastest developers.

The East Asia crisis

This is not the place for an extended exegesis either of the crisis' cause or its depth, and I have spoken extensively about these matters elsewhere. Nevertheless, there are important lessons to be learned from the crisis concerning the design of development strategies. These lessons have not been completely lost on the world over the past year, even if they have at times become, in my view, somewhat muddled.

To show how views about development have begun to change because of the crisis, it is worth thinking back to 1997. How much the world has changed in but a short year! A little more than a year ago, in Hong Kong, there was a debate about extending the IMF charter to include a mandate for capital market liberalization. Critics of hedge funds were seen as financial Luddites who wished to reverse the course of history and the inevitable domination of free markets. Countries that encountered economic problems were widely chastised for failing to follow the dictates of the physicians of the modern market economy: they had failed to regulate their financial institutions, they were guilty of crony capitalism, they lacked transparency, they lacked governments that were committed to reform.

Now, a year later, we see things from a more balanced perspective. Yes, good financial institutions are important, and all countries should strive to strengthen their institutions. Yes, transparency is important, not only for the effective working of the economy, but also for there to be meaningful democratic governance. Yes, crony capitalism undermines not only the economy but democratic processes. Reforms in these areas are essential, and the attention that the East Asia crisis brought to these issues is one of the silver linings in the East Asia cloud. All of these issues mark gaps in the Washington consensus as traditionally applied, and hence are clearly welcome topics for discussion that the crisis helped bring to the fore. But events and analysis in the intervening year have cast a new light on many of these issues:

- We now realize that for every borrower there is a lender; and the lender is as much to blame as the borrower. Indeed, to the extent that the foreign banks were *marginal* lenders, they deserve even more of the blame: foreign lenders to Korea's highly leveraged firms (or to banks that had themselves made extensive loans to highly leveraged firms) *knew* that these enterprises debt-equity ratios were far higher than any financial analyst would have called prudent. Yet supposedly well-managed banks, supervised by supposedly sophisticated regulatory authorities, made these loans. Moreover, these loans were not driven by government pressure. Nor was there any evidence of government pressures associated with the real estate loans in Thailand. Is there a suggestion that in some countries bad loans result only from crony capitalism, while in others, they result from the natural working of market processes?

- The difficulties of regulating financial institutions (including banks) has been brought home most forcefully by the bailout of Long-Term Capital Management, the huge hedge fund which reportedly before its crash had an exposure of more than a trillion dollars. The bailout has raised a lot of questions that put a new perspective on the charges in East Asia. Did the bailout represent crony capitalism, given that one of the partners in the hedge fund was a former vice-chairman of the Federal Reserve Board? Did the regulators really not realize the size of the threat? And if so, what does this say about the supervisory capacity of supposedly the most sophisticated regulators in the world, with the longest tradition of regulation, extending for almost a century and a half? If not, what does this say about their understanding of financial markets? Or was the defense of the government role – the threat of contagion – just a cover-up? While Federal funds were allegedly not involved, did the discretionary regulatory powers provide implicit threats (of tighter supervision in the case of non-cooperation) and promises (of regulatory forbearance if the bailout proved costly)? Was there a deliberate attempt by all participants to restrict transparency, by not revealing to the market all the relevant information?

- Statistical studies have thrown doubt on many of the conventional explanations. While macroeconomic policies may not have been perfect in the crisis countries, Korea at least shows essentially no evidence of an overvalued exchange rate. Transparency on average (at least as gauged by standard measures) was no worse than in other countries that did not experience a crisis; the crisis countries of East Asia had had three decades of remarkable growth, yet, if anything, transparency had *increased* rather than decreased prior to the crisis. Moreover, the last major set of crises had occurred in countries with seemingly high levels of transparency and advanced institutional structures: the Scandinavian trio of Finland, Norway and Sweden.

- Other statistical studies suggested a different culprit: excessively rapid financial and capital market liberalization, unaccompanied by corresponding strengthening of financial regulation (which, as we have just commented, is extraordinarily difficult even in more advanced countries). And indeed, the rapidity of the change in investor sentiment, reflected in changes in risk premia, and the associated massive change in capital flows were of a speed and magnitude that few countries could have withstood. Could even the United States have withstood a change of this magnitude, which relative to its GDP would have meant a reversal in flows of $700 billion?

- The fact that today countries like Argentina, as well as other countries that have for some years followed sound economic policies, are now being battered has further undermined confidence in the international financial architecture.

These observations have reinforced a close look at the intellectual coherence and econometric evidence in support of the arguments for unfettered capital market liberalization, a position which is increasingly being recognized as being based more on ideology than on science. While the evidence concerning the risks which such liberalization brings is overwhelming, the evidence concerning the benefits is far more scanty. In a lecture I delivered in Fiesole on Thursday, I outlined not only this evidence, but also the theoretical reasons why these results should not come as a surprise. Indeed, the arguments for bailouts, as well as the presence of bailouts themselves, provide overwhelming support for the view that there may be marked discrepancies between private and social net returns to short-term capital movements. These discrepancies at the very least call for a review of feasible government actions to redress this market failure, which has imposed such huge costs on millions and millions of people (though, to be sure, some of these costs might have been reduced if the crisis-response policies had been better designed).

III. THE PRINCIPLES OF THE NEW DEVELOPMENT STRATEGY

The new development strategy takes as its core objective *development, the transformation of society*. It recognizes that an integral part of successful development is the increase in GDP per capita. But this is only part of the story, and even this will not be achieved unless the country adopts a broader development focus. If successful, the new development strategy will not only raise GDP per capita, but also living standards, as evidenced by standards of health and literacy. It will reduce poverty – our goal should be its elimination, a goal that the more successful economies have actually attained (at least by the *absolute* poverty standard). It will be sustainable, strengthening the environment and ensuring real societal transformations.

The discussion is divided into three sections: what development strategies are, and how they differ from *plans*; how we can catalyze *society-wide* change; and why *participation and ownership* are crucial.

THE CONCEPT OF DEVELOPMENT STRATEGIES

Corporations have increasingly found corporate strategies of use in guiding their thinking and longer-term investments. Development strategies need to be thought of in the same light, rather than as the detailed programming models and development plans of the past, which were derived from a core faith in central planning. Development strategies, while less detailed than these planning documents, are in many ways more ambitious, for they set out a strategy not just for the accumulation of capital and the deployment of resources, but for the transformation of society.

68

A development strategy needs to set forth the *vision* of the transformation, what the society will be like ten to twenty years from now. This vision may embrace certain quantitative goals, such as a reduction in poverty by half, or universal primary education, but these are elements in the transformation process, not the vision of the transformation itself.

This vision needs to include a view of the transformation of institutions, the creation of new social capital and new capacities, in some cases to replace traditional institutions that will inevitably be weakened in the process of development. In other cases, the new institutions will contain within them elements of the old; there will be a process of evolution and adaptation. Some of these transitions may be difficult, either to articulate or to implement: how will societies that have traditionally discriminated against women achieve a higher degree of equality at the same time that they maintain traditional values?

A development strategy has sometimes been likened to a blueprint, a map of where the society is going. But this metaphor is misleading, and understanding why helps us to see the difference between plans of the past and development strategies of the future. The development process is too difficult for us to write down today a blueprint or a map of where the economy will be going over the next ten years, let alone a quarter of a century. Doing so requires too much information, knowledge that is not currently available. In the past, planning documents have failed to take into account virtually any of the major uncertainties facing the development process. While in principle, a development plan could map out how the economy would respond to the myriad of different contingencies that might occur in the coming years, in practice this is seldom done. By contrast, a development strategy is a living document: it needs to set forth how it is to be created, revised and adopted, the process of participation, the means by which ownership and consensus is to be obtained, how the details will be fleshed out.

The development strategy fulfils several functions as it sets forth its vision for the future.

Development strategies and priorities

All societies are resource-constrained; poor countries even more so. Beyond general resource constraints are the constraints on the capacity of government, the limitations on the number of issues which it can pursue. While there are many pressing needs, it is imperative that the development strategy set priorities. A key aspect of prioritization is an awareness of sequencing: what tasks have to be done before other tasks. It may, for instance, be essential to establish a competition and regulatory framework before privatization; or it may be essential to establish a financial regulatory framework before capital market or financial sector liberalization.

Development strategies and coordination

In traditional economic theory, prices perform all the coordination that is required in an economy. But this requires a full set of markets – an assumption that patently is not satisfied in less developed countries. Having a sense of where the economy is going is essential: if, for instance, an economy is to move to the "next" stage of development, the appropriate infrastructure, human capital and institutions all have to be in place. If any of the essential ingredients is missing, the chances of success will be greatly reduced. Not only must there be coordination of different agencies within and levels of government, there must be coordination between the private sector and the public, and between various parts of the private sector.

The kind of coordination provided by the development strategy is markedly different, both in spirit and detail, from the kind envisioned (but never actually achieved) in indicative planning. While indicative planning saw itself as a substitute for missing markets, attempting to provide detailed coordination of input and output decisions of various industries, development strategies focus more on the broader vision, including entry into new technologies or new industries.

Development strategies as consensus builders

The process of constructing a development strategy may itself serve a useful function, in helping build a consensus not only about a broad vision of the country's future, and key short- and medium-term objectives, but of some of the essential ingredients for achieving those goals. Consensus-building not only is an important part of achieving political and social stability (and avoiding the economic disruption that comes when claims on a society's resources exceed the amount of available resources), but also leads to an "ownership" of policies and institutions, which in turn enhances the likelihood of their success.

CATALYSING SOCIETY-WIDE CHANGE: BEYOND ENCLAVES AND PROJECTS

If the transformation of society is at the heart of development, the question becomes how to bring these changes about. One of the major roles of the development strategy is to serve as a catalyst, for example by identifying the areas of a country's (dynamic) comparative advantage. Identifying these areas and publicizing such information is a *public good*, and as such is a responsibility of government.

Transforming whole societies

To be effective, this attempt to serve as catalyst will need to embrace the ambitious goal of encouraging *society-wide* transformation. Earlier, we noted that all too often, development efforts succeeded in transferring technology without transforming societies, in the process creating dual societies with pockets of more advanced technology but little more. In a sense, duality – in which only isolated enclaves are developed – represents a failure of the development process. Our goal is to understand in part what went wrong, why these enclaves did not serve as "growth poles", catalysts of development beyond their narrow confines.

The same could be said about many development projects. A project may be "good" in the sense that it yields high project returns, but it may have little development impact. Of course, high returns are better than low, but if benefits do not spread to the broader society, then the project cannot be judged a true success.

In some cases, the lack of development impact may result from *fungibility*: a country has a range of projects that it wishes to undertake, some with high social returns and some with low, perhaps even negative, returns (sometimes because they are designed primarily to enrich the ruling elites). The country "sells" the good projects to the aid donors,

71

which allows it to shift its own resources from those projects to others that have low social returns. Ascertaining the *additionality* associated with a project – what occurred that would not otherwise have happened – is often difficult if not impossible. But in any case, we should be aware that the marginal contribution may be far different than it appears at first blush.

Part of the government's role as a catalyst is to undertake projects that can lead to *social learning* – that is, projects from which the country can draw widely applicable lessons, for instance about the viability of an industry. The benefit of the investment is not just the direct returns from the project, but also what can be learned for other projects from its success or failure. Because these learning benefits cannot be appropriated fully by private agents, there will be too little of this kind of experimentation within the private sector. A critical aspect, then, of the government's decision to undertake a particular project should be whether it can be *scaled up*. A project that succeeds only because of massive investment of resources that could not be mobilized more generally, or only because it requires an input which is not generally available, is not a good candidate for scaling up.

To make this point more concrete, let me suggest a couple of examples. A project that provides more textbooks to a school may, for instance, be able to increase the effectiveness of that school, but if there are no resources available to provide similar textbooks to all schools, the project will have very limited development impact. By contrast, a project that develops a new curriculum, one that is better suited to the conditions of the country and motivates children and their parents more effectively, can have nationwide impact, as we have seen in Colombia. A project that demonstrates that local participation in education and local control of rural schools increases school effectiveness (as in El Salvador) can easily be replicated nationwide (or indeed, even worldwide), with limited additional resources. Indeed, such local involvement can itself be a catalyst for community-based development efforts that go beyond education. There are strong *externalities* associated with such projects. Not only do others learn *directly* from how the project itself performs, but in the process of learning to interact to address educational problems, the community learns how to deal with other issues as well, how to engage each other in a process of consensus formation. This concern with scaling up must be at the core of government's involvement with projects, if that involvement is really to have the desired transformative effect.

72

PARTICIPATION, OWNERSHIP, AND THE ROLE OF OUTSIDERS

The development strategy approach also has clear implications for where the locus of development must be, as I will explain in this section.

Why imposing change from the outside cannot work

This much seems clear: effective change cannot be imposed from outside. Indeed, the attempt to impose change from the outside is as likely to engender resistance and barriers to change as it is to facilitate change. At the heart of development is a change in ways of thinking, and individuals cannot be forced to change how they think. They can be forced to take certain actions. They can be even forced to utter certain words. But they cannot be forced to change their hearts or minds.

This point was brought home forcefully at a recent meeting of finance ministers and central bank governors from the countries of the former Soviet Union. It struck me that all could articulate perfectly the requirements of sound macro-policy, and that each announced that he subscribed to those policies 100 per cent – including those whose practices deviated markedly from the professed beliefs.

Indeed, interactions between donors and recipients may sometimes actually impede the transformation. Rather than encouraging recipients to develop their analytic capacities, the process of imposing conditionalities undermines both the incentives to acquire those capacities and recipients' confidence in their ability to use them. Rather than involving large segments of society in a process of discussing change – thereby changing their ways of thinking – excessive conditionality reinforces traditional hierarchical relationships. Rather than empowering those who could serve as catalysts for change within these society, it demonstrates their impotence. Rather than promoting the kind of open dialogue that is central to democracy, it argues at best that such dialogue is unnecessary, at worst that it is counterproductive.

73

Ownership and participation

Thus, key ingredients in a successful development strategy are *ownership* and *participation*. We have seen again and again that ownership is essential for successful transformation: policies that are imposed from outside may be grudgingly accepted on a superficial basis, but will rarely be implemented as intended. But to achieve the desired ownership and transformation, the process that leads to that strategy must be participatory. Development cannot be just a matter of negotiations between a donor and the government. Development must reach deeper. It must involve and support groups in civil society; these groups are part of the social capital that needs to be strengthened, and they give voice to often-excluded members of society, facilitating their participation and increasing ownership of the development process. By involving these groups, the process of strategy formulation may be able to elicit the commitment and long-term involvement that is necessary for development to be sustainable. Ownership and participation are also necessary if the development strategy is to be adapted to the circumstances of the country; our research shows that projects with higher levels of participation are in fact more successful, probably in part because those projects make fewer erroneous assumptions about the needs and capabilities of beneficiaries.

Outside agents, including donors, can encourage ownership through persuasion, that is, through presenting evidence, both theoretical and empirical, that particular strategies and policies are more likely to bring success than other approaches. But the degree of ownership is likely to be even greater when the strategies and policies are developed by those within the country itself, when the country itself is in the driver's seat.

Some, in their enthusiasm for ownership and participation, have implied that these participatory processes by themselves would suffice. But while individuals within a community may actively participate in discourse about what to do and how to do it, there must be more to this process than simple discourse. First, for participation to be fully meaningful, it should be based on knowledge; hence the crucial role of education. Second, merely calling for participation does not resolve the issue of *incentives*: individuals (and groups of individuals or organizations) need to be motivated to be involved. In particular, it will be difficult to sustain participation if participants sense that they are not being listened to, that their views are not taken into account in decision-making. What is required, then, is participation in a process that constructs institutional arrangements, including incentives. Institutions, incentives, participation and ownership can be viewed as complementary; none on its own is sufficient.

Participation and ownership are crucial, then, and it is clear that the involvement of outsiders cannot take the place of this local ownership. Nevertheless, as I will discuss later, outsiders do have a role in facilitating the process, and in assisting in the provision of resources and knowledge.

The need for inclusion and consensus-building

One of the obstacles to successful development has been the limited ability of some countries to resolve conflicts. The ability to resolve disputes is an important part of social and organizational capital. Reforms often bring advantage to some groups while disadvantaging others. There is likely to be greater acceptance of reforms – a greater participation in the transformation process – if there is a sense of equity, of fairness, about the development process, a sense of ownership derived from participation, and if there has been an effort at consensus formation. Numerous examples (such as Ghana) have shown the importance, for instance, of consensus formation in achieving macroeconomic stability. By contrast, a decision to, say, eliminate food subsidies that is imposed from the outside, through an agreement between the ruling elite and an international agency, is not likely be helpful in achieving a consensus – and thus in promoting a successful transformation.

IV. THE COMPONENTS OF A NEW DEVELOPMENT STRATEGY

While the details of a development strategy will differ from country to country, one constant is that since a development strategy outlines an approach to the transformation of society, it must address *all components* of society.

75

Loci of development

In particular, a strategy must include components aimed at developing the private sector, the state (the public sector), the community, the family and the individual. The different components of the development strategy are intricately interrelated. For instance, at the center of the strategy for the development of the individual is education; but enhancing skills is also critical for the private-sector strategy, and the increase in wages for women that results from improved female education has a strong bearing on the family.

(a) Private sector development. In the past, too often development strategies focused on government; this was natural, given that to a large extent, the "plan" was a plan for *public* action, a blueprint for the government. But given the broader role that we see for *development strategies*, it is natural to begin our discussion with the private sector, which will, after all, typically be at center stage.

A key objective is the creation of a strong, competitive, stable and efficient private sector. Among the elements of strategies which advance that objective are

- A legal infrastructure, providing (and enforcing) competition laws, bankruptcy laws, and more broadly commercial law;

- A regulatory framework which encourages the private provision of infrastructure where possible, which maximizes the extent of feasible competition, and which ensures that where competition is not possible, there is not abuse of market power;

- The government provision of infrastructure, where private infrastructure does not occur;

- A stable macroeconomic framework;

- A stable and effective financial system, which requires a regulatory framework that not only ensures safety and soundness, but also enhances competition, protects depositors, creates confidence that there is a "level playing field" in securities markets by protecting investors from abuses, and identifies underserved groups within society;

- An adjustment strategy, a strategy for the elimination of those distortions in the economy that interfere with the efficient deployment of resources.

The failure to establish some of the key institutional predictions to a market economy is perhaps one of the factors contributing to the limitations in success of the transition to a market economy of many of the countries of the former Soviet Union. The failure to establish a sound legal and regulatory environment for banks, securities markets and the financial sector more broadly is now recognized to have played a large role in the East Asia crisis. Indeed, the importance of the financial sector for development had been reflected not only in the World Bank's research, but in the Strategic Compact that was formulated well before the East Asia crisis occurred.

If the private sector is to flourish, the environment must be conducive to private-sector development. But much more is also required, including notably an educated, healthy workforce.

(b) Public Sector Development. A sector to which the development strategy should pay particular attention is the public sector. After all, if the government cannot manage its own affairs, how can it be expected to manage (or even affect in an appropriate way) the affairs of others? The key question behind the strategy for the public sector is to identify the role of the government – both what the government should do and how it should do it. And the question should not be whether a particular activity should be carried on in the public or private sector, but how the two can best complement each other, acting as partners in the development effort. Related issues include what tasks should be undertaken at what level of government, and how governments can most effectively interact with "civil society", creating the conditions that are most conducive to the transformation of the whole society.

Central ingredients to the public sector strategy are (i) a focus of the public sector on the unique functions that it must perform, such as: creating the enabling environment for the private sector, discussed in previous paragraphs; ensuring that health and education are widely available; and spearheading the drive to eliminate poverty; (ii) a strengthening of the capabilities of the public sector, including the development of an effective civil service, and a restructuring of the public sector, to make more effective use of incentives and of market and market-like mechanisms; and (iii) a matching of both responsibilities and modes of operation to the capabilities of the State.

(c) Community development. While certain activities are most effectively undertaken at the national (or international) level, much of life centers around communities, and communities are often the most effective vehicle for bringing about the transformation of society. National governments are simply too remote, and the opportunities for meaningful participation are too limited. Well-designed development projects (such as those that have been financed through social funds) can be a catalyst for community development. Participation at the community level allows the project choice to reflect the needs and preferences within the community, and the project design to reflect the local information, ensuring that local conditions and circumstances are taken into account. Equally important, local participation engenders commitment, which is necessary for project sustainability over the long run. And participation in the project itself becomes part of the transformation process. There is growing evidence concerning the relationship between participation and development effectiveness.

(d) Family development. A major determinant of success in raising income per capita is population growth, which stems from decisions made within the family. Another major determinant is female education, also a decision made within the family; the impact of female education is reflective of the key role that women play in educating the next generation. During the key formative years of a child, the family is responsible not only for education, but for nutrition and health. More broadly, we have become increasingly aware of the importance of family development, of what goes on within the household. And just as we have become aware of the power of the family as an instrument for development, we have also become aware that in many parts of the world, there are frequent instances of dysfunctional behaviors, including within-family violence.

(e) Individual development. In the end, the transformation of society entails a transformation of the way individuals think and behave. Development entails the empowerment of individuals, so that they have more control over the forces that affect their lives, so that they can have

a richer, healthier life. Education and health are at the center of efforts at individual development.

Resources, knowledge, and institutions

We have provided a framework for thinking about development strategies that focuses on five levels – the private sector, the government, the community, the household and the individual. A second cut at the development strategy approach emphasizes not the levels on which it operates, but what it must provide:

(a) Resources. As I noted earlier, development entails more than resources: returns to capital, even defined broadly to include human capital, depend heavily on the availability of complementary inputs such as a well-managed economic environment and well-functioning institutions. Nevertheless, it is clear that resources are an important ingredient in development. A development strategy must outline plans for developing physical capital and human capital, as well as preserving natural resources; plans for encouraging saving and investment, and for filling the gap between the two; plans for schools and for financing them; plans for using and renewing natural resources.

(b) Economic Management. One of the defining characteristics of less developed countries is a paucity of resources, which is why it is all the more important that the resources that are available are well deployed. Comprehensive development strategies must set out to identify the most important distortions in the economy, and how they are to be addressed, taking full account of the social costs and distributional impacts of policies.

But the ingredients in economic management need to be broader than the traditional lists, which focused largely on liberalization, privatization and macro-stability.

(c) Knowledge management. As we have noted repeatedly, development requires closing the gap not only in "objects", in human and physical capital, but also in knowledge. Knowledge and capital are in fact complements: improved knowledge enhances the return to capital, while additional capital provides the opportunity to make use of recently

acquired knowledge. Incorporating knowledge into the development strategy requires creating capacities to absorb and adapt knowledge (through investments in human capital and in research institutions), investing in technologies to facilitate the dissemination of knowledge, and creating knowledge locally, and absorbing and adopting global knowledge. Thus, a development strategy needs to outline a strategy of knowledge management. The World Bank increasingly thinks along these lines, conceiving of itself as a *knowledge bank*, with one of its central tasks being to help countries to close the knowledge gap. It can provide the cross-country experience that, when melded with local knowledge, makes possible effective choices of development strategies.

(d) Sector and sub-national strategies. In many cases, it is useful to narrow one's focus from the whole economy to a sector, to some industry (the health care sector, or agriculture), to some region, to cities (an urban strategy), or to the rural areas. The cities represent an arena in which a cluster of concerns jostle together forcefully – infrastructure, the environment, health, finances. In some ways, cities are microcosms of the economy as a while, and integrated solutions to a city's problems may provide insights into integrated solutions for the economy as a whole. Moreover, many cities have been more successful in achieving modernization than rural areas, and it is thus natural to focus particularly on cities in trying to achieve societal transformation.

(e) Social and organizational capital. Another form of capital, beyond physical capital, human capital and knowledge, is also essential for a successful transformation: social and organizational capital, which includes the institutions and relations that mediate transactions and resolve disputes. I will elaborate a bit on this point, because it is too often given short shrift in policy discussions. Traditional societies often have a high level of organizational and social capital, though this capital may not be of a form that facilitates change. But in the process of development, this organizational and social capital is often destroyed. The transformation may weaken traditional authority relationships, and new patterns of migration may sever community ties. The problem is that this process of destruction may occur before new organizational and social capital is created, leaving the society bereft of the necessary institutional structure with which to function well.

Social and organizational capital cannot be handed over to a country from the outside. It must be developed from within, even if knowledge from outside about key ingredients can facilitate the creation of this social/ organizational capital. The pace of change and the pattern of reforms must be adapted to each country's ability to create social/organizational capital. This factor may, in fact, be the most important constraint on the speed of transformation. China has demonstrated that a country can absorb enormous amounts of capital quickly. In the early stages of de-velopment, the needs for roads, schools, energy, telecommunications and other elements of the infrastructure are huge, and it is hard to believe that more resources could not be productively used. But simply providing these ingredients does not constitute development.

There has been much talk of late about capacity-building. The (relatively) easy part of capacity-building is providing the human capacity, the education, the skills, the knowledge required for development. The hard part of capacity-building is the development of the organizational/ social capital, the institutions that enable a society to function well. There are many dimensions to this:

- The enabling environment for the private sector, which includes markets and the legal infrastructure that is necessary for markets to function well;

- The knowledge environment, which enables new knowledge to be absorbed, adapted to the circumstances of the country, and put to use;

- The policy environment, which includes the capacity to make key decisions concerning development strategies;

Consistency, coherence and completeness

We have described the various pieces that constitute an effective devel-opment strategy from two points of view: the levels on which it must operate and the building blocks that it must provide. But the whole is more than the sum of the parts, and the parts must not only be consistent with each other, but must also must fit together, and together set forth a road map – a vision of the future combined with a framework for realizing that vision.

The development strategy envisioned here is not a one-year plan, or even a five-year plan. The fruits of enhancing nutrition or education of a pre-school child will not be fully developed until a decade or more later. The vision must be long-term, while at the same time pointing to actions to be taken today. To be meaningful, the vision and actions must be set within a coherent framework, which requires setting priorities, encouraging partnership, and taking into account the global and regional environment.

Priorities. We know that so much is needed for successful development, including the actions listed above and more. But given limitations on our resources – including our and the developing country's administrative capacities – we need to set priorities. We, and developing country governments, need to focus on leveraging – on identifying areas where their limited actions can have large-scale effects, and where absence of requisite action on their part can have disastrous effects. Although the particular priorities will differ from country to country, there are some common elements.

- Among the most important is *education*, because without education a country cannot develop, cannot attract and build modern industries, cannot adopt new growing technologies as rapidly in the rural sector. But most fundamentally, if development represents the transformation of society, education is what enables people to learn, to accept and help engender this transformation. Education is at the core of development.

- *Infrastructure* – and in particular communications and transportation – is vital for the conduct of business in the modern world. It is also necessary to reduce the sense of isolation of those in developing countries, which is one of the most crippling aspects of underdevelopment. But today, we realize that much of the infrastructure can be provided privately, provided that the government establishes the appropriate regulatory/legal environment. Doing so must be given a high priority.

- *Health* – because an unhealthy population cannot be a productive labor force, because a basic standard of health should be viewed as a fundamental human right, because it is unconscionable that diseases that could be eradicated or least controlled continue to afflict millions of those in the less developed would, often robbing them of any human dignity.

* *Knowledge* – because, like education, it enriches the human spirit, and because, like education and health, it leads to a more productive society. The power of knowledge is enormous: with increased knowledge, the output that can be produced with limited amounts of resources can be multiplied by orders of magnitude.

* *Capacity-building* – because in the end, successful development, a successful transformation, must come from within the country itself, and to accomplish this, it must have institutions and leadership to catalyze, absorb and manage the process of change, and the changed society.

Partnership and country assistance strategies

The country's own development strategy provides, then, the overall framework for thinking about a country's plan for change. Within that framework, various donors, including the World Bank, can act as partners in the development effort by identifying where they can be most effective. These roles will include not only transferring capital, but also providing knowledge that is essential for development and capacity building.

But partnership goes beyond the country and the aid donors. Recall that development entails transformation of the whole society; hence the whole society must be engaged. The development strategy needs to outline how this engagement will occur. It should describe, for instance, the roles of the local business community and civil society.

Consistency with the global and regional environments

We have emphasized that all five components of the development strategy are interrelated; for instance, strategies for the private sector must be complemented by strategies for the public sector; strategies at the national

83

level must be complemented by strategies at the community level. At each level, the strategy must be consistent with the environment within which it is embedded, at levels above and below. And all of the strategies are embedded within an ever-changing global environment. This global environment has opened up new opportunities – vast international markets for goods, so that countries need not be limited in their growth to domestic demand, and the possibility of vast flows of international capital to complement domestic resources. But these opportunities have been accompanied by new challenges. For example, heavy dependence on exports of goods or imports of capital exposes a country to the vicissitudes of markets abroad, such as a foreign economic downturn that may close off opportunities for exports or a sudden change in investor sentiment that may reduce sharply the capital inflows from abroad. The magnitude of these risks may depend little on how well the country manages its own economy. It takes strong government actions, and strong economic institutions, to weather these storms – and even then there may be large costs to the economy. For many less developed countries, the impacts may be – and, experience has shown, frequently are – disastrous. An essential part of the new development strategies must be to take advantage of the new global environment while at the same time reducing the country's vulnerability to the inevitable shocks that are associated with global engagement.

All countries, developed and less developed, share our planet, and thus must husband together our globe's scarce resources, including the atmosphere. The preservation of our atmosphere – avoiding the build-up of carbon – is an example of an international public good, the benefits of which accrue to all people. A development strategy needs to set forth a vision of how these international collective needs are to be addressed.

There is another aspect of global development, which becomes particularly important when one sees development through the lens of a societal transformation. We have seen that some countries have had remarkable success in making that transformation, and that there is much those who are in the early stages of a transition can learn from those experiences. As more successes (and failures) occur, these successes (and failures) have impacts on others, as each extracts the lessons that can be learned from each of the experiences. The spreading of experiences no doubt played a role in the successive development of the countries within East Asia.

At the same time, many countries' economic strategies, even more narrowly defined, must be set within the context of developments within their region. This is especially true of small countries, and even more so of land-locked countries, for whom access to markets is critical. But it is not only transportation issues that have to be dealt with on a regional level. There is, for instance, a myriad of environmental and natural resource issues (most notably dealing with water) that can only be addressed at a regional level.

V. LEARNING FROM OPENNESS: TRADE, FOREIGN CAPITAL AND THE NEW DEVELOPMENT STRATEGY

Where does openness to the outside world fit into this vision of a new development strategy? Our new understanding of development as a transformation of society – rather than just the accumulation of physical or even human capital – gives us a lens with which to examine this question. It reveals that trade can play a crucial role, although not through the mechanisms that economists have traditionally stressed.

Trade and the development transformation

Let me take a moment to explain this. In the standard textbook model of international trade, openness to foreign goods is supposed to bring benefits primarily through its effects on the market price of imported goods. If Indonesia produces midsize automobiles domestically at a cost of $40,000 each but can import them at $20,000 apiece, then opening to auto imports yields a net gain in welfare: the increase in consumer surplus more than offsets the fall in profits enjoyed by Indonesian manufacturers. Indonesia can then move the resources formerly employed in producing cars – the idle labor, human and physical capital and land – and shift them into an industry in which the country has a comparative advantage (textiles, in the classic story). Barring terms-of-trade effects, the resulting increase in efficiency will allow Indonesia to be better off as a result of trade liberalization, even if we don't assume that foreign countries respond with market-opening of their own. The magic of comparative advantage is that a poor country benefits from trade even if, in absolute terms, its productivity is lower than its trade partners across the whole range of goods.

This standard model tells an important tale, but one that is far from the whole story. There is much more going on, in ways that contribute directly to the transformation of society. Consider the gaps between the standard Hecksher-Ohlin trade model and what we see in practice. First, both rigorous empirical research and country experience suggests that the growth effects of engagement in the global marketplace are far larger than would be predicted by the standard model. Most specifications of empirical growth regressions find that some indicator of external openness – whether trade ratios or indices of price distortions or average tariff level – is strongly associated with per-capita income growth. And countries (especially small, poor ones) that have tried autarky have typically found themselves lagging far behind in development, for reasons that apparently stem in part from their closed borders. Yet the standard Hecksher-Ohlin model predicts gains from trade that are relatively small, consisting only of the well-known Harberger triangles in the supply-demand diagrams. Clearly, something is missing from the standard story.

A second problem is that industry-level evidence is also inconsistent with the standard model. Recall that in that model, trade causes economies to shift intersectorally, moving along their production frontier. But in reality, the main gains from trade seem to come from an *outward shift* of that production frontier, with little intersectoral movement. In essence, trade makes it possible for the economy not just to consume a given basket of goods at lower cost, but also to *produce* a given pre-opening set of goods at lower cost. (And any increase in quantities can be explained by the producer's Harberger triangles.)

What is going on here? The evidence suggests strongly that opening up to the outside world leads to an improvement in the technology of production. When I say "technology", I have in mind something far broader and more important than the technical blueprints that lie behind the production of any given good. "Technology" here means anything that affects the way in which inputs are transformed into outputs – not just blueprints, but also market and non-market institutions and modes of organizing production. A major difference between developed and less developed countries is the difference in the efficiency with which inputs are transformed into outputs; trade reduces the discrepancy.

If what we are concerned about is the transformation of society, then we must adopt policies that ensure that openness leads to that broad transformation. It is crucial that trade and foreign direct investment not be confined to small enclaves, even if those enclaves give a temporary boost to our statistical measures of national output. For example, a wealth of gold resources in an area far from a country's population base might well be successful at attracting FDI and increasing mineral exports, but may well do little to spur development over the long term. In designing policies to spur openness and capture its potential benefits, we need to focus on realizing the transformative power of interaction with the outside world. To put it succinctly, our goal should be *not a dual economy, but a developed economy.*

Both trade and foreign direct investment have important roles here. Our understanding of how these roles work remains incomplete, but it is growing. I've already spoken a bit about trade. FDI is of similar importance, because when capital enters a country through direct investment, it typically comes in a package with management expertise, technical human capital, product and process technologies and overseas marketing channels – all of which are in scarce supply in the typical developing country. Evidence suggests that if the society puts in place the appropriate complementary policies and structures, FDI can give a boost to the technological level and growth of the host country. The fears about FDI in the 1960s and 1970s were based largely on the notion of FDI as an enclave phenomenon; in its more modern incarnation, which is typically better integrated into the surrounding society, FDI is something to attract, not to fear. International competition among multinationals has become more robust, so that the foreign corporation receives fewer monopoly rents and the host country gets a larger share of the benefits from investment.

Implications for the international architecture and financial flows

In recent months, the rethinking and soul-searching that has followed the global financial crisis has led to much discussion of how to redesign the international financial architecture. The new development strategy that I have outlined here has important implications for that design process. How, for example, should we think about short-term capital? First, note

87

that short-term capital is especially volatile, as the experience of the past year has reminded us repeatedly. Even as FDI flows have largely continued unabated, short-term capital flows have completely reversed in many of the crisis countries. Second, short-term capital has none of the added benefits brought by FDI – benefits that seem ancillary in the old view of development as accumulation of capital, but that are recognized as *central* when we view them through the lens of the new development strategy. With today's volatility of short-term capital, one cannot make good long-term investments based on this short-term capital. But equally important, short-term capital does not in itself bring development transformation. (Similarly, hedge funds don t bring development, especially if they go bankrupt.) Indeed, in societies with high domestic saving rates and hence relatively low quality of marginal investments, short-term capital may retard that transformation. The high development costs exacted by abrupt capital-flow reversals – the lost years of education, the rise in infant mortality, the job losses – can easily swamp any marginal benefit derived from such flows, as happened in East Asia.

Implications for the developed countries: what are their responsibilities?

It is clearly in the interest of developing countries to engage fully with the world through trade and through attracting foreign direct investment. But the trade policy agenda for the developing world – or at least the agenda advocated for developing countries by the West – has in recent years suffered from its single-minded focus on liberalization through reduction of trade barriers *in those countries*. To complement this argument, important as it is, we need to ask also; what responsibilities does the *developed* world have in the area of trade policy? It is not for me to lay out all those responsibilities here, but let me suggest several developments that have clearly helped delay the progress toward transformative development through openness:

- First, the Uruguay Round trade agreement – for all the benefits it brought to the world's consumers, producers, and taxpayers – did too little to ensure the opening of markets to developing-country exports. Consider the empirical estimates of net benefits by region, calculated just after the agreement was signed: according to these estimates, sub-Saharan Africa was a net *loser* as a result of the Uruguay Round. To be sure, Africa failed to gain largely because it did too little to liberalize its own barriers to trade, thus depriving itself of the opportunity to lower costs and spur efficiency and innovation domestically. But the Round also offered relatively little in the way of new market access for the products that Africa is most able to export. As suggested by the experiences of East Asia's economies, much of the learning opportunity offered by trade takes place in export markets, as developing-country firms build relations with sophisticated customers and compete head-to-head with the best producers in the world. Success in export markets requires learning, and the export champions can then bring these lessons home to apply in the domestic market. Note that I am not claiming here that lack of market access is the only, or even most important, barrier to African exports. African countries can still do much to make life easier for exporters, whether by improving communications infrastructure, revamping transportation facilities, or reducing unnecessary bureaucratic obstacles to exports. But market access is one area where the developed world is uniquely positioned to give a boost to the development transformation that I have called for.

- Second, and a related point, is that we must continue working to stem the tide of the new protectionism in the West. As you know, the last two decades have seen a rise in the use of creative new measures to block imports. Examples include nuisance anti-dumping claims, lodged under laws that often make little economic sense; countervailing duties that similarly lack objective justification; and barriers to genetically altered products, which are likely to become steadily more important as developing-country exports make greater use of those products. Developed countries often have the luxury of large and well-paid legal and lobbying industries in their capitals, industries that can be quite innovative in devising new means of restricting competition. From an equity standpoint, it is essential that we stamp out these innovations as energetically as we work to lower developing-country barriers to trade.

- Third, international protection of intellectual property rights (IPRs) should strike a balance between the interests of producers and users. Those users include not only many firms and consumers within the developing world – who are more often technological adapters and users than innovators – but also the academic community throughout the world (developed and developing). Yes, it is important to give incentives to innovators by ensuring them a return on their investment in R&D. But we must remember that knowledge is a crucial input into production processes, whether in agriculture or high-tech industry, and that unlike physical inputs into production, knowledge can be shared *ad infinitum* without any additional cost. Thomas Jefferson likened the creation of knowledge to the lighting of a candle in the darkness: many other candles can draw their light from that first candle without diminishing its power or brilliance. Excessive protection of IPRs may end this virtuous cycle of knowledge transmission and regeneration in the developing world. There is no easy answer, but that should not stop us from asking questions. It is for this reason that we have devoted a section in this year's *World Development Report* to the issue of intellectual property rights.

In all these cases, we should seek to construct not just good policies, but also a sense that the process by which policies are devised is itself *fair and open*. Without such a sense of fairness, the developing world will retreat from its reforms of recent decades. Worse still, the perception of hypocrisy reinforces the sense of unfairness: even as the more developed countries preach the doctrines of openness, they engage in restrictive practices. Even as they preach that countries must undertake the painful measures of liberalization – which may entail losses of jobs and industries – developed countries use anti-dumping and safeguard measures to protect their own industries that are adversely affected. Moreover, they do so even when their economies are at full employment, so that the risks of extended unemployment are minimal, in marked contrast to the situation in many less developed countries, where unemployment is high and safety nets are inadequate. And even as the developed countries dismiss the political problems facing less developed countries, they justify their own resort to these protectionist measures as necessary to overcome even worse protectionist sentiments within their own countries.

As I said in my Fiesole speech earlier this week, the pendulum of opinion has swung before, and it now risks swinging too far back in opposition to openness. Our task is to lessen the momentum of this pendulum swing, by increasing the equity of the international architecture for trade and finance. Retreat from openness in the developing world would unacceptably delay the development transformation that it so sorely needs.

VI. CONCLUDING COMMENTS

We have learned in the last half-century that development is possible, but also that development is not inevitable. We have learned that development is not just a matter of technical adjustments, but a transformation of society.

In my opening remarks, I referred to the disillusionment with the Washington consensus, which provided a set of prescriptions that failed to foster this development transformation. That consensus was too narrow both in its objectives and its instruments. I have tried in this lecture to set out the foundations of an alternative paradigm to the Washington consensus. In a way, what I have said is far from revolutionary: within the World Bank and the development community more broadly, there has been increasing attention over recent decades to issues of health and education, and we have moved beyond measures of GDP to look at lifespans and literacy rates. We have recognized the importance of economic security, and stressed the creation of safety nets. There has been a growing consensus behind the objectives of democratic, equitable and sustainable development. Here, I have tried to argue that the whole is greater than the sum of the parts, and that successful development must focus on the whole – the transformation of society. We are well prepared for this task, precisely because we have increasingly taken within our ambit a broader range of issues – even though all too often we have underemphasized important components, such as the role of competition and financial markets and the institutional infrastructure more broadly.

But I have also tried to argue here that a successful development transformation affects not only what we do, but how we do it. Yes, this broader perspective affects the strategies and policies, but it also affects the processes. It argues for openness, partnership and participation, words that too often sound like appeals to the politically correct nostrums of the day. I have tried to argue that there lies behind these words a theory of development, as well as evidence that these processes can lead to more successful development efforts.

Honesty, however, requires me to add one more word. In calling for a transformation of societies, I have elided a central issue: transformation to what kind of society, and for what ends? Further, some have worried that development will destroy traditional values. In some cases, there will be a clash between science and traditional beliefs. But development today often focuses on the preservation of cultural values, partly because these values serve as a cohesive force at a time when many other such forces are weakening. Maintaining social organization and enhancing social capital are part of the key to successful development transformations. Moreover, it is important to note that much of the progress that is associated with successful development – the mothers who do not have to see their children die in infancy, who see the opening of minds to new knowledge and the increased opportunities – reflect almost universally held values.

But there is a further reason that I believe in openness in trade and openness in process: these contribute to a more open, democratic society. For me, these are values in their own right.

REFERENCES

Deininger, K., and L. Squire. 1996. "A New Data Set Measuring Income Inequality." *World Bank Economic Review* 10(3), 565–591.

Finger, J. M., ed. 1993. *Anti-Dumping: How It Works and Who Gets Hurt.* Ann Arbor: University of Michigan Press.

Harrison, G. W., T. F. Rutherford and D. G. Tarr. 1995. "Quantifying the Uruguay Round." In W.Marti, and LA. Winters, eds., *The Uruguay Round and the Developing Economies."* World Bank Discussion Paper 307.

Romer, P. 1994. "New Goods, Old Theory, and the Welfare Costs of Trade Restrictions." *Journal of Development Economics* 5–38.

Sachs, J. D. and A. M. Warner. 1995. "Economic Reform and the Process of Global Integration." *Brookings Papers on Economic Activity* 1–95.

Stiglitz, J.E. 1997. "Dumping on Free Trade: The US Import Trade Laws." *Southern Economic Journal* 64:2 (October), 402–424.

———. 1998. "More Instruments and Broader Goals: Moving Toward the

Post-Washington Consensus." Presented as the WIDER Annual Lecture, at the World Institute for Development Economics Research in Helsinki (January).

Williamson, J. 1990. *Latin American Adjustment: How Much Has Happened?* Washington, DC: Insitute for International Economics.

——. 1997. "The Washington Consensus Revisited." In L. Emmerij, ed *Economic and Social Development into the XXI Century.* Washington, DC: Inter-American Development Bank, 48–61.

World Bank. 1997a. *China 2020: Development Challenges in the New Century.* Washington, DC: World Bank.

——. 1997b. *World Development Report 1997: The State in a Changing World.* New York: Oxford University Press.

——. 1998. *World Development Report 1998/99: Knowledge for Development.* New York: Oxford University Press.

Wolfensohn, J.D. 1998. "The Other Crisis." World Bank/IMF Annual Meetings Address (6 October).

Chapter 3

Redefining the Role of the State

What should it do? *How* should it do it?
And *how* should these decisions be made?

Paper presented at the Tenth Anniversary of MITI Research Institute
Tokyo, March 1998

Both the past praise and the current criticism of the East Asian miracle have brought the question of the role of government to the forefront. While the economies were growing quickly, incomes were rising, literacy rates were increasing and poverty was dwindling rapidly[1], scholars were quick to note that in almost every one of the East Asian cases, government played a far more active role than typically envisaged in what has come to be known as the Washington consensus[2]. Governments went beyond the conventional prescriptions of sound macro-economic policies, including low deficits and inflation. They put markets at the center of their development strategies, but they were not loath to intervene in markets, or, to use Robert Wade's expression, to "govern markets".[3] The East Asian states set out to create and regulate institutions which promoted savings and helped allocated resources, including scarce investment. They promoted investments in infrastructure, human capital and the advancement of technology.

The recent turmoil in East Asia has, in some circles, cast doubt on the public-private partnership that characterized the region's development strategy. The accusations of "crony capitalism", overbearing state direction of investments and lack of transparency have, in some minds, discredited government involvement in development. I would argue that the critics have been too harsh – after all, the past achievements in accumulating savings, promoting investment, and developing human capital cannot simply be erased. In historical perspective, financial crises and economic downturns are not a new phenomenon in capitalist economies. Furthermore, several countries in the region, most notably China[4] and Taiwan (China) seem to have weathered the storm quite well.

Nevertheless, the depth of the crisis in countries such as Korea, Thailand, Malaysia and Indonesia does provoke questions.

We have much to learn from East Asia and the East Asian model, perhaps even more as we set about trying to ascertain not only the lessons of their remarkable growth, but also the lessons of their current crisis.

The discussion of the role of government is vital for improving our development strategy. There is a growing consensus that governments can play a vital role in successful development efforts, but we also recognize that the wrong kind of government intervention can be highly detrimental. We have recognized that the scope and effectiveness of government activities, rather than simply the size of the government's budget or personnel, is the key issue. Within a given size range, government's effectiveness can vary widely with the scope of its activities: they can do too much of some things and too little of others, and redirecting the state's efforts could produce benefits on both accounts. These are all important issues.

I wish to focus this paper, however, on the more fundamental question which underlies this discussion: "How are decisions about the role of the state made?" The processes of government itself affect the answers to questions about the size and scope of the state. Improving these processes, an effort in which I have been involved over the past half decade, may provide the most enduring way of making progress in the other areas. Critics of government interventions which claim that such interventions are inevitably welfare reducing, and simply attempts by one group to enhance their welfare at the expense of others, are at best unproven, and at worst untrue. The question is, "Are there ways of designing governmental institutions which enhance the likelihood of, if not ensuring that, public interventions are welfare enhancing?"

Part I of this paper will review current thinking on the appropriate role of the state, while in Part II I put forward five new propositions for improving the processes which underlie government actions.

THE ECONOMIC ROLE OF THE STATE

An enquiry into the appropriate role of the state must begin with the question, "In what ways is the state different from other organizations in society?" The answer relates to the nature and source of its powers.

The state and its representatives are the sole basis of the legitimate use of compulsion both to do certain things (such as being drafted into the armed forces) and not to do certain things (such as selling drugs). Membership in the "state" is a default condition, defined automatically for those meeting certain qualifications such as birth or residence. The state's jurisdiction extends to all of those residing within its boundaries or who accept citizenship within the state.

These extensive powers are matched by certain limitations. First is the inherent inability to make credible commitments. The state's unique powers of compulsion lead it to be the enforcer of contracts, but leave it without an entity to enforce its contracts and allow it to demonstrate its commitment to certain policies. The state can impose certain obligations on itself, including an obligation to fulfil its contracts, but no government can impose obligations on its successors or even do much to stop itself from reneging on previous commitments. While Buchanan emphasized the role of constitutions, there are wide areas where the Constitution provides insufficient commitment. Governments can commit themselves weakly by imposing rules which affect transactions costs, but this imperfect commitment mechanism entails trade-offs in terms of future flexibility. These transactions costs may provide for stability, but can also inhibit governments' ability to adapt quickly to changing circumstances.

Our political systems have created further restrictions to prevent potential abuse of government powers. The regulations associated with government procurement and civil service are some of the most notorious examples of this "red tape". Both are usually designed to ensure equitable treatment of all citizens and to prevent some groups from using the powers of the state to enrich themselves at the expense of others, but both inhibit the government's ability to function efficiently. The political process also defines the rules by which those in decision-making positions are chosen and the process by which actions can be undertaken. The common system of passage by Parliament and approval by the Executive, for example, is, again, designed to prevent the abuse of power, but often makes decision-making slow and cumbersome.

The view from the market: Three conservative propositions

Many critics of the government base their beliefs on premises about the market: first, that markets, by themselves, yield efficient outcomes; and second, that efficiency is more important than, say, distribution between persons or generations.[5] Based on these judgments, critics of government have argued

i.   Government is unnecessary because anything the government can do, the private sector can do better;
ii. Government is ineffective because anything the government does, the private sector can and will undo;
iii. The incentive structures inherent in public institutions imply that government actions generally decrease societal welfare, or, at the very least, inhibit productive economic activity by taking resources away from one group and giving them to another, often less deserving, group.

Recent advances in welfare economics have highlighted several shortcomings in these market-focused propositions for the role of government by pointing out new conditions under which markets are not Pareto efficient. Externalities (such as associated with pollution or innovations) and public goods are not the only factors that create stumbling blocks for an otherwise market efficient economy. Imperfect information and incomplete markets – an extremely common condition – have been added to the list of factors which give rise to problems in the market economy.[6] It is now recognized that imperfections of information (about individuals or evaluations of public goods, for example) prevent Coasian bargaining from adequately resolving externality problems. (See Farrell, 1987, Stiglitz, 1994, Dixit and Olson, 1997.) There never was a presumption that markets yielded an optimal societal or generational distribution of income and now there does not seem to be any basis for the presumption that markets yield efficient outcomes.

The fact that markets do not achieve efficient outcomes, of course, does not automatically mean that government intervention can improve upon matters, which is why these *conservative* propositions need to be dealt with through an assessment of *government* powers and limitations.

From the vantage point of our analysis, we can see that the first proposition is simply not true: government has powers that the private sector does not have. The second proposition is even more obviously wrong. True, there are some highly idealized models, such as those involving the neutrality of money, in which the proposition of government ineffectiveness may have some limited validity. More generally, however, whenever governments take actions or have rules that change relative prices or redistribute income, and whenever the private sector has imperfect information concerning government actions, the state's policies cannot be fully undone.[7]

The third proposition is the most difficult to deal with. Certainly, there is no general proposition concerning the efficiency of actions which emerge from political processes. There are good reasons to believe that public and private interests are far from perfectly aligned. Indeed I have argued elsewhere (Stiglitz, 1994) that the principal agent problems which arise in the public sector are, in many respects, not dissimilar to those which arise in large corporations in the private. In both cases, the rewards of managers are at best only loosely linked to performance. Managerial rent seeking within the private sector (Shleifer and Vishny, 1989, and Edlin and Stiglitz, 1995) can be every bit as problematic as rent seeking in the public.[8] There have been important instances in which government actions have been welfare-decreasing. Nevertheless, as a historical proposition, it is also the case that government has played a significant positive role in the countries with the most successful development strategies, including the United States and the countries of East Asia.

Market failure, public failure, and new views of the role of government

While market failure theories dominated thinking about the role of government in the decades following the proof of the fundamental theorems of welfare economics, public failure theories began to dominate discussions in the Reagan/Thatcher era. The public failure theories can be thought of as an elaboration of the Third Conservative proposition above. It was asserted that

  i.   Special interest groups would, without constitutional bars, seek to establish market impediments that generate rents;
  ii. The opposing public interests were too diffuse to successfully oppose the special interests. While aggregate costs might

exceed aggregate benefits for society, a public goods problem arose when costs were much more diffuse than benefits;

iii. Competition for rent-seeking tended to dissipate the rents, but the rent dissipation simply added to the waste.

While there is plenty of evidence to suggest that rent seeking was important, these propositions do not seem to adequately describe the process. First, there is a curious intellectual inconsistency: while many conservatives seemed to argue that Coase's theorem (or what might more appropriately be called Coase's conjecture) worked well in the private sector, it seemed to have no sway in the public. Inefficiencies within that sector did not seem to get "bargained out". Second, it was simply assumed that there was perfect competition in rent-seeking. In reality, however, competition in rent seeking was every bit as imperfect as competition elsewhere in the economy. There are quite general theorems which established that if there were even epsilon sunk costs, even strong potential competition was not enough for the dissipation of imperfect competition rents. (See Stiglitz, 1987.) Third, rent-seeking activities tend to be concentrated in certain sectors, such as trade and agriculture, although there are clearly opportunities for significant rents elsewhere. Understanding why these are not pursued, or at least not successfully pursued, may provide important new insights into the rent-seeking process.

State and society: An interactive partnership

The first attempts to combine the previous analyses of market and government failures resulted in efforts to assign separate tasks to the public and private sectors. In earlier discussions, some sectors were thought of as largely within the domain of the public sector, others as largely in the jurisdiction of the private. Today, however, the question is posed somewhat differently: "How can government and the private sector act together, as partners, or, in the more technical jargon of economics, in a complementary fashion?"

One can ask this question about the financial sector, for example. Lending activity should clearly be primarily the responsibility of the private sector. Yet there is a large public role. Government has helped create new institutions, where the private sector failed, for one reason or another, to address needs adequately. The role of government in the mortgage market in the United States, in establishing long-term credit institutions in Japan or in establishing thick bond markets elsewhere, are just a few examples of this activity. Government is also needed to regulate financial institutions, not only to ensure competition, but also to maintain the safety and soundness of the financial system.[9]

The general theory of this "partnership" has recently been set out.[10] The government can change the "game" that the private participants are playing in ways which are welfare-enhancing. While older literature focused on dissipative rent-seeking, this newer work has emphasized how governments can create rents which enhance incentives for, say, prudential behavior in the financial sector, or more generally for wealth creation. The rents associated with access to foreign exchange and credit which were distributed to those firms who were most successful in exporting provided much of the spur that led to the success of East Asia (see World Bank, 1993). Not only can government actions thus improve the behavior of market participants, but the government actions themselves can be shown to be "incentive compatible", that is, under plausible hypotheses concerning government objectives, such actions can be shown to be in the interests of the government itself.

Improving the performance of the public sector

As understanding concerning what the appropriate role of government is has increased, attention has turned to a new question: how to improve the performance of the public sector. It is now recognized that government can avail itself of many of the incentive mechanisms that the private sector uses. Government can use markets and market-like mechanisms.

   i. It can use auctions both for procuring goods and services and for allocating public resources;
   ii. It can contract out large portions of government activity;
   iii. It can use performance contracting, even in those cases where contracting out does not seem feasible or desirable;
   iv. It can design arrangements to make use of market information. For instance, it can rely on market judgments of qualities for its

procurement (off-the-shelf procurement policies); it can use information from interest rates paid to, say, subordinated bank debt to ascertain appropriate risk premiums for deposit insurance.

NEW ISSUES

Today, I want to push the discourse on the role of the state a little bit beyond the basic what and how, by pushing the discussion one step back to ask, "What can we say about the process by which these decisions get made?" It is natural that our discussion should have evolved to this point. In the early stages of the discussion of the role of the state, we had hoped to be able to derive simple rules – the provision of defense is the responsibility of government, the production of steel is the responsibility of the private sector. As the debate has advanced, however, the hard questions, those that the rules do not cover, have surfaced. When confronted with the question of "What to do where there is a market failure, or at least the potential of a market failure, but where it is not obvious that government interventions will improve matters?", for example, the maxim "Undertake the public action if it improves, or is expected to improve, social welfare" is of little help. Reasonable people may disagree in their judgments, and special interests will always claim that the actions which are intended to help them are really in the general interest. This is the area where policy debates center.

Thus, the question which we need to ask is, "Are there processes or rules of decision-making which are more likely to result in decisions which are in the public interest, rather than in the private use of public interest?" My remarks are largely based on close observation of the political process in the United States over a long period of time, but particularly in the last five years. During this period, I had frequent occasions to observe special interest groups. The question I asked was, "How could their influence be curbed?"

Part of the answer – reform of campaign finances – has been noted repeatedly in recent public discussions in the United States. Reducing the need to raise such levels of funds (e.g., by providing free air time to those who are willing to limit campaign fund-raising); subjecting contributions to more sunshine; and restricting the level and sources of contributions, or of the actions which elected officials can take on donors' behalf or in the area where they have received contributions, would all be helpful in reducing the influence of special interests.[11] Here, however, I want to focus on some strategies that have not received as extensive discussion.

Many of the issues I will be discussing in this section – participation in decision-making, virtues of consensus processes versus more self-interested advocacy processes – are often approached from a broader philosophical perspective. Many of those who believed in consensus processes put greater emphasis on the notion of community, an emphasis which is somewhat foreign to traditional economic approaches which take a self-interested, rational, individual as the basic unit of analysis. In this case, interactions with others matter only to the extent that they satisfy the individual's own preferences. Many outside the very individualistic Anglo-American cultures would emphasize the importance of these communitarian values.

I want to base my discussion here not on these statements of values, but on other grounds, on positive economics and instrumental bases. I discuss five general propositions for improving governance.

Proposition 1 for a better government: Restrict government interventions in areas in which there is evidence of a systematic and significant influence of special interests.[12]

The first strategy is to reduce the allure of "rents" by limiting government action in areas where special interests have had strong sway, and where the benefits of special interest legislation are limited. There are several difficulties in such a strategy. First, existing interest groups are unlikely to relinquish the rents that they have gained.[13] Second, government's inability to commit makes such "abstinence" policies difficult to maintain and the transactions costs required for even imperfect commitment may create unforeseen problems in the future. That is why some of the most significant progress in these areas has occurred in the context of international trade negotiations.[14]

The important question to ask in identifying the areas which government should avoid is, "Would the adoption of rules prohibiting (or making it more difficult for government to take) action in these areas bring with it benefits that exceed the obvious costs?" I can mention several areas where "abstinence" might be beneficial. As I noted before, there are some specific areas where rent-seeking special interests tend to gain a foothold. Although I and most other economists are convinced that while there are some instances in which trade impediments might be desirable in a world of benevolent leaders, trade interventions in practice predominantly reflect special interests and are welfare decreasing. One of the reasons that trade interventions may be more frequent is that one side of the interventions – the loss of profits of the "outside" producers – is not represented in the political process, while the gain in profits of the "inside" producers is represented. By contrast, in commodities which are purely domestic, both losers and winners are represented and the gains from price increases to producers are just offset by the losses of users. Agriculture may represent another extreme case where the users (consumers) are highly diffuse (virtually everyone in society is a consumer) while the producers are highly concentrated.

Many of the interventions in both agriculture and trade take the form of restrictions to competition rather than explicit subsidies. These interventions help enforce cartels and cartel-like arrangements which enhance the industries' profits at the expense of consumers. Special interest groups have become adroit both in cloaking their pleas under the mantle of general interest and in developing euphemisms which hide the restrictive nature of the desired interventions. The milk industry in the United States, for example, refers to its request for a cartel arrangement as "self-help".

Proposition 2 for a better government: There should be a strong presumption against government actions restricting competition; and there should be a strong presumption in favor of government actions which promote competition.

Policy-makers should concentrate on enhancing competition. Government restrictions on competition, almost always associated with a decrease in welfare, are one of the most common symptoms of undue influence by special interests. Although most would agree that promoting competition and acting as a "referee" in the market economy are key government roles, the state often succumbs to pressure to reduce competition. In some cases, the most vocal special interest groups are not firms but workers. Thus, in the United States, while there is vibrant competition between public and private institutions in the provision of higher education, such competition is severely restricted at the elementary and secondary level. This class of interventions marks the subversion of the general

103

good to the particular good as the government succumbs to pressure to protect certain groups from competition.[15]

Just as few are explicit in their search for special interests benefits, few are explicit in their attempts to reduce competition. Subsidies to ethanol, for example, continue under the guise of promoting the "general interest" by reducing environmental damage and dependency on foreign oil. In fact, the fuel is economically inefficient and bad for the environment.[16] Similarly, many groups claim to seek protection from "unfair" or "disruptive" competition. This is particularly important in the so-called unfair trade laws – such as the anti-dumping laws. The presumption underlying these laws seems to be that any firm that undercuts domestic producers must only succeed in doing so by engaging in some unfair trade practice. The standards for unfair international trade laws are completely different than those associated with antitrust laws, the domestic equivalent. Domestic firms have increasingly used the dual standard as protection from foreign competition.[17] The correlation between government actions and the electoral cycles is also perhaps noteworthy. Impending elections appeared to influence the US decision to restrict Mexico's "unfair" undercutting of America's tomatoes in 1996. Mexico had simply succeeded in importing improved technology for growing tomatoes, especially tomatoes that were robust enough to survive shipping.

Proposition 3 for a better government: There should be a strong presumption in favor of openness in government and against secrecy.

Secrecy, or restricted information, is often used by government officials to restrict outside participation in decision-making. The resulting exclusivity of the decision-making process increases both the influence and the rents to be had for government officials. Limitations on information, in effect, restrict competition in the decision-making process.

Increasing openness can be a powerful tool in reducing the influence of special interests and improving government performance. First, sunshine is a strong antiseptic that often discourages, or at least increases the cost of, the more outrageous forms of special interest. Second, secrecy makes it more difficult to correct errors and to evaluate officials. Indeed, concern about exposure of mistakes may be even a greater motive for secrecy than concern about hiding the influence of special interest groups. Third, secrecy creates rents for those who have information, giving them something to exchange. While the exchanges between government officials and the press are seldom monetary, the exchanges which occur are no less iniquitous. It is not only the occasional puff piece extolling the virtues of the provider of the information but, more importantly, the distortions in information which are harmful. Finally, secrecy means that information is often revealed in a less continuous process. Just as large adjustments associated with fixed exchange rates lead to more economic instability, so too do large, sudden, blasts of information.

Government officials have always sought to find a rationale for the secrecy which creates information rents to be exchanged with the press and those willing to make campaign contributions (their clientele) and protects them from criticism for mistakes. How often have we heard the tantalizing "If you only knew what I knew, but regrettably, I can't tell you,"? Secrecy creates the aura of authority that is essential for the effective exercise of power. The emperor may have no clothes, or far fewer clothes than is generally recognized, and part of the objective is to keep that secret.

In economic matters, however, governments have recently come up with a new and powerful rationale for secrecy: discussions (of anything) may disturb markets. It is ironic that many of those who most ardently put forward this argument are those who *believe* in the importance, and presumably rationality, of markets. Their support of secrecy seems at odds with this belief, for rational markets should be related to the basic fundamentals which are seldom altered in important ways by the pronouncements of the beliefs of one government official or another. In fact, the fundamentals *do* seem to be what ultimately matters. In the United States, Alan Greenspan's attempt to let a little air out of what he worried was the stock market's bubble by referring in December 1996 to the market's irrational exuberance demonstrated that even statements (other than actions, or explicit announcements of actions) from those who have a central role in policy making have little permanent effect. The remark moved the market only slightly – a downward blip that lasted no more than a couple of days, with no discernible effect thereafter.[18]

Almost all information gets revealed eventually. The issue whether it is revealed in "big" packages or slowly along the way. As I suggested, the former strategy may indeed create more instability than the latter.

Proposition 4 for a better government: Government should encourage the private provision of public goods, including through non-governmental organizations, not only as mechanisms for the creation of effective competition to itself, and therefore putting discipline on itself, but also as an effective way of conveying voice.

Earlier I argued that there should be a strong presumption in favor of actions which promote competition and against those which restrict competition. This commitment to competition should extend to the political arena as well. Actions which increase participation in the political process should be encouraged, those which decrease it should be discouraged.

One of the reasons that I have so strongly opposed secrecy in government is that it increases the barriers to effective participation in the political process. More generally, the large natural barriers to entry limit the effective competition in expression of citizens' interests and contribute to the power of narrow interest groups. The size of the national polity and the automatic membership in the state prevent the use of exit and choice to convey information.[19] As I noted before in my discussion of government failures, there are serious free rider problems in the expression of preferences when policy costs are diffuse and benefits concentrated. Restricted information flow further increases the costs of individuals' and diffuse groups' participation.

Government can intervene in this area to provide a public good: voice. They can take a more pro-active stance in encouraging more widespread public input on policy-making. One way of doing so is to ensure that the voices of those who come together collectively to express a view, through the myriad of non-governmental organizations which are playing an increasingly important role in our society, are heard. The distinction between rent-seeking interest groups and voice-conveying citizens is not always clear[20] and increasing the numbers of participants and degree of competition would ensure more balanced signals of societal preferences.

While government encouragement of NGOs would increase the extent of public participation, I know of no general propositions supporting the conclusion that, short of complete participation, those most likely to participate would be fully representative of the views of society as a whole. On the contrary, they are more likely to be the groups with the greatest degree of self-interest (to benefit the most from particular government actions). NGOs may be more effective at conveying the

106

intensity of feelings of certain groups within the population than in conveying a sampling of the whole population's views. While it is important for the political process to reflect the *intensity* of views of some groups, government policy making must take into account the potential non-representativeness of those most forcefully exercising "voice".

Proposition 5 for a better government: Governments need to achieve a balance between expertise and democratic representativeness and accountability.

Openness needs to extend to the areas which have typically been the realm of experts. In order to do this, the experts have to explain themselves better (reduce the "secrecy" or "shrouding" effect of technical jargon) and also be more open to the wider political realm in order to get a sense of the kind of goals toward which they should apply their expertise.

Expertise is important. One of the widely noted limitations of participatory mechanisms (including electoral mechanisms) is that the decisions may not adequately reflect "expertise", and as a result the decisions may not have their intended effects or may not be the most efficient way of achieving the intended objectives. For instance, lay views concerning environmental hazards are not closely linked to scientific views of the risks incurred.[21] If decisions about resource allocations for mitigating environmental risk were left to participatory processes, there would be a marked discrepancy between perceived and actual risk reduction.

In innumerable instances, the political process has recognized these limitations. Indeed, within the United States, the early debates about republican forms of government versus direct democracy centered on similar issues of information and expertise (though not necessarily in that language.) In the United States most regulatory powers have been delegated to an independent board, typically bipartisan, though accountable to Congress and the executive branch. Although not perfect, restrictions on communication between these boards and other government branches and limitations on movement to and from the private sector help prevent the experts from being captured by particular interests. This independence is one example of the "abstinence" strategy I mentioned in proposition 1: these are areas where rents could easily be created and the government (or at least the responsive, democratic government) has limited its role in these issues. The independent boards take on a quasi-judiciary role, though much of their work is more in the nature of delegated legislation, filling out the technical details of the regulatory framework.

Achieving a balance between representativeness and independence, however, is not an easy task. Experts – particularly the experts chosen to serve on these independent agency boards – are typically drawn from a non-representative sample. Those who are knowledgeable about an industry are more likely to have worked in the industry. The major exception are academics. In any case, expertise creates its own biases.

Perhaps the most egregious departures from representativeness have been in the area of monetary policies.[22] Many countries have set up independent central banks which are only loosely accountable to elected officials. The fact that politicians are judged largely on the performance of the economy creates a curious situation where elected, representative politicians are dependent on appointed experts. With many of the appointed representatives appointed by previous administrations, the current administrations cannot even be held accountable for the quality of its appointments. The rationale for this independence, that the setting of macro-economic policies is too important to be left to politicians, may make sense as a prophylactic for populist policies in situations where short-run economic irresponsibility is a possibility, but it is weaker in those countries where huge and persistent deficits have greatly reduced the scope for discretionary policies.

One can argue that central bank independence would be a good thing in those countries which are prone to electorally-driven spending. The facts that politicians are accountable to the economy and the electorate is relatively naïve strengthen incentives for quick fixes.[23] But one can also say that independent central banks are not the only or even the most effective way to ensure responsible monetary policy.[24] There is some evidence that voters in countries with histories of hyperinflation and unpleasant crises will vote responsibly – i.e. not push for more jobs when there is a chance for repeated inflation (Stokes, 1996). Also, the need to maintain the confidence of international capital markets may discipline politicians.

The basic argument for more representativeness in monetary policy-making is that economic policy involves important choices that do not have just technical answers. Though central banks often draw heavily upon bankers for their officers and boards, central banks are not just concerned with banking. The actions they take are central for macro-economic policy, and the behavior of the economy both in the short run and the long. The central bankers typically have little knowledge of these broader macro-economic policy issues which should be their central concern. Although technical expertise is important in macro-economic policy, there are a number of trade-offs (between inflation and growth, for instance) that are a matter of values. The values – and special interests – of the banking community typically differ markedly from that of the country as a whole.

Moreover, it is striking the extent to which "expert" judgments are affected by special interests: those who have more to lose from inflation and less to lose from an increase in the unemployment rate typically see less of a trade-off (less of a gain in employment, say, from a slight increase in inflation) than those who have less to lose from inflation and more to lose from an increase in unemployment. In this case, excessive reliance on "expertise" clearly inhibits competition in the public's expression of preferences.

While some central banks have achieved a reasonable degree of expertise in their main mission (macro-stability and growth), many (to say the least) do not even draw upon the best expertise in their economy or cultivate expertise outside the affected industries, e.g., within academia or think tanks. This is particularly the case for monetary policy, the main concern of central bankers. Indeed, central bankers typically do not have even the training that makes them suited for judging the macro-economic consequences of their policy decisions – arguably their central concern. This is a case where there may even be a conflict between the relevant expertise for decision-making in the national interest and the expertise of vested interest groups. In any case, it is certainly the case that one could achieve a high level of expertise which was at least as high as that achieved today in many, if not most, central banks, which was more representative of the national interest and affected parties and which would combine professional judgments with values that are more in accord with society as a whole. Interestingly, though greater independence of the central banks may be associated with greater stability of prices, there is little evidence that economies with more independent central banks have achieved higher levels of performance in what really matters, the performance of economic activity, either in the rate of growth or the level of economic stability.[25] These results should not be surprising: the banking community, overwhelmingly represented within central banks, is more concerned with price stability than employment stability. Thus, that they have achieved objectives more in accord with their own values and interests should not come as a surprise.

Indeed, in some cases, actions which do not reflect broader views of society can give rise to political and social disruptions which interfere with the functioning of the economy. To be sure, the "experts" entrusted with the management of monetary policy should, in principle, take the costs of those disruptions into account, even if the political and social ramifications are not expressly part of their "objective function". Nevertheless, in many cases they do not. One might well ask why they do not. Surely, there are systematic relationships between, say, economic policies and unemployment, unemployment and the probability of disruption, and the possibility of this disruption leading to political turmoil which can seriously undermine, say, the restoration of confidence in the economy. Indeed, political officials within a country typically have a far better sense of these political consequences than do those who might fly into the country for a brief visit.

Perhaps the reason for the seeming proclivity to ignore these important dimensions is the observations made earlier and elsewhere (see Stiglitz, 1998) of the correlation between values and economic judgments: those who worried more about inflation, for instance, systematically saw a NAIRU in the United States that was higher than those who were more concerned about unemployment. This simply reinforces the conclusion of the difficulties of separating out expertise from values, and therefore reinforces the importance of achieving a degree of representativeness in boards entrusted to bringing expertise to public decision making.

The propositions in context

The five propositions provide loose guidelines for thinking about some of the government weaknesses I mentioned in the beginning of the paper. Many of these limitations of government cannot be "solved", but our response to them can be made more balanced.

Civil service systems, for example, represent constraints intended to ensure against the abuse of power; but those same constraints often interfere with the ability of government to hire the best people and pay them competitive wages. The problem, as I noted in my 1989 Amsterdam lecture, can be viewed as one of information: outsiders cannot tell whether the government official is paying a high wage to some employee a) as an "efficiency wage" designed to elicit better performance or lower turnover; b) because he has to attract the individual as c); the employee is actually highly efficient and the wage adequately reflects marginal contribution; or d) the higher wage is simply a payoff to a friend. This last case represents a private abuse of public power; a redistribution from the taxpayers to this particular individual. In the private sector, on the other hand, if the owner of a firm decides to pay a higher wage, there is a presumption that there is a good economic rationale for doing so. In any case, when mistakes or inefficient arrangements are made, only the owner of the firm bears the cost.

Similarly, in procurement, restraints are imposed to reduce the potential abuses of power. But there are high costs to these constraints. By one estimate, the cost of making jet engines for the government are a third higher than the cost of making identical engines for the private sector, simply because the government imposes a host of regulations to ensure that it is not cheated. A high price is paid to prevent abuse.

In many of these areas, there is a sense that the government has lost a sense of balance and is now paying too high a price for preventing abuses. The persistence of the red tape can be explained by another recognized "government failure": politicians have a concentrated interest in ensuring that "mistakes" do not occur under their watches, while the diffuse public pays for the mistake-avoidance regulations. The reliance on processes is one way which government officials seek to avoid blame. If something goes wrong, they can at least claim that they had followed well accepted procedures. It would be nice if the electorate could commit itself to judging mistakes in a more balanced way.

Such a commitment is unlikely, however. Part of the problem has to do with Proposition 3 and provides a further argument against the excessive secrecy that cloaks so much of government decision making in so many countries. The electorate only observes outcomes and seldom has the information required to assess whether reasonable actions were undertaken. Better information – including less secrecy – might enable better judgments to be made, and thus lessen biases towards risk avoidance on the part of officials. The other part of the problem, however, has to do with the difficulty of a diverse electorate arriving at an agreement as to what constitutes "reasonable actions."

We are discovering now that there are less costly ways of reducing the incidence of mistakes by relying on market mechanisms. If the government contracts out its janitorial services – a form of increasing participation – it can accept the lowest bid. It then doesn't have to worry about what it pays individual janitors.

Political processes and societal cohesion:
consensus versus advocacy

Most of the propositions have to do, in one way or another, with participation in decision making. Secrecy seeks to exclude all but a small group; non-governmental organizations seek to expand those actively involved; the discussion of expertise versus representativeness is a debate about the extent to which decision making should be delegated to special sub-groups within the population.

There is a related issue: the manner in which decision-making occurs, in particular whether it is a consensus-seeking or advocacy process in which one side or another wins, can have a major impact on social cohesion and thereby affect political, social and economic stability. Decisions arrived at through consensual processes have a higher degree of *permanence*, and a higher probability of *success*. If individuals believe that those decisions are arrived at in a fair way and believe that they have been able to participate meaningfully in the decision, they are more likely to support the decision, that is, work to make sure that it is carried out and executed in a way which maximizes the likelihood of success. By contrast, policies arrived at through an exclusionary process or an advocacy process in which the majority wins and shows little regard for the losing minority set up the opposite dynamic. Losers work to reverse the decision and will take the first opportunity that they can to vote for a change. Because a decision is more likely to be reversed if the program is a failure, they may work to undermine its success; at the very least, they will not strive to ensure that it is successful. In anticipation of this, the majority may put into place all sorts of impediments to change, impediments which may not only be directly costly, but which impede change in response to unforeseen future events.

Effective consensus processes require openness. The argument

112

that consensus will be undermined by conflictual discussion has been put forward as a reason to suppress discourse and in extreme cases maintain secrecy, but it overlooks that fact that *competitive* advocacy processes are the best way to bring out opposing arguments and encourage a balanced consideration of policies' costs and benefits. A mark of a mature democracy is that it values and understands the importance of debate and discussions, not only before decisions are made, but after. The intent of the discussion is not to undermine the last decision, but to set the stage for the next. And in an ever changing society, there will be a "next" decision. The problems society faces are complex, and the more open discussion that occurs, the greater the chance that a better consensual decision will be arrived at, one which better incorporates the information about preferences of more citizens and one which has a deeper level of commitment of the various participants.[26]

Inclusion is also an essential part of the consensual process. While economists have long sought policies which are Pareto improvements – policies which benefit everyone, or at least harm no one – they have also long recognized that few changes actually benefit everyone. Changes which leave out major groups in society, however, are unlikely to receive widespread support. Thus, egalitarian policies, in which the fruits of growth are shared widely, are essential. Part of the success of East Asia is that they developed a growth strategy which was *inclusive*.

CONCLUDING REMARKS

This brings me back to the theme with which I began this lecture: the lessons to be learned from East Asia, both the successes over the past three decades and the problems over recent months.

It seems that many of the factors identified as contributors to East Asian economies' current problems are strikingly similar to the explanations previously put forward for their success. Strong financial markets, which were able to mobilize huge flows of savings and allocate them remarkably efficiently[27], have turned into weak financial markets which are blamed for their current problems. Addressing information problems in an effective way, including business-government coordination, were considered a hallmark of these economies' success; but this coordination is now viewed as political cronyism and lack of transparency is viewed as one of the main failings. Openness to international markets was hailed as one of the grounds of their success, yet insistence on eliminating barriers in capital and trade flows is an important ingredient in many of the IMF programs. Macro-stability including low inflation was agreed to be one of the key ingredients of the East Asian economies' remarkable performance, yet the Korea IMF program included a provision requiring the establishment of an independent central bank whose sole focus was price stability. Promoting competition, especially through export-oriented policies was hailed as one of the central pillars of their stellar performance, yet lack of competition in the business conglomerates is seen as one of their critical failings.

We seem to be ignoring the fact that this is a single crisis against a record of thirty years of remarkable growth. Although a significant setback, the current turmoil does not seem likely to permanently reverse the gains of the past quarter century. We are unjustifiably treating the occurrence of a crisis as compelling evidence of a fundamentally malfunctioning economy. No economy since the beginning of capitalism has escaped fluctuations. The historical record, in fact, shows that East Asia has had *ever* such fluctuations than other parts of the world – hardly evidence of a striking vulnerability in the economies. In the last three decades, Indonesia and Thailand have not had a single year of negative growth, and Korea and Malaysia have only had one each. In contrast, the United States and United Kingdom have had six years each of negative growth over the same period. History also suggests that, over the long run, East Asian governments' investment strategies were reasonably successful. Even if one accepts Young and others' growth accounting results as evidence that total factor productivity growth was not higher in Asia than anywhere else[28], one has to admit that total factor productivity growth was also not lower than elsewhere. However one looks at the econometric results, it is obvious that *the government system of reallocation had managed to allocate a larger percentage of GDP investment than had been achieved anywhere else in the world without any decrease in aggregate efficiency.*

The complete transformation of public discourse on East Asia demonstrates that pundits are inclined to hyperbole and to simple explanations of complex phenomena. The reality of East Asia's past success and current turmoil is probably somewhere in between the two extremes. One can see this, for example, by examining the strident accusations of "crony capitalism". True, business-government interaction in the region (the so-called Japan, Inc.and Malaysia, Inc.) always included the danger that the fine line between consensus building and collusion, between partnership and political cronyism, would be crossed. Indeed, those concerns were one of the reasons that many of us hesitated in suggesting that other countries follow all aspects of the East Asian model. Nevertheless, on balance, while there may have been some misallocation of resources as a result of abuses of power, the strength of the East Asian system outweighed the risks for many years. Perhaps the gains from improved coordination exceeded the losses from misguided investments. In any case, only an ideologue would claim that *but for their system of close government and business cooperation* they would have grown even faster.

A comparison of the East Asian countries with the United States also suggests that a more balanced, broad discussion should replace the current superficial, ahistorical coverage. I have often been struck by the similarities between the strategies pursued by East Asia and the United States, including the role that the government undertook in promoting universal education, in advancing technology and in creating and regulating financial markets.

The governments were both involved in successful industrial policy. The US government's active role in promoting economic expansion into the West, granting huge blocks of land to railroads, can be seen as an early business-government collaboration. This was a collaboration which resulted in a few individuals accumulating huge amounts of wealth, with more questionable benefits to society more generally. Perhaps a less questionable policy was the US government's financing of the first telegraph line between Baltimore and Washington, in 1842, an example of what today would be called *pre-competitive* innovation. Many observers also argue that a strong and effective industrial policy has been hidden in our defense policies over the half century since World War II.

In both cases, the creation of deep financial institutions has been lauded as a source of their success, but neither has been fully successful in ensuring stability of the financial sector. The United States was the first country in the world to establish a national regulator, the Office of the Comptroller of the Currency, in 1863; but this did not succeed in eliminating the relatively frequent financial panics which beset the country. And while the reforms in 1933 – including the establishing of national deposit insurance – eliminated panics, they did not eliminate crises, with the last being but nine years ago. The current crisis in East Asia reinforces the necessity of government taking a large role: financial sector problems can give rise to systemic effects, with significant adverse effects on the entire economy.[29]

Though there are many similarities in policies in the United States, there were also differences, of course, with policies pursued in several East Asian countries. Apart from its promotion of universal education and the opportunities afforded by the opening up of the West, the United States did little to promote a more egalitarian distribution of income. To be sure, American mythology emphasized the Horatio Algers of the world, but the reality may have been closer to that portrayed in Harrington's *Other America*. Many East Asian countries took deliberate measures – such as land redistribution and wage compression – to increase the degree of equality and reduce the most obvious manifestations of inequality. I have already referred to their success in reducing poverty. East Asia, contrary to the predictions made by Kaldor and Kuznets, showed that development could occur without high levels and marked increases in inequality.[30] It succeeded in rapid development with levels of inequality that were comparable to, and in some cases lower than, those in the United States.[31] These egalitarian policies brought with them a sense of inclusion and a degree of political and social stability so necessary for successful economic growth.[32]

In this more balanced perspective, we can see both strengths and weaknesses of government intervention. We can better identify the specific problems which have contributed to the East Asian turmoil without overshooting and condemning the role of government altogether. It is interesting to note that some of the current failures seem to be a result of governments discontinuing some of the activities that had ensured their growth over the past three decades. Thailand, for example, had a sound bank regulatory system which restricted lending to real estate. The government both realized the vulnerability that this lending created and believed that directing credit away from speculative real estate and towards more productive plants and equipment was an essential part of an effective growth strategy. These restrictions were eliminated, however, under the influence of those who claimed that such restrictions interfered with economic efficiency. Thailand's response to demands for financial

116

market liberalization was not accompanied by an equal emphasis on strengthening regulatory/supervisory structures. It seems fairly clear that too little government, not too much, was the problem.

Some journalists and even economists have suggested that not all proposed reforms are germane to the crisis. Some, such as Martin Feldstein[33], have explicitly addressed this issue. For instance, it has been suggested that Korea alter its monetary policy to focus exclusively on price stability. Including such reforms seemed unnecessary in Korea, a country which had not even had a history of high inflation, and indeed, in which inflation in the past year had been brought down from five and a half to four per cent. One may recall that in the United States there were earlier vehement' public and, I think, effective, arguments against the proposed reforms to change the Federal Reserve's mandate to an exclusive focus on price stability. Feldstein has argued that going beyond measures that are directly related to the crisis and into matters which reflect social values represents an intrusion into democratic processes which may even be counterproductive for the reform process. By contrast, ongoing dialogue redefining programs in light of changing circum-stances may enhance credibility and support within a country. If my earlier analysis on the importance of consensus formation has any modicum of truth, major reforms are unlikely to be achieved or maintained without social consensus and a policy of open debate.

It also seems clear, however, that lack of transparency contributed both to the vulnerability of the financial system in East Asia and the magnitude of the downturn. In the midst of growth euphoria, accounting details might be ignored, but in the midst of a crisis, they become central.[34] High debt equity ratios may, for a time, fuel rapid economic growth by allowing the economy to expand without the deeper institutional infra-structure required for robust capital markets. As we have seen in recent experience, they can also make countries more vulnerable to shocks. The fact that the private sector opted for these risky conditions and chose to ignore accounting details and have high debt equity ratios is not, however, the result of government intervention. These choices, like the decisions made in Bangkok and in Dallas to invest excessively in commercial real estate, were made by individual firms.

But these private decisions were nonetheless affected by government: governments failed to provide an adequate regulatory structure for banks[35] that included regulations providing appropriate risk assessments of highly indebted firms[36] and restricting excessive real estate lending[37]; they failed to put into place the legal and regulatory structure required for vibrant capital markets (including protection of minority shareholders and the kinds of protections provided by the Securities and Exchange Commission)[38]; they did not encourage or enforce effective accounting standards[39]; and they did not take actions to mitigate the systemic risks that these private decisions can lead to.[40] One can also accuse the United States, European, Japanese and other creditor country governments of being lax in their duties. The East Asian governments did not force banks in these countries to make the incremental loans that further increased East Asian firms' debt-equity ratios. In short, governments' omissions, more that commissions[41], appear to account for the current problems in East Asia.

To be sure, governments in East Asia have not followed all of the maxims I have listed as part of good government. They promoted competition in some areas, but restricted it in others. Export sectors were competitive, but non-traded sectors often were not. Leaders promoted dialogues and consensus in some areas, but did not have sufficient transparency and openness in others. The checks and balances which reduce the likelihood of abuses were in some cases absent and in others muffled. The balance between consensus and advocacy may have been tilted too far in one direction. Nevertheless, these circumstances are changing even in the midst of crisis. Korea, for example, had its first democratic transition of power after an open election with an active debate on key issues. Consensus on a wide set of reforms supported quick enactment of legislation.

These problems, as well as the enormous successes over the preceding three decades, provide a framework for re-examining the role of the state, for re-asking the questions, not only of what the government should be doing, but also how it should do it, and perhaps most importantly – and most durably – how these decisions are made.

NOTES

1. In Indonesia, so extensively criticized in the press recently, charges of so-called "crony capitalism" have obscured the fact that in two decades, the poverty rate has been reduced from over 60 per cent to 11 per cent.

2. See Williamson (1990) for a list of the Washington consensus principles. There is by now a large literature detailing the ways in which East Asia diverged from some of these policy norms, but this is not the occasion to review this literature. For some of my personal views, see Stiglitz (1996a and 1996b). For some more comprehensive views, see World Bank (1993).
3. Wade (1990).
4. China, in particular, departed from standard doctrines in its transition from socialism to "market socialism with a Chinese character". As Russia and other transition economies retracted the state and focused on privatization as a first step to competition, for example, China put off restructuring of the state-owned enterprises and focused instead on encouraging the growth of new private businesses to compete with the public enterprises, eventually forcing a restructuring on their part. Nevertheless (or perhaps consequently), its development performance has been impressive. China alone accounted for nearly two-thirds of the increase in incomes of low-income countries during the previous two decades, though it accounted for but 40 per cent of the low-income countries population, and 25 per cent percent of aggregate incomes at the beginning of the period. If China's 30 provinces were treated as independent data points (and most have populations of tens of millions of people), the 20 fastest growing units in the world over the last two decades would all be in China (World Bank, 1997).
5. The absence of an emphasis on distribution may stem from a simple lack of concern about distributional issues or from the belief that the adverse effects of redistribution are so great that the costs exceed the benefits.
6. More precisely, markets are not even constrained Pareto optimal where due attention is paid to the costs of information and of establishing markets. See Greenwald and Stiglitz (1986).
7. Even the proposition concerning monetary neutrality is valid only under highly restrictive conditions. For instance, if the government has a rule which increases the money supply in different amounts in different states of nature (keeping the mean increase in money supply fixed), then the demand for money will be affected (so long as there is not risk neutrality), and hence the price level, and real money supply will be affected differently in different states of nature, and hence the level of capital accumulation. See Greenwald and Stiglitz (1986).
8. There is, however, one fundamental difference: increases in capital values from good managerial values are typically partially captured by managers in private corporations (since to some extent, managers participate in the increase in the value of the firms which they manage),while increases in the "capital value" of public enterprises are more difficult for public managers to capture. (In practice, private managers may capture a relatively small fraction of the increase in capital values. See Jensen and Murphy, 1990.)
9. For a fuller articulation of the role of government in this sector, see Stiglitz (1992). There are further roles for government in consumer protection and in ensuring that underserved groups have access to credit.
10. See Hellman, Murdock, and Stiglitz (1995), Hellman and Murdock (1995), Aoki, Murdock and Okuno-Fujiwara (1997).
11. It is ironic that ethics laws prohibit officials from owning shares of stocks in companies that might be affected by the decisions taken, but do not prohibit elected officials from receiving money from the same companies.
12. Some people go further: restrict all government interventions into the market,

including industrial policy. This broader set of restrictions is more problematic. I have tried to state here a set of propositions with which most economists, regardless of their ideological persuasion, would agree.

13. Replacing the current below-market prices for grazing permits with auctions, for example, would have been good for the budget, good for economic efficiency and good for the environment. Not surprisingly, however, it was strongly resisted by ranchers. Interest groups fearing a reduction in rents are also likely to to resist seemingly Pareto-improving changes which make these rents more visible and hence more vulnerable to attack. Farmers did not oppose the conversion of the United States milk cartel and other distortionary agricultural programs into welfare equivalent lump sum payments because they would be worse off in the short run, but because the increased transparency made the abolition of the implicit and explicit subsidies more likely. See Stiglitz (1998).

14. The international trade mechanisms seem to have served as a more effective commitment mechanism than domestically-imposed transactions costs. Those resisting opening up trade or abandoning farm support programs outside of international trade negotiations sometimes liken it to unilateral disarmament. But this is wrong: one of the most widely accepted propositions in economics is that in competitive markets, a country which lowers its trade barriers benefits itself.

15. This example also illustrates the difficulty of separating private from public interests. The advocates of public schools point out their role, for instance, in social integration. What disrupts that perspective, however, is the fact that the public monopoly has given rise to social segregation based on residence; suburban schools are often, or perhaps typically, far less integrated than urban private schools, especially urban parochial schools. The concern about the separation of church and state can and has been handled in other ways, for example by restricting teaching of religious subjects to certain periods.

16. Ethanol's viability in the U.S. requires huge subsidies - in some cases close to a dollar's worth of subsidy for a dollar's worth of ethanol. Worse still, producing ethanol requires a large amount of energy so that the net reduction of oil imports as a result of ethanol production is far less than the ethanol usage itself. Ethanol derivative additives also increase the volatility of gasoline and thus add to air pollution and reduce fuel efficiency.

17. Thurow (1985) has noted that "if the [anti-dumping law] applied to domestic firms, the top 20 firms in the Fortune 500 would have been found guilty of dumping in 1982". Discussed in Stiglitz (1997a).

18. I sometimes joke that the announcement of my leaving the chairmanship of the Council of Economic Advisers had a larger and longer effect! Of course, this also underscores the point that these market movements are as much random occurrences as anything else.

19. Hirschmann (1970). On a local level, however, where citizens can move between jurisdictions, exit and choice can provide market-type signals to governments. This idea, the so-called Tiebout hypothesis, is one of the predominant rationales for decentralization. While the analogy between choices among communities, suggested by Tiebout (1956), and the choice of private goods in conventional markets is suggestive, there are fundamental differences between the two which make the optimality of resource allocations arising from competition among communities far less likely (or valid under far more restrictive conditions) than optimal resource allocation in purely private markets. See Stiglitz (1983).

20. In the United States, for example, the Association for the Advancement of Retired People provides a forceful expression of voice for the aged; but it is a special interest group which has impeded reformers in key public entitlement programs for the elderly, blocking reforms which are necessary for the continued fiscal solvency of the country.
21. Slovic, Layman and Flynn (1993), EPA (1987).
22. Stiglitz (1997b).
23. There is a large literature documenting the proclivity for shortsighted policies, especially when the electorate exhibits myopia, perhaps based on its lack of understanding of the long-run consequences of current policies. See, for example, Dornbusch and Edwards (1991).
24. Indeed, the statistical evidence correlating independent central banks with more stable monetary policies may be as much a reflection of the fact that societies that are more concerned with inflaction choose to have independent central banks, and these central banks reflect societal preferences, as it has to do with the actual effect of independent central banks. See Posen (1993). For instance, Russia had an independent central bank, which was a major source of inflationary pressures, seemingly against the will of the elected government; and India has had a long tradition of stable macro-policies without an independent central bank.
25. Alesina and Summers (1993). The fact that those objectives have little impact on real values (economic growth and stability, as reflected in real growth rates and unemployment) also shouldn't come as a surprise, given the evidence on the weak connection between the two. More generally, economic systems adapt to greater price stability, and may, for instance, undertake greater leverage, making the real consequence of any variation in inflation and nominal interest rates all the greater. See Greenwald and Stiglitz (1986).
26. There are some obvious exceptions to this generalization, in societies in which there are fundamental cleavages in values, where open discussion may reveal the depth of those cleavages. For the most part, however, among those committed to making democratic societies work, even the recognition of depth of those cleavages may be useful in discouraging the majority from attempting to impose its values on the minority.
27. There is strong evidence of significant correlations between the depth of financial markets and economic growth. See King and Levine (1993). Levine (1997) contains a comprehensive summary of recent work.
28. Young (1994) and Kim and Lau (1993). However, there are good reasons for not taking these studies seriously. Rodriguez-Clare and Hammond (1993).
29. And there might well have been another crisis after 1989, had the United States not had the good fortune of falling long-term interest rates in 1993, a result of deficit reduction. Given the excessive holding of long-term government bonds (a result of a misguided regulatory policy which treated these long-term bonds as safe assets, in spite of the obvious capital asset risk) had a budget deal not been made, interest rates are likely to have soared, and banks would have found themselves without adequate net worth. Would the United States then have been accused of lack of regulatory transparency or of political cronyism, as a result of the close connections between the regulatory authorities and the banking community which may well have induced this misguided regulatory policy? For a more extensive discussion, see Stiglitz (1997b).
30. Kaldor (1963) had argued that high levels of inequality were necessary to generate

high levels of savings. East Asia showed that even the relatively poor could save at high rates, provided there was the right institutional structure. Japan, for instance, created postal savings banks, providing a safe and convenient vehicle for financial savings. Kuznets (1955) posits that inequality will rise and fall in a U-shaped pattern during development.

31. The average US Gini index for 1947-1991 is 35.28, barely below the 36.18 average of the much faster-growing East Asian economies. Taiwan (Province), China, Indonesia, Japan and Korea, in fact, had lower average Gini indices (thus less inequality) over approximately the same period (Deininger and Squire, 1996).

32. World Bank (1993), Birdsall and Sabot (1993), Campos and Root (1996).

33. Feldstein (1998).

34. Transparency was important partly because lenders could not distinguish between good and bad borrowers, and thus withheld credit from all borrowers. But one has to keep a perspective on this as on other issues: the last set of financial crises occurred in Scandinavia, a set of countries with the general reputation of having the "cleanest" governments with the highest degree of transparency.

35. Though here too one must keep one's perspective: if one criticizes banks in the affected countries for making bad lending decisions, equal fault must be assigned to the banks and regulatory authorities in the developed countries. These banks presumably had better risk management systems, and these loans were more frequently marginal loans, added on to the debt that the companies had previously accumulated from domestic borrowers. While the systemic risk of these loans to the lending countries is no doubt less, the fact that several of the major lending countries urged international actions can best be justified as a reflection of a judgment of a broader systemic risk.

36. But again, the mistakes of Asia need to be put in perspective: as I noted above, the risk assessments employed in the United States clearly did not reflect the asset value risk associated with long-term government bonds.

37. Indeed, some of the countries had had more effective regulations, which were rolled back under pressure for financial sector liberalization, under the argument that these restrictions interfered with the efficient allocation of resources.

38. Though, to be sure, many developed countries still do not have adequate protections.

39. In the United States, accounting standards are set by the private sector, not the government; but fraud, disclosure and other protective laws have provided a strong impetus for their widespread adoption.

40. Again, many of the countries have been subjected to pressure to reduce interventions that were designed to or had the effect of mitigating these risks. These policies are now being looked at in a far more favorable light.

41. To be sure, certain government policies contributed to the problem: the seemingly pegged exchange rates in several countries may have contributed to a perception of less exchange rate risk associated with foreign borrowing that there really was. But one must not confuse policies which may be misguided with policies which underlie the current crisis. While government decisions to undertake a particular industrial project may or may not be misguided, such decisions probably played a second order effect in exposing the country to the current vulnerabilities.

REFERENCES

Alesina, A., and L. Summers. 1993. "Central Bank Independence and Macroeconomic Performance: Some Comparative Evidenc." *Journal of Money, Credit, and Banking* 25(2), May.

Aoki, Masahiko, Kevin Murdock and Masahiro Okuno-Fujiwara. 1997. "Beyond the East Asian Miracle: Introducing the Market-Enhancing View" in M. Aoki, H. Kim, and M. Okuno-Fujiwara (eds.), *The Role of Government in East Asian Development*. Oxford: Clarendon Press.

Birdsall, Nancy, and Richard Sabot. 1993. "Virtuous Circles: Human Capital Growth and Equity in East Asia." Background Paper for *The East Asian Miracle*. World Bank Policy Research Department, Washington, DC.

Campos, Edgardo, and Hilton Root. 1996. *The Key to the East Asian Miracle*. Washington, DC: Brookings Institution.

Deininger, Klaus, and Lyn Squire. 1996. "A New Data Set Measuring Income Inequality." *World Bank Economic Review,* 10(3): 565–91.

Diebold, F., and G. Rudebusch. 1992. "Have Postwar Economic Fluctuations Been Stabilized?" *America Economic Review* 82(4): 993–1005.

Dixit, Avitash and Mancur Olson. 1997. "Does Voluntary Participation Undermine the Coase Theorem?" Princeton: Princeton University, Press.

Dornbusch, R., and S. Edwards. 1991. "The Macroeconomics of Populism." In Dornbusch and Edwards (eds.), *The Macroeconomics of Populism in Latin America*. Chicago: University of Chicago Press.

Edlin, A., and J. Stiglitz. 1995. "Discouraging Rivals: Managerial Rent-Seeking and Economic Inefficiencies." *American Economic Review.* 85(5): 1301–12.

Environmental Protection Agency (1987). *Unfinished Business: A Comparative Assessment of Environmental Problems*. Washington, DC: EPA.

Farrell, Joseph. 1987. "Information and the Coase Theorem." *Journal of Economic Perspectives* 1(2): 113–29.

Feldstein, Martin. 1998. "Refocusing the IMF." *Foreign Affairs* 77(2), March/April, 20–33.

Greenwald, B., and J. Stiglitz. 1986. "Externalities in Economics with Imperfect Information and Incomplete Markets." *Quarterly Journal of Economics* May, 229–264.

Harrington, Michael. 1962. *The Other America: Poverty in the United States*. New York: Maxwell Macmillan International.

Hellmann,Thomas, Kevin Murdock, and Joseph Stiglitz. 1995. "Deposit Mobilization through Financial Restraint." Stanford Graduate School of Business Research Paper 1354, July.

Hellmann, Thomas, and Kevin Murdock. 1995. "Financial Sector Development Policy: The Importance of Reputational Capital and Governance." Stanford Graduate School of Business Research Paper 1361, December.

Hirschman, Albert O. 1970. *Exit, Voice, and Loyalty: Responses to Decline in Firms, Organizations and States*. Cambridge, Mass. Harvard University Press.

Jensen, Michael, and Kevin Murphy. 1990. "Performance Pay and Top-Management Incentives." *Journal of Political Economy* 98(2), April: 225–64.

Kaldor, Nicholas. 1963. "Capital Accumulation and Economic Growth." in Friedrich Lutz and Douglas Hague (eds.), *Proceedings of conference Held by the International Economics Association*. London: Macmillan.

Kim, Jung, and Lawrence Lau. 1993. "The Sources of Economic Growth of the East Asian Industrialized Countries." Paper presented at a Conference on the Economic Development of Republic of China and the Pacific Rim in 1990 and Beyond, Stanford University, California.

King, Robert G., and Ross Levine. 1993. "Finance and Growth: Schumpeter Might Be Right." *Quarterly Journal of Economics,* 108(3): 717–38.

Kuznets, Simon. 1955. "Economic Growth and Income Inequality." *American Economic Review* 45(1): 1–28.

Levine, Ross. 1997. "Financial Development and Economic Growth: Views and Agenda." *Journal of Economic Literature* 35(2), June, 688–726.

Posen, Adam. 1993. "Why Central Bank Independence Does Not Cause Low Inflation: There is No Institutional Fix for Politics." In Richard O'Brien, ed., *Finance and the International Economy*, vol. 7 New York: Oxford University Press for the Amex Bank Review. 41–54.

Rodriguez-Clare, Andres, and Peter Hammond. 1993. "On Endogenizing Long-Run Growth." *Scandinavian Journal of Economics* 95(4): 391–425.

Shleifer, A., and P. Vishny. 1989. "Management Entrenchment: The Case of Manager-Specific Investments." *Journal of Financial Economics* 25(1): 123–39.

Slovic, Paul, Mark Layman and James Flynn 1993. "Perceived Risk, Trust and Nuclear Waste: Lessons from Yucca Mountain." In R. Dunlap, M. Kraft, and E. Rosa (eds.), *Public Reactions to Nuclear Waste*, Durham, N. C.: Duke University Press.

Stiglitz, J.E. 1983. "The Theory of Local Public Goods Twenty-Five Years After Tiebout: A Perspective" In *G.R. Zodrow (ed.),Local Provision of Public Services: The Tiebout Model After Twenty-Five Years*, G.R. Zodrow (ed.), 17–53 Academic Press.

———. 1987. "Technological Change, Sunk Costs, and Competition." *Brookings Papers on Economic Activity*, 3. (Special issue of *Microeconomics*, M.N. Baily and C. Winston, eds., 1988, 883–947.)

———. 1989. "The Economic Role of the State: Efficiency and Effectiveness." In A. Heertje, ed., *The Economic Role of the State*. London: Basil Blackwell.

———. 1992. "The Role of the State in Financial Markets." *Proceedings of the World Bank conference on Development Economics 1993.* Washington, DC: World Bank.

———. 1994. *Whither Socialism?* Cambridge, MA: MIT Press.

———. 1996a. "Some Lessons from the East Asian Miracle."*World Bank Research Observer,*11(2), August, 151–77.

———. 1996b. "Financial Markets, Public Policy, and the East Asian Miracle." with M. Uy. *World Bank Research Observer,* 11(2), August 1996, 249–76.

———. 1997a. "Dumping on Free Trade: The US Import Trade Laws" *Southern Economic Journal.* 64(2): 402–424.

———. 1997b. "Central Banking in a Democratic Society." Presented as Tinbergen Lecture, Amsterdam, Netherlands, October.

———. 1998. "The Private Uses of Public Interests: Incentives and Institutions." *Journal of Economic Perspectives,* 12(2): 3-22.

Stokes, Susan. 1996. "Public Opinion and Market Reforms: The Limits of Economic Voting." *Comparative Political Studies* 29(5), October.

Thurow, Lester. 1985. *The Zero-Sum Solution: Building a World-Class American Economy.* New York: Simon and Schuster.

Tiebout, C. 1956. "A Pure Theory of Local Expenditures." *Journal of Political Economy,* 64(5): 416–424.

Wade, R. 1990. *Governing Markets: Economic Theory and the Role of Government Intervention in the East Asian Economies*. Princeton, N.J.: Princeton University Press.

Williamson, John. 1990. "What Washington Means by Policy Reform" in John Williamson, ed., *Latin American Adjustment: How Much Has Happened?* Washington, DC: Institute for International Economics.

World Bank. 1993. *The East Asian Miracle*. New York: Oxford University Press for the World Bank.

World Bank. 1997. *China 2020*. Washington, DC.

Young, Alwyn. 1994. "The Tyranny of Numbers: Confronting the Statistical Realities of the East Asian Growth Experience." *Quarterly Journal of Economics*, 110 (August): 641–80.

Chapter 4

Whither Reform? –
Ten Years of the Transition

Paper presented at the Annual Bank Conference
on Development Economics
Washington DC, April 1999

INTRODUCTION

This century has been marked by two great economic experiments. The outcome of the first set, the socialist experiment that began, in its more extreme form, in the Soviet Union in 1917, is now clear. The second experiment is the movement back from a socialist economy to a market economy. Ten years after the beginning of the transition in Eastern Europe and the Former Soviet Union, how do we assess what has happened? What are the lessons to be learned? Surely this is one of the most important experiments in economics ever to have occurred, a massive and relatively sudden change in the rules of the game. As rapidly as the countries announced the abandonment of communism, so too did western advisors march in with their sure-fire recipes for a quick transition to a market economy.

A decade after the beginning of the transition in Eastern Europe and the Former Soviet Union (FSU), and two decades after the beginning of the transition in China, the picture is mixed. Each country started the course of transition with a different history, a different set of human and physical endowments. Some had lived under the yoke of central planning and authoritarianism for most of the century, while in others it was imposed only in the aftermath of World War II. Those countries bordering Western Europe with encouraging prospects of European Union integration were clearly in a different position than the land-locked countries of Mongolia and the former Soviet republics in Central Asia.[1] Counterfactual history – what would have been but for the policies that were pursued – is always problematic, and no more so than when there are so many variables with which to contend. Yet the disparity between the successes and failures is so large that it calls out for interpretation and explanation, and in any case, the public debate has already begun.

The contrast between the strategies – and results – of the two largest countries, Russia and China, may be instructive. Figure 1 shows that over the decade beginning in 1989, while China's GDP nearly doubled, Russia's GDP almost halved; so that while at the beginning of the period Russia's GDP was more than twice that of China's, at the end it was a third smaller.[2] Not only did Russia stagnate during this past decade, but Figure 2 shows how it succeeded in turning the theoretical tradeoffs of inequality and growth on its head – in the process of shrinking its GDP, Russia also doubled its inequality (as measured by the Gini coefficient). Recent data contained in the 1999 *World Development Indicators* paint an even bleaker picture, with poverty – defined as $4 a day – rising from two million to over 60 million people by the middle of the decade.

The titles of some recent books by leading advisors in the transition process are telling – *How Russia became a Market Economy* or *The Coming Boom in Russia*. While those who had advised Russia on its transition path constantly predicted that it was on the verge of success – virtually declaring victory just a short while before its recent crash – the shortfall should have been apparent. Yes, Russia had succeeded in "privatizing" much of its industry and natural resources, but the level of gross fixed investment – a far more important sign of a burgeoning market economy – had fallen dramatically over the last five years [EBRD 1998]. Russia was fast becoming an extractive economy, rather than a modern industrial economy.

Standing in marked contrast with these failures has been the enormous success of China, which created its own path of transition (rather than just using a blueprint or recipe from western advisors). It succeeded not only in growing rapidly, but in creating a vibrant, non-state-owned collective enterprise sector. While investment in manufacturing in Russia stagnated, that in China was growing by leaps and bounds. Critics of such comparisons point out the marked difference in starting points – China's income was far lower, and so there were more opportunities for catch-up. On the contrary, however, I would argue that China's challenges were greater, for it had to manage the challenges of transition and of development simultaneously. China did better than countries of comparably low income, while the countries of the FSU and Eastern Europe, by and large, did worse than countries of comparable income.

Figure 1: Russian and Chinese Gross Domestic Product*

*Measured in constant 1987 US$.
Source: Statistical Information and Management Analysis (SIMA)
database.

Figure 2: Russian Growth and Inequality

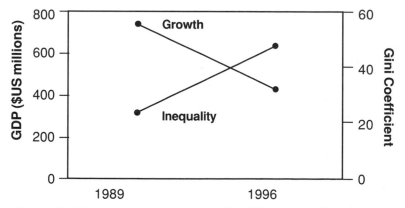

Source: World Development Indicators, 1999. The GDP is measured in constant 1987
$US and chart represents generated trendline between 1989 and 1996 data points.

The question that we need to ask is, why the failures? Not surprisingly, those who advocated shock therapy and rapid privatization argue that the problem was not too much shock and too little therapy, but that there was too little shock. The reforms were not pursued aggressively enough. The medicine was right; it was only that the patient failed to follow the doctor's orders! Other defenders of the recommended reform programs argue that the failures were not in the design of the reforms, but in their implementation. One of the Russian reformers recently quipped that there was nothing wrong with the laws they enacted except non-enforcement.

I want to argue here, however, that the failures of the reforms that were widely advocated go far deeper – to a misunderstanding of the very foundations of a market economy, as well as a failure to grasp the fundamentals of reform processes. I will argue below that at least part of the problem was an excessive reliance on textbook models of economics. Textbook economics may be fine for teaching students, but not for advising governments trying to establish a new a market economy – especially since the typical American style textbook relies so heavily on a particular intellectual tradition, the neoclassical model, leaving out other traditions (such as those put forward by Schumpeter and Hayek) which might have provided more insights into the situations facing the economies in transition. (But, as I shall argument below, the failings of textbook economics are far greater: with few exceptions, they fail even to incorporate insights concerning corporate governance, a concern of mainstream economics from Marshall [1897] to Berle and Means [1932] and a major focus of modern information and transactions costs economic.) A part of the problem also rose from confusing means with ends: taking, for instance, privatization or the opening of capital accounts as a mark of success rather than a means to the more fundamental ends. Even the creation of a market economy should be viewed as a means to broader ends. It is not just the creation of market economy that matters, but the improvement of living standards and the establishment of the foundations of sustainable, equitable and democratic development.

Finally, while due obeisance was paid to "political processes" – and insights into the political process were often put forward in justification of particular courses for reform – in fact, little understanding of these political processes was evidenced. In hindsight, it is clear that many of the political forecasts of those involved in the reform process were far from clairvoyant; many worries seem, by and large, not to have materialized, while political developments which should have been of concern were not anticipated. Nor can one separate "principles" from how they are, or are likely to be, implemented. Policy advisers put forth policy prescriptions in the context of a particular society – a society with a particular history, with a certain level of social capital, with a particular set of political institutions, and with political processes affected by (if not determined by) the existence of particular political forces. Interventions do not occur in a vacuum. How those recommendations are used, or abused, is not an issue from which economists can simply walk away. And this is especially so in those instances where one of the arguments for the economic reforms is either failures in the political process or their impact on the political process itself.[3] It is time for the doctors to rethink the prescription.[4] But in doing so, they will have to take the patient as he is today, not as he might have been had history taken a different course. The point is not to refight the old battles, but to learn the lessons of the past, to help guide the future.

PART I: MISUNDERSTANDINGS OF MARKET ECONOMIES

In my book, *Whither Socialism?* (1994), I argued that the failure of market socialism arose in part from a failure to understand what makes a actual market economy function – a failure arising in part from the neoclassical model itself. If the Arrow-Debreu (AD) model (1954) had been correct, then market socialism might have fared far better. But while the AD models capture one essential aspect of a market economy – the information conveyed by price signals, and the role that those price signals serve in coordinating production – the information problems addressed by the economy are far richer. Prices do not convey all the relevant information. I want to suggest here that those advocating shock therapy, with its focus on privatization, similarly failed because they failed to understand modern capitalism; they too were overly influenced by the excessively simplistic textbook models of the market economy. But we should be less forgiving of those failures. While Hayek and Schumpeter had earlier in the century developed alternative paradigms, views that had not been well integrated into the mainstream of the Anglo-American tradition, by the time the post-socialist economies faced their transition, the modern theory of information economics had shown the striking limitations of the AD model, and used the tools of modern economic analysis to illustrate forcefully the problems of corporate governance that Marshall (1897), Keynes [1963 [1926]], Berle and Means [1932], Galbraith [1952], March and Simon [1958], Baumol [1959], Marris [1964] and many others had written about over the course of the twentieth century.

In the following paragraphs, I want to review what I see as the major ways in which what, for want of a better term, I shall refer to as the "Washington consensus" doctrines of transition, failed in their understandings of the core elements of a market economy.[5] In the second section of this talk, I shall focus more sharply on the *reform strategy*, that is, on views about sequencing and pacing.

Competition and privatization

Standard neoclassical theory argues that for a market economy to work well (to be Pareto efficient), there must be both competition and private property (the "Siamese twins" of efficient wealth creation). Both are required and, clearly, if one could wave a magic wand and instantaneously institute both, one would presumably do that. The issue however, concerns choices: if one cannot have both, should one proceed with privatization alone?

While those pushing for privatization pointed with pride to the large fraction of state enterprises that were turned over to private hands, these were dubious achievements. After all, it is easy to simply give away state assets, especially to one's friends and cronies; and the incentives for doing so are especially strong if the politicians conducting the privatization exercise can get a kickback, either directly or indirectly as campaign contributions. Indeed, if privatization is conducted in ways that are widely viewed as illegitimate and in an environment which lacks the necessary institutional infrastructure, the longer-run prospects of a market economy may actually be undermined. Worse still, the private property interests that are created contribute to the weakening of the state and the undermining of the social order, through corruption and regulatory capture.

Consider the incentives facing the so-called oligarchs in Russia. They might well have reasoned: democratic elections will eventually conclude that our wealth is ill-begotten, and there will thus be attempts to recapture it. They might have been induced to pursue a two-fold strategy: on the one hand, to use their financial power to gain sufficient political influence to reduce the likelihood of such an event; but, assuming that that strategy is inherently risky, to use the other hand to take at least a significant part of their wealth out of the country to a safe haven. Indeed, the "reform" advisors facilitated this process by encouraging – in some cases even insisting – on the opening of capital accounts.[6] Thus, the failure of privatization to provide the basis of a market economy was not an accident, but a predictable consequence of the manner in which privatization occurred.

Privatization alternatives

Those advocating rapid privatization faced the quandary that there were no legitimate sources of private wealth within the country with which privatization could be accomplished. Governments thus faced essentially four alternatives – a sale of national assets abroad; voucher privatization; taming "spontaneous" privatization; or what I shall call for want of a better term "illegitimate" privatization. The latter was the route Russia chose after 1995 in the notorious "loans-for-shares" scheme.[7] The government can allow private entrepreneurs to create banks, which can lend these private parties money with which to buy the enterprises (or in the loans-for-shares deal, lend to the government, with the shares of government enterprises as collateral). Whoever got the banking license got a license to print money, and the license to print money is a license to acquire government enterprises. While the corruption was somewhat roundabout – and the process was less transparent than if the government had simply given the nation's assets to its friends – there is in fact little distinction between the two processes.

Since the whole process was widely viewed as illegitimate, this "robber baron" privatization put market capitalism to even greater disrepute than perhaps the indoctrination of the communist era. And since there was no presumption that those who thereby acquired the assets were particularly good managers, there was no reason to hope that the assets would be better deployed than they had previously been. To be sure, some who advocated this process worried little about either the political impact or the managerial incompetence: they believed that there were strong incentives in play for an "aftermarket" – so that the assets would eventually be sold to those who could best manage these enterprises. The hope was that these new "robber barons" would at least conduct a good auction. But this process failed for several reasons: first, there remained the underlying problem – where were the internal managerial teams with the requisite capital? Worse still, the declining confidence in the economy and the government made the country even less attractive to foreign investors. The oligarchs found that they could extract more wealth from asset stripping than from redeploying assets in a way that would provide the foundations of wealth creation.

The voucher schemes proved little more successful, with the Czech Republic (at first taken as a model) providing the clearest illustration of the underlying problem of corporate governance, the public good of corporate management, which I will consider later.

Perhaps trying to discipline spontaneous privatization might have offered the greatest hope: breaking up the large enterprises into smaller units which might have provided a basis for more effective governance by the stakeholders, a possibility I turn to later in this essay.

Creative destruction

An essential part of the transition to a more efficient economy is the redeployment of resources from less productive to more productive uses. Moving workers from low productive employment to unemployment does not, by itself, increase productivity. Indeed, productivity is lowered, and some productivity is better than none. The movement into unemployment is a costly and inefficient intermediate stage – one could only defend it if there were no better way of moving workers directly from a low productivity job to a higher productivity job. A crude form of Say's law (with little empirical basis) was often put forward: a large supply of idle workers will create a demand, partly by facilitating downward pressure on wages.

But any student of the process of enterprise creation and entre-preneurship would have expressed concerns, especially in regions like the FSU, where there was little history of market-oriented entrepreneurship.

For entrepreneurship to succeed, certain skills need to be developed in practice, skills which those in the FSU had no opportunity to develop. They had acquired skills in evading government regulations, in arbitraging away some of the inefficiencies in government regulations for private profit, and in operating at the interstices between the legal and illegal world. But that is a far different kind of enterprise from creating new businesses and competing in the international market place.

Entrepreneurship also requires capital. As noted above, few had the necessary capital – especially after inflation eroded what little savings people had accumulated. The banking system had no experience in screening and monitoring loans – it was wrong even to think of these banks as "banks" in the Western sense. The language here confused both those in the country and Western advisers. But in any case, few of the enterprises actually got into the business of providing funds to new, small enterprises, and thus, even under the best of conditions, entrepreneurship was stifled. Where, then, were the new jobs for those forced out of existing employment?

Bankruptcy, or the credible threat of it, is a crucial part of a market economy. The institution of bankruptcy, like its inverse of entrepreneurship, had little or no precedent in the socialist countries. The institution of bankruptcy had to be created. A variety of available models for bank-ruptcy codes had evolved over centuries in the market economies, and each was integrated into the specifics of its economy. A transplant to an alien environment could hardly be expected to take root quickly – particularly in the absence of an independent and competent judiciary, trained in and sympathetic to the basic tenets of bankruptcy. Those who hoped that newly drafted and "installed" bankruptcy codes would drive industrial restructuring have been much disappointed.

Moreover, as is so often the case, there is no "one best way"; all bankruptcy systems involve genuine tradeoffs between creditor and debtor rights. Systems need to be tailored to the local environment.[8] For instance, one relevant feature is the speed with which assets can be re-engaged in productive use. In countries with little entrepreneurship, poor social safety nets, and little tradition of labor mobility, we must expect a tilt towards debtor-oriented bankruptcy.[9] Moreover, we should not think that much industrial restructuring will come out of bankruptcy courts; the real restructuring is usually done to keep companies out of formal bankruptcy. I will later consider a range of such restructuring actions.

Entrepreneurship and bankruptcy, entry and exit, must be seen as two sides of the same coin of economic change. The advice to "just enforce the bankruptcy laws" or "just harden the budget constraint" is not good advice where there is little culture of new business creation. Both parts of Schumpeter's phrase "creative destruction" must be remembered.[10] Even long-standing market economies do not get out of deep depressions, where many firms qualify as bankrupt, by forcing large numbers of firms into bankruptcy. Vigorous programs of employment creation and maintenance, through promotion of entrepreneurship and/or by Keynesian stimuli, must go hand in hand, if not precede, bankruptcy-induced restructuring.

Social and organizational capital

It has long been recognized that a market system cannot operate solely on the basis of narrow self-interest. The informational problems in market interactions offer many chances for opportunistic behavior. Without some minimal amount of social trust and civil norms, social interaction would be reduced to a minimum of tentative and distrustful commodity trades. Behind these social norms stands the machinery of the law which itself stands apart from the market.

> Property systems are in general not completely self-enforcing. They depend for their definition upon a constellation of legal procedures, both civil and criminal. The course of the law itself cannot be regarded as subject to the price system. The judges and the police may indeed be paid, but the system itself would disappear if on each occasion they were to sell their services and decisions. Thus the definition of property rights based on the price system depends precisely on the lack of universality of private property and the price system. ... The price system is not, and perhaps in some basic sense cannot be, universal. To the extent that it is incomplete, it must be supplemented by an implicit or explicit social contract. (Arrow 1972, 35.)

The information requirements for, and transactions costs involved in, implicit and explicit contract enforcement are typically different, so that the two should best be thought of as complements rather than substitutes. The problem in the economies in transition was that both enforcement mechanisms were weak: the state's legal and judicial capacities were limited, while the very process of transition – high institutional turnover, high shadow interest rates and short time horizons – impairs the effectiveness of implicit contracts. Thus, even if institutions did not need to be created, the very process of transition provides impediments to the workings of a market economy.

Arrow, Hirschman (1992), Putnam (1993), Fukuyama (1995), and others have argued that the success of a market economy cannot be understood in terms of narrow economic incentives: norms, social institutions, social capital and trust play critical roles.[11] It is this implicit social contract, necessary to a market society, that cannot be simply legislated, decreed or installed by a reform government. Some such "social gluc" is necessary in any society. One of the most difficult parts of a transformation, such as the transition from socialism to a market economy, is the transformation of the old "implicit social contract" to a new one. If "reformers" simply destroy the old norms and constraints in order to "clean the slate" without allowing for the time-consuming processes of reconstructing new norms, then the new legislated institutions may well not take hold. Then the reforms will be discredited and the "reformers" will blame the victims for not correctly implementing their ill-considered designs.

One variation on this theme is to blame the failure of the shock therapy reforms on corruption and rent-seeking at every turn (e.g., Åslund, 1999). But while rent-seeking and corruption were important, there was more to the failure than that (and indeed, if rent-seeking were the sole problem, then the reductions in rents asserted by Åslund should have been accompanied by a soaring of national output.) Moreover, corruption and rent seeking may itself have been increased by the manner in which the reforms were conducted, which both destroyed the already weak social capital and enhanced opportunities and incentives for such activities.[12]

The social and organizational capital needed for the transition cannot be legislated, decreed, or in some other way imposed from above.[13] People need to take an active and constructive role in their self-transformation; to a large extent, they need to be in the driver's seat. Otherwise the reform regime is only using bribes and threats to induce outward changes in behavior insofar as behavior can be monitored – but that is not transformation.[14]

In market economies, firms may be seen as local non-market solutions to collective action problems where transaction costs inhibit coordination by market contracts (Coase, 1937). In the new post-socialist market economies, as in the established market economies, the primary example of extensive (i.e., beyond the family) social cooperation in daily life is found in the workplace. Thus entrepreneurial efforts that arise out of or spin off from existing enterprises may be particularly effective in post-socialist societies in preserving "lumps" of social and organizational capital. Once dissipated, organizational capital is hard to reassemble, particularly in environments with little entrepreneurial experience. Other social organizations that might incubate and support entrepreneurial efforts include local township governments,[15] unions, schools, colleges, cooperatives (housing, consumer, credit and producer co-ops), mutual aid associations, guilds, professional associations, churches, veterans' associations, clubs and extended family groups. Creativity and experimentation should be the order of the day to remobilize social resources particularly in the slow-starting transitional economies of the former Soviet Union.[16]

The post-socialist separation of ownership and control

Given the difficulties in reassembling organizational capital once it is dissipated or destroyed, it is particularly important to promote entre-preneurial restructuring in existing enterprises. The need for fundamental enterprise restructuring has not been lost on the swarms of Western advisors, but their advice has sometimes contributed as much to the problem as to the solution.

In retrospect, one of the remarkable features of the body of Western advice given to post-socialist economies ("Washington consensus"), especially as they approached the issue of privatization (see above), is the absence of attention to the separation of ownership and control. The intellectual framework often seems to be a curious pre-Berle-Means[17] world where "private ownership" and control of the enterprise are essentially the same thing – as if the small or medium-sized closely-held corporation was the norm. Yet the salient feature of the large companies in the Anglo-American economies has been what Berle and Means called the "separation of ownership and control". Keynes, even earlier, made the same point.

> One of the most interesting and unnoticed developments of recent decades [written in 1926] has been the tendency of big enterprise to socialize itself. A point arrives in the growth of a big institution – particularly a big railroad or big public utility enterprise, but also a big bank or a big insurance company – at which the owners of the capital, i.e., the shareholders, are almost entirely dissociated from the management, with the result that the direct personal interest of the latter in the making of the great profit becomes quite secondary. (Keynes, 1963.p. 314.)

The divergence of interests between the managers and shareholders in large publicly-traded corporations has been a major source of the economics of agency contracts.[18] Yet the hard lessons of the separation of ownership and control, and the resulting agency problems, have received insufficient attention in the standard Western advice in spite of much discussion of "the corporate governance problem". Let me give you a few examples of "fine phrases".

"Clearly Defined Private Property Rights"

Instead of trying to control managers in state-owned companies with better incentive contracts, the standard advice is to privatize and let "private property rights" provide the natural incentives – "like in the West". Yet the separation of ownership and control in large Western companies means that the control function is not allocated on the basis of "clearly defined private property rights". The ownership of shares, like the ownership of bonds, is indeed clearly defined; the shareholder can buy, sell or hold those rights. But those rights do not "add up" to a real ownership-based control of the company when the shareholders are atomized and dispersed. One way to express this point is to recognize that the management of a publicly held company with disperse ownership is a public good[19] – and as in the case of any public good, there will be an undersupply. Another way of putting the same point is that the market for managers – the process of take-overs – is highly imperfect, and does not in general ensure that the company will be managed by those who will ensure that the assets yield the highest returns.[20]

"Controlling Private Owner"

When the problems of dispersed shareholding were recognized in operating companies, then the suggested solution was usually to have a "controlling private owner" in the form of an investment fund – as in the standard form of voucher privatization promoted by the Washington consensus and modeled essentially on the Czech voucher privatization program. One obvious problem with this "solution" is that the voucher investment funds had an even greater "corporate governance" problem than the companies in their portfolio. The funds' shares were held by a broad cross-section of the entire population of citizens. Thus the shareholders' influence on the fund management was essentially nil. Yet the controlling investment fund idea was "sold" by the standard Washington consensus as a "solution" (rather than a worsening) of the corporate governance problem.

"Natural Incentives of Private Ownership"

In economics, as in politics, it is a good idea to "follow the money". Who has the economic interests ("cashflow rights") normally associated with corporate ownership? The standard theory is that the economic interests are attached to share ownership. The shareholder enjoys the economic return to ownership in two ways: dividends on shares and capital gains on shares when sold. But when there is a separation of ownership and control, then the controlling agent is partly or almost wholly disconnected from those "natural incentives of ownership". The effects of the separation are aggravated when there is pyramiding.

An actual case is point in the Czech voucher privatization scheme. The voucher investment funds were limited to at most a 20 per cent stake in a portfolio company, and the funds were controlled by fund management companies receiving 2 per cent of the asset value under management. That fund management company's economic interest in the portfolio company is 0.4 per cent (20 % x 2 %). If two funds with the same management company each have a 20 per cent interest, then we have a 0.8 per cent economic interest. Other variations allowed 30 per cent maximum holdings and three per cent fund management fees for a 0.9 per cent economic interest. Moreover, these returns are gross to the fund manager. If the fund manager must expend any costs, say in devising and implementing a restructuring plan for a portfolio company, then those costs would have to be subtracted to get the net return to the fund management company.

Let me ask you. If you had control of an economic asset but could only extract say 0.9 per cent through a certain channel, would you tend to use that channel or to find a more "efficient" channel for extracting value? At least in retrospect, no one should be surprised that the Czech investment funds found other channels to extract or "tunnel" value out of the portfolio companies.[21] After all, one does not need a lot of sophisticated economics to figure out that if the controlling interest must pay over 99 per cent tax on money taken out one door, then there will be a determined search for another door to get the money out.

"Better Management Contracts"

It will be said, perhaps the answer lies with better regulations and well-designed incentive contracts for the controlling fund managers. But let us now step back and take stock. If a government had such incredible monitoring and enforcement powers to overcome such disincentives, why not apply those powers directly in corporatized state-owned enterprises and then privatize later in a better thought-out way?

One of the main points of "privatization" was to use the "natural incentives of private ownership" instead of the more contrived incentives of management contracts (e.g., in SOEs). Yet we have come full circle. We have seen that the rapid privatization schemes promoted by the standard Western advice (voucher privatization with investment funds) did not establish or lead to controlling owners motivated to restructure enterprises towards long-term economic success. The current advice has ended up focusing on better regulations and management contracts to try to get those in control (e.g., the Czech fund management companies) to act like "private owners" – since the standard form of privatization didn't do that job. It is time to rethink that "standard" type of privatization.

Reducing agency chains: Stakeholder privatization

A modern market economy is based on highly developed agency relationships. One of the most important ways in which real economies diverge from textbook models is in the problems of asymmetric information, imperfect monitoring and opportunistic behavior. Accordingly some of the most important economic institutions arise to alleviate agency problems, such as the legal machinery to enforce shareholder rights and other stakeholder rights, liquid stock markets and open-end investment funds(so investors can "vote with their feet"), the legal framework of competition policy, the entire monitoring system of accounting and auditing, and lastly the ethos of managerial professionalism. In the more stable and developed market economies, long multi-stage chains of agency relationships have developed (e.g., workers are agents for managers who are agents for shareholders such as mutual funds whose shares are held by pension funds which act as agents for their beneficiaries such as workers). But in earlier stages of development, market economies had much shorter agency chains.

These agency institutions need to grow incrementally and evolve over decades. If one tries to just set up a market economy overnight with such extended and concatenated agency relationships, then the superstructure may collapse in dysfunction. That is what has happened in Russia and the former Soviet Union. The elites who have had the roles of institutional agents representing broad constituencies in the FSU have, in many cases, not been able resist grabbing what they can.[22] The elites have betrayed society's trust in them on a massive scale. Those who would enforce the agency relationships and other legal obligations are too often themselves part of the problem.

That is why it is time to rethink the elaborate agency chains we have been trying to "install" in the former Soviet Union. Think for a moment why we condemn oligarchs and managers for asset stripping and looting that leads to the demise of an enterprise. One might say that they are within their legal rights as shareholders. Yet we nonetheless condemn them because of the direct impact on the livelihoods of workers and indirect impact on the economic life of the local community and on the prospects for related parties such as suppliers and customers. By bringing in the interests of these other parties in evaluating the looting, we are in effect identifying these other parties as *stakeholders* in the enterprise.

The stakeholders all have implicit contracts signifying long-term relationships with the enterprise. It is these stakeholders who are ultimately harmed as an "externality" by the agents' betrayal of the extended agency relationships in the transitional economies.

If the pyramided agency relationships are not functioning and it will take many years to build the supporting institutions, then perhaps it is best to shorten the relationships so that those who are monitoring are the ultimate stakeholders who are hurt by the looting and malfeasance. Instead of A trying to get B to get C to do something for A, the pyramided agency relationships should be shortened as much as possible. Shortening one stage means A trying to get B to do something for A. The most dramatic and self-enforcing arrangement is the unification of principal and agent so that A helps him- or herself directly. Then "corporate governance" becomes a more manageable problem, if not a solved problem. There is no corporate governance problem with unified principal and agent in the family farm or small owner-operated business. In general, we might reason that the shorter the agency chain, the easier it is to resolve the corporate governance problem.[23]

This is a strategy of *privatization to stakeholders*, which could be seen as a way to generalize the owner-operated business or family farm to medium-sized and larger firms (see below on decentralizing large firms).[24] Since the stakeholders, by definition, have a long-term economic relationship to the enterprise, they have broader interests in the firm and another channel through which to exert their corporate governance on the management.[25] Their cooperation is necessary for the firm to function so this "hold-up power" gives the stakeholders a way to exercise "corporate governance" as part of their day-to-day business relationships rather than through external legal machinery. They are not unrelated absentee shareholders who see the enterprise only as a "property" (perhaps to be quickly harvested) or who are dependent on agency chains and intermediary institutions to exert their influence.[26]

This general strategy would push towards decentralization. The idea is to push decision-making responsibility down to the levels where people can more directly control their agents or where peer-monitoring can operate – without presupposing the elaborate institutions of monitoring and enforcement that will take many years to develop. There is usually corruption also at decentralized levels but centralization keeps control too removed from the discontents that can lead to change. As David Lilienthal, past Chairman of the Tennessee Valley Authority, put it:

> [C]entralization to avoid unsavory local influences surely deprives the people of the chance to draw their issues locally and to clean up their own local inadequacies. The fundamental solution is to crowd more, not less responsibility into the community. Only as the consequences of administrational errors become more local-ized can we expect citizens to know which rabbit to shoot. (Lilienthal 1949, 89–90.)

This strategy would also entail energizing some of the more subdued segments of the population such as the workers and their unions. If oligarchs and/or managers are looting an enterprise and destroying people's future jobs, then any national pride in being "long suffering and enduring" is quite misplaced. Those who are being hurt should have the information and the organizational capacity to vigorously protect their interests, not just to depend on some reform elite to act in their best interest.[27] The same holds for local governments as well as suppliers and customers – all of whom are stakeholders in the enterprise being looted. The cooperation of the stakeholders is necessary for the enterprise to function and the interests of the stakeholders are harmed when the enterprise is looted. Therefore stakeholder privatization coupled with stakeholder empowerment will tend to reunite the *de facto* control rights and *de jure* ownership rights in a self-enforcing system of corporate governance. Since the strategy of shortening agency chains leads in the direction of devolution to ultimate stakeholders, let us step back and look at the role of bankruptcy and decentralization in restructuring – particularly in the larger firms.

Restructuring and bankruptcy

Industrial restructuring to improve competitiveness has proven one of the most difficult and intractable parts of the transition process. Hopes that privatization would lead to restructuring "by the market" have been widely disappointed. Part of the blame, as I have noted, should be assigned to privatization methods that created little incentive for restructuring as opposed to "tunnelling" value out of firms. But part of the blame should also be assigned to a failure to understand the nature of the restructuring process in the context of economies in transition.

One fundamental error (similar to one which we have encountered in the past couple of years in East Asia) is a failure to distinguish between what is required in the case of restructuring a single firm within a well functioning market economy, and restructuring virtually an entire economy, or at least the manufacturing sector of an economy.

Systemic reorganization is different from reorganization when a single firm has a problem. When a single firm is restructured in an economy operating at full employment, firing underemployed workers has beneficial effects, partly because those workers get quickly redeployed to more productive uses. When, however, there already is massive unemployment, firing workers moves them for a situation of underemployment to no employment – not necessarily a transfer that leads to an overall increase in the productivity of the economy, though it may improve the balance sheet of a particular firm. In the economies in transition, many bad investment decisions had been made. The issue facing a country,given its capital stock, was not, in the short run, whether it wished it had a different capital stock; there was no magic wand by which it could convert its inefficient steel mills into efficient aluminum smelters. The question was, given its capital stock, what was the best way to employ its workers. To be sure, even in the short run some rearrangements in the labor force were desirable; some firms should be hiring workers, some firing workers: this is an on-going part of the process of any dynamic economy. But it cannot be the case that all firms are overstaffed – except if at the same time new firms can be *and are being* created to absorb the workers let go.[28]

It is particularly important to recognize that there was no reason to believe that the inherited financial structure of the firms in the economy in transition at the beginning of the process had any inherent "merit," simply because finance under the socialist regime played a completely different role. Banks did not have the job of screening and monitoring. A high debt-equity ratio – leading a firm to a situation where it could not meet its obligations – thus had no informational value; it did not convey information even about the incompetence of the chief financial officer.[29]

By the same token, when there is systemic bankruptcy, selling off assets may make little sense: who is there to buy them? And even when it is possible that some firm could more effectively utilize the asset, if capital market imperfections are rampant – so that the firm that should be expanding does not have access to capital – it may not find it possible to obtain the funds to purchase the asset. The rearrangement of assets in the presence of a systemic problem is thus far more difficult than in the case of an isolated weak firm.

Thus, financial restructuring was necessary, but a weak financial position had far different implications than in an ongoing market economy; and the prospects of fundamental improvements in the underlying structure of the economy from disposing of assets, in the presence of systemic bankruptcy, were far bleaker.

Restructuring through decentralization, reconstitution, and recombination

There was a form of restructuring that was important – but unfortunately, with few exceptions, such restructuring was not the focus of attention – and that is restructuring to decentralize decision-making. Indeed, it seems to me that there is a rather general model of restructuring which suitably describes successes in a wide variety of contexts. Consider a centralized organization that is encountering consistent failure in its tasks. It could be a unit of government or an economic enterprise. The "iron law of oligarchy"[30] has done its work so the organization is centralized, ossified and stagnant. Those who have power in the organization want to maintain its structure to preserve their power and perquisites.

New and complex situations call for experiments; not one but many experiments. The need for many parallel experiments to see "what works" implies decentralization so that the smaller units can operate with some independence.[31] Risk is diversified since a bad decision by one unit does not entail the same for the other units. Decentralization means vertically and/or horizontally disintegrating a large firm into separate semi-autonomous teams or profit centers within a federal structure[32] – or perhaps a split into more independent business units (e.g., spin-offs which could be confederated and/or partly owned by the mother firm). Decentralization can improve incentives (by linking actions of individuals and smaller units to rewards) and accountability, and harden budget constraints – eliminating the cross subsidies that often exist in large organizations.

New managers are needed in the decentralized parts. This devolution is the hardest part of the process since it entails the central management giving up a good part of its power to the decentralized or spun-off units under younger middle managers. Yet it is key. Restructuring for a market economy entails a sea-change away from the strategy of keeping or conglomerating together the largest units possible to be more successful in lobbying for subsidies. Instead of the slogan "United we stand; divided we fall", the slogan might be "Centralized, we go to the ministry; decentralized, we go to the market."

One can argue that it is best if the pressure for the center to cede power to the decentralized units to begin the process of re-constitution comes from the constituent stakeholders (e.g., workers, creditors, and other parties with stable relationships to the enterprise), those who will lose if the organization is not successfully restructured. Their participation and involvement in the restructuring decisions will lead to better execution of the restructuring plans (since the stakeholders will have more "buy-in" and "ownership" of a plan they helped devise).

The fundamental fact is that much of the relevant knowledge is, in fact, decentralized; that the well recognized failures of central planning – having at least in part to do with the inability of the central planner to gather and disseminate relevant information – can apply with equal force within a large organization; and that simply calling the organization a "firm" does not by itself provide the constituent parts with incentives to transmit information to the center, nor does it endow the "firm" with the ability to process that information, nor does it provide a clear mechanism for the central headquarters to convey instructions to its constituent parts, nor does it provide the incentives for those parts (and the individuals within them) to respond in the desired manner.

Following the decentralization, the new units can experiment to probe their environment, to test their capabilities and to accumulate local knowledge. The connection or loop between experiment and feedback is, under decentralization, now much tighter so the learning process can proceed apace. Benchmarking and world quality standards provide a Hirschmanian pacing mechanism to drive the learning.[33] Real decentralization within an enterprise means that the units can now buy supplies and sell outputs outside the firm whereas before they were in effect restricted to a monopoly supplier or buyer within the firm. It also means the new units should bear the costs of their failure just as they

147

may reap the fruits of their success. These competitive possibilities will expose vulnerabilities within the various units to induce learning and change.

Thus decentralization along with the benchmarking and outside competition (like "export promotion" in the international arena) could be seen as social learning mechanisms to drive the process of recombination and restructuring.[34] Thus, the horizontal discussions between the units should be seen not simply as "best practice fora" but as part of the "constitutional" process of rebuilding the organizational relationships from the ground up.[35] This is the process of rebuilding social capital, to which so little attention was paid in the process of transition.

We have so far illustrated the general model of restructuring through decentralization, reconstitution and recombination by applying it to a large and presumably distressed firm. The model helps to explain why successful restructuring is so rare in post-socialist countries (as well as elsewhere). The center refuses to decentralize power to start the new process of learning and reconstitution. The center clings to the hope that some new master restructuring plan (coupled no doubt with "new machinery" as a technological fix) will solve the problem. If the government is to foster restructuring in troubled firms, then it needs to find ways to promote restructuring through decentralization, reconstitution. Where enough constituent units have the leadership (e.g., middle managers) and initiative to strike out on the restructuring path, then the government can help to devise ways to lift the dead hand of the center (i.e., the failed managers clinging to centralized power) so the process of renewal can go forward.[36]

PART II: MISUNDERSTANDINGS OF THE REFORM PROCESS

Early in the decade, there was much discussion about the proper pacing and sequencing of reforms in the transition economies. In both cases, political and economic considerations were invoked to justify alternative strategies. I have already referred to some of the debates concerning key economic issues – like corporate governance – where the neoclassical model had been found wanting; and the lacuna had only been grasped in the last fifteen years, and evidently, not even then by many of the reformers. But traditional economic theory has even less to say about the dynamics of transition than it has to say about equilibrium states; and yet it was issues of dynamics of transition that were central to the debate over pacing and sequencing.

In the next sections, I will take up the issues of sequencing and pacing in turn.

Sequencing and pacing of reforms

There was always the facile recommendation that "everything is important" and "everything should be done at once." But real choices are always necessary given the real limitations on any government's time, focus and resources. One of the theories was to start with the "low hanging fruit" – the easy pieces – to build up the momentum of reform before taking on the harder pieces. Even if there were no other theories, governments will tend to take the easy pieces first anyway. In any case, this approach was widely used.

The particular context in which I will look at the issue of sequencing is *privatization*. There were three different perspectives: (a) Proceed with privatization as fast as one can; it is more important that privatization occurs than how it occurs; (b) Proceed with privatization as soon as one has put into place an appropriate framework for privatization itself, but do not wait for an appropriate legal structure, including a regulatory and competition framework, to be in place (since government failure is much more important than market failure); and (c) Only proceed with full privatization when there is the appropriate legal framework in place.

There were, in fact, arguments put forward in favor of each of these strategies. Consider the first approach. Underlying it was the Coasian idea that the initial private owners didn't matter too much as "the market" would soon reallocate the assets to the efficient owners. One of the strong arguments for rapid privatization was that it would create powerful political forces that would move forward the broader agenda of economic reform. Fearing a reversion to a communist state, one needed not only to lock up what successes one could, but to create a political force in favor of the market economy. Still another argument was that waiting until a legal structure was in place would result in long delays. Privatization, at least in a formal sense, can be done quickly while it will take years to build up the regulatory framework for competition and the legal system to enforce it. One needed to "grab" the low hanging fruit, "take advantage of the window of opportunity" in every way that one could.

149

In contrast to the argument that one should take the "low hanging fruit" is the view that reforms have strong complementarities. Privatization is no great achievement – it can occur whenever one wants – if only by giving away property to one's friends. Achieving a private, competitive market economy, on the other hand, is a great achievement, but this requires an institutional framework, a set of credible and enforced laws and regulations. Do this, and the larger politically-sensitive privatizations can be attended to when the needed institutional infrastructure is ready, while in the meantime stakeholder-oriented privatization of small and medium-sized firms (which have less potential for abuse and require simpler regulatory structures) can go forward apace.

Those who worried about the sequencing and pacing of reforms were also concerned that without the appropriate reform strategy the likelihood of success was limited; and a failure of reform could indeed undermine its sustainability. Success, rather than speed, was of the essence. Indeed, failures could be reinforcing: if reforms were not viewed to be sustainable, then investors would not have an incentive to make the long term commitments required for growth; one could get caught in a low level equilibrium trap. Successful transition strategies had to have the property of time consistency, including political sustainability.

What have we learned? Some of the most telling lessons relate to the political process itself. One of the problems in the theory is that the interest groups do not sit still in the midst of the reform process. And the reform can create new political forces. The early reforms, the "low hanging fruit", can – and in many cases did – create new interest groups, often associated with the "reformers", that would then add their decisive weight to block the later reforms. Several examples might be cited.

- It is doubt easier to start the process of privatizing banks by privatizing the early ones to domestic groups. The new domestic private banks would then be able to stabilize themselves before allowing foreign competition by selling other banks to foreigners or by allowing direct entry of foreign banks. The problem in the strategy is that the private groups owning the first privatized banks will use their political clout to prevent the foreign sales or entry.

- Many countries, in effect, adopted the policy to "privatize now, regulate later", Here again, the early privatizations into an essentially unregulated environment created a strong vested interest to block the later attempts at regulation in the case of natural monopolies, or to create a competitive market, in the case of those industries where competition was viable.[37]

While privatization was supposed to "tame" political intrusion in market processes, privatization provided an additional instrument by which special interests, and political powers, could maintain their power. For instance, in a variety of dubious arrangements, political allies of the reformers "bought" assets (e.g., with money borrowed from the government or from the banks to which the government gave charters), with part of the "profits" generated thereby being recycled to support the political campaigns of the reformers.

The Coasian argument that there would quickly be a reallocation of assets to "efficient" producers failed in part because there was no genuine secondary market for the same reasons that there was no real primary market – so the assets were more "looted" than resold.

But there was a further problem in the "Coasian" approach. It is important for sustainability not only that property rights are clarified but *how* they are clarified. Suppose there are several parties with ill-defined claims on "pieces of a pie". One strategy would be assign "clear property rights" to some party (probably on political grounds) and then let them trade. But the other parties would probably reject the assignment and sabotage the "solution". This "solution" ignored the whole process of discussion and agreement that could bring "buy-in" so that the resulting agreed-upon property rights might "stick" and be respected. In that alternative negotiated settlement between the stakeholders, the exact *ex ante* shares would be unclear, but all parties would have an incentive to come to some agreement that could then be sustained so that business could go forward. But when those who received the "clear" property rights by fiat or connivance did not view those rights as secure – and could not, since there was little perceived legitimacy to them – it made more sense for them to engage in asset stripping than in wealth creation, precisely the strategy that was in fact pursued.

151

The grabbing hand of the state:
the velvet glove of privatization

One of the theories that promotes privatization independently of a competitive or even regulated environment is the "grabbing hand" theory of the government.[38] The state is seen as the primary source of the problems: interfering in state firms and preying on private firms. The emphasis is on government failure, not market failure.[39] Privatization of enterprises and depoliticization of economic life are the overarching policy goals.

> The architects of the Russian privatization were aware of the dangers of poor enforcement of property rights. Yet because of the emphasis on politics, the reformers predicted that institutions would follow private property rather than the other way around. (ShleiferndVishny,1998,11.)

Not only were regulatory and corporate governance institutions supposed to arise on their own account, but the proponents of this theory even saw it actually happening in Russia. "Institutions supporting corporate governance, such as the banking sector and capital markets, are also developing rapidly in part because of the profit opportunities made available by the privatized firms." [Shleifer and Vishny 1998, 254, note 4]

Historians may well wonder how the programs implemented by the architects of the Russian privatization could have led to the present system of economic oligarchy and disorganization. The grabbing hand theory sees the state as being irredeemably corrupt – while the private sector is viewed through rose-colored glasses. Yet the resulting program of transferring assets to the private sector without regulatory safeguards ("depoliticization") has only succeeded in putting the "grabbing hand" into the "velvet glove" of privatization. The "grabbing hand" keeps on grabbing with even less hope of public restraint. The rapid liberalization of capital accounts allowed the aforementioned "banking sector" to spirit tens of billions of dollars of loot out of Russia each year while the architects of capital account liberalization negotiated more billions of international debt. Economic and political forces – incentives – are at play, with far different outcomes than predicted by the proponents of the grabbing hand theory (some of whom are still arguing that, ten years after the beginning of the process, with output plummeting and inequality soaring, we are being too hasty in reaching a judgment). And why should we be surprised? It is not the first time that strong vested interests have used political processes to maintain and strengthen their economics interests. What is remarkable about this episode is that economists, who should have known better, had a hand in helping create these interests, believing somehow – in spite of the long history to the contrary – that Coasian forces would lead to efficient social outcomes.

Clothing the grabbing hand in a velvet glove does not solve the underlying problem of irresponsible power, public or private. That is why I have urged a strategy of decentralization to push power down to the levels where people can use local institutions (e.g., enterprises, associations, unions and local governments) to protect their own interests and marshal their resources incrementally to rebuild functioning institutions on a broader scale.

This brings us to the larger debate about the methods and pace of institutional change.

The modern debate: Shock Therapy versus Incrementalism

The standard Western advice, such as what I have called the "Washington consensus", took what Hirschman (1973, p. 248) called an ideological, fundamental and root-and-branch approach to reform as opposed to an incremental, remedial, piecemeal and adaptive approach. I have no great quarrel with "shock therapy" as a measure to reset expectations quickly, say, in an anti-inflation program. The controversy was more about the attempted use of a shock therapy approach to "install" institutions – where it might more aptly be called a "blitzkrieg" approach. Historically, the shock therapy approach to changing institutions is associated with Jacobinism in the French Revolution and (ironically) with Bolshevism in the Russian Revolution.

There is an "Austrian" tradition of criticism of the Jacobin-Bolshevik approach to institutional change. Karl Popper's criticism (1962) of utopian social engineering and Friedrich Hayek's critique (1979) of the Jacobinic ambitions of scientism gave this tradition its modern Austrian flavor but the roots go back at least to Edmund Burke's (1937 [1790]) attack on Jacobinism in the French Revolution. Peter Murrell (1992) has explicitly used that tradition in his critique of the shock therapy approach. A major theme in my own professional work is that informational problems coupled with human fallibility make the actual world we deal with strikingly different from the models of conventional neoclassical economic theory.[40] Indeed many of the intuitions and informal arguments of the Austrian school find their precise formulation in the new information economics. Thus it is no surprise that I have always had misgivings about the shock therapy component of the Washington consensus, at least as applied to institutional change.

The irony of it all is that the modern critique of utopian social engineering was based particularly on the Bolshevik approach to the transition from capitalism to communism, and the shock therapy approach tried to use many of the same principles for the reverse transition. It is almost as if many of the Western advisors just thought the Bolsheviks had the wrong textbooks instead of the whole wrong approach. With the right textbooks in their briefcases, the "market Bolsheviks" would be able to fly into the post-socialist countries and use a peaceful version of Lenin's methods to make the opposite transition.

But we belittle the issue by seeing it only as an intellectual question of overlooking the Austrian or information economics critique of utopian social engineering. One deeper origin of what became known as the "shock therapy" approach to the transition was moral fervor and triumphialism left over from the Cold War. Some economic Cold Warriors seem to have seen themselves on a mission to level the "evil" institutions of communism and to socially engineer in their place (using the right textbooks this time) the new, clean, and pure "textbook institutions" of a private property market economy. From this Cold War perspective, those who showed any sympathy to transitional forms that had evolved out of the communist past and still bore traces of that evolution must themselves be guilty of "communist sympathies". Only a blitzkrieg approach during the "window of opportunity" provided by the "fog of transition" would get the changes made before the population had a chance to organize to protect its previous vested interests. This mentality is a reincarnation of the spirit and mindset of Bolshevism and Jacobinism.

Since, for better or for worse, much of the "great debate" has been carried on in metaphorical terms, I will summarize the "battle of the metaphors" in the following table (1).

Table 1: "Battle of Metaphors"

	Shock Therapy	Incrementalism
Continuity vs. Break	Discontinuous break of shock–razing the old social structure in order to build the new.	Continuous change–trying to preserve social capital that cannot be easily reconstructed.
Role of Initial Conditions	The first-best socially engineered solution that is not "distorted" by the initial conditions.	Piecemeal changes (continuous improvements) taking into account initial conditions.
Role of Knowledge	Emphasizes explicit or technical knowledge of end-state blueprint.	Emphasizes local practical knowledge that only yields local predictability and does not apply to large or global changes.
Knowledge Attitude	Knowing what you are doing.	Knowing that you don't know what you are doing.[41]
Chasm Metaphor	Jump across the chasm in one leap.	Build a bridge across the chasm.
Repairing the Ship Metaphor	Rebuilding the ship in dry dock. The dry dock provides the Archimedian point outside the water so the ship can be rebuilt without being disturbed by the conditions at sea.	Repairing the ship at sea. There is no "dry dock" or Archimedian fulcrum for changing social institutions from outside of society. Change always starts with the given historical institutions.
Transplanting the Tree Metaphor	All-at-once transplantation in a decisive manner to seize the benefits and get over the shock as quickly as possible.	Preparing and wrapping the major roots one at a time (*nemawashi*) to prevent shock to the whole system and improve changes of successful transplantation.[42]

The Chinese were not historically immune to this mentality but they seem to have "got it out of their system" in the Great Leap Forward and the Cultural Revolution. They learned the hard way where that Bolshevik mentality would lead. When they came to choose a path to a market economy, they chose the path of incrementalism ("crossing the river by groping for the stones one at a time"[43]) and non-ideological pragmatism ("the question is not whether the cat is black or white, but whether or not it catches the mice"). They had the wisdom to "know they didn't know what they were doing" so they didn't jump off a cliff after being assured by experts that they would be jumping over the chasm in just one more great leap forward.

In contrast, the Russians have tended towards a more Jacobinic reform regime guided by prophets armed with clean textbook models. They have learned the hard way to appreciate the old saying: "It's not so much what you don't know that can hurt you – but what you know that ain't so."

The CDF and the presumption for participation

What is the alternative strategy for change? As social and organizational capital turns out to be so fragile and like Humpty-Dumpty, hard "to put back together again", one can argue that it is best to start with existing social institutions and try to induce their incremental transformation – rather than trying to eliminate them "root-and-branch" in order to start with "a clean sheet of paper".

> An unwillingness to start from where you are ranks as a fallacy of historic proportions; .... It is because the lesson of the past seems to be so clear on this score, because the nature of man so definitely confirms it, that there has been this perhaps tiresome repetition throughout this record: the people must be in on the planning; their existing institutions must be made part of it; self-education of the citizenry is more important than specific projects or physical changes. (Lilienthal 1944, p. 198.)

Why were the reformers so unwilling to start from where they were? Perhaps the simplest explanation is that the post-Soviet reformers saw anything that grew organically out of Soviet or Russian reform attempts as still bearing the stigma of communism. They wanted to make a clean break by using the "window of opportunity" to jump over the abyss to an "advanced model" as in the Western textbooks.

We should be clear: there were risks everywhere. The critics of gradual reform worried that the forces at play – the old vested interests – would somehow manage to reassert themselves, unless their power was broken. They worried, too, that the momentum – and the people's taste – for change was limited, and one had to seize the opportunity while one could. Alternatively, there is a long history of gridlock in democratic societies, and for a society in desperate need for change, such gridlock too would prove disastrous.

Perhaps nowhere did these conflicting fears and anxieties play out so much as in the debate over stakeholder (local) privatization, sometimes referred to as "spontaneous" privatization. The term spontaneous might have suggested a natural evolutionary process; a Hayekian might have seen these privatizations as a natural (efficient?) social response to the unfettering of central controls. For decades prior to the actual collapse of communism in 1989–90, reformers had worked in East Europe and in the Soviet Union itself to decentralize power away from the state. Various models of decentralized socialism were promoted starting in Yugoslavia in the early 1950's and eventually in many of the countries within the Soviet bloc to a lesser degree. In the late 1980's the "destatization" and decentralization spread to the Soviet Union. Some measures of independence and "self-accounting" were extended to state enterprises. New ownership forms such as cooperatives and collective ownership by work collectives were legalized. "The Law on Leasing set up a legal basis for gradual evolution of state ownership: work collectives could now lease enterprises from the state and run them as more or less private entities, according to the market logic." (Plekhanov 1995, p. 38.) These ownership forms were not imposed on managers and workers by the state. They represented the results of experimentation and collective efforts to wrench more control over their lives from the state.[44] By the beginning of 1992, some ten thousand enterprises had become leasehold enterprises.[45] Reformers who recognize that real transformation requires participation and involvement would have welcomed this reform momentum and would have helped it push all the way to full privatization. Yet the Western-oriented reformers took the opposite course. In Russia, the leasing movement was stopped dead in its tracks in favor of voucher privatization. Throughout the countries of the former Soviet Union, official announcements emphasized that voucher privatization was necessary to speed up the process – while there were unofficial and private admissions that the leasing movement had to be stopped in order to have something left to go into the voucher auctions.

The leasehold firms, like the TVEs in China or the self-managed firms in Yugoslavia, were far from "perfect" by Western standards. A large literature had detailed both the strengths and weaknesses of the Yugoslavian model, and suggested reforms that would improve their performance. *A priori*, one would have thought that the chances of improving upon the flawed decentralized ownership forms were at least as good as the chances of designing new privatization schemes *de novo*. But rather than working to improve these ownership forms, to prevent abuses and to channel these spontaneous energies, the reformers in country after country of the FSU tried to stop dead the "flawed" and "imperfect" bottom-up movements in favor of the top-down voucher programs based on textbook models of publicly-traded joint stock companies. Why? Partly they feared that docile or naïve workers would let local managers and party bosses strip the assets and weaken or destroy the firms. Partly they felt that reforms under the new political regime should be far more dramatic than the "constrained" evolution that the old structure had allowed. Some undoubtedly approached the reform process with a central planners mentality: how could one "control" a spontaneous privatization process?

Politics and political dynamics were discussed – but political dynamics are even harder to forecast than economic dynamics; the fact that so few foresaw the dynamics of the breakdown of the Soviet empire should have instilled a sense of humility; and the forecast record in the process of transition seems to have fared no better. Sustainable development requires widespread support; such support inevitably is engendered by a history of successes. Had the economics of reform fared better, perhaps so too would have the politics. But today, in Russia, there appears little support for the so-called reformers, and the reforms – at least in the form that they took in recent years. (This does not, however, mean that there is no support for the "market economy" or that the spirit of entrepreneurship has been quashed. The opposition seems to be to the particular manner in which the reforms were conducted.) The reformers claim, to be sure, that it was politics that hindered them: it inhibited the reforms from occurring at the pace and in the manner which they recommended. But this claim has a certain unconvincing ring to it: Remember, one of the key arguments for the pace and sequencing of reforms recommended was that it was best *given the political situation*. Clearly, the advocates of shock therapy misjudged the politics.

In the first part of this paper, I also argued that they misjudged the economics. They underplayed the importance of social, organizational and informational capital; they underestimated the impediments to the creation of new enterprises; and perhaps most importantly, they paid too little attention to the issues of corporate governance. For instance, on the voucher model, real "corporate governance" of the firms would reside in the voucher investment funds sometimes staffed by the political allies of the reformers. (With the later loans-for-shares scheme, this theme of privatizing to provide favors for political allies was "perfected" even if corporate governance was not.) But even when politics did not get involved (and the political involvement should itself be viewed as endogenous, a consequence of opportunities and incentives provided by the process itself), we have seen that there were strong *a priori* arguments to expect that voucher privatization schemes would face severe corporate governance problems. Stakeholder privatization too could have faced corporate governance problems – after all, "public good" and "free rider" problems arise at the local level as well as the national. But if the local communities are provided with appropriate incentives (as they were in China), there is at least a prospect that local communities will evolve ways of addressing the issues (as they did in China).

The hardest questions concerning the reform process take us beyond economics, beyond politics, to issues concerning evolution and change in and of society – issues which were given short shrift in the early debate, and about which we have insufficient evidence to make statements with the confidence that we would like. More research, particularly from the more dispassionate viewpoint of history, is needed to understand the turbulent decade we have just been through. But I do think we can draw some tentative lessons about the methods inducing institutional change – or at the very least, let me put forth some tentative hypotheses. There are certain areas of macro-economic management where central government-initiated action should be the norm. At the other extreme, there are vast domains of institutional transformation that are well outside the reach of central government dictates. And there are, of course, gray areas in between. But economic development and transition is more a matter of institutional transformation than of day-to-day economic management. To be sure, societal transformation inevitably entails collective action, but such collective action can take place both within and outside government, and both at the national and local levels. The central level will inevitably play a large role, but perhaps most effectively by creating environments in which evolutionary processes – including local experimentation – can best occur.

Thus the Comprehensive Development Framework[46] argues for a presumption in favor of inclusion, popular participation and involvement. Given a choice between the momentum of bottom-up involvement in "flawed" reforms and top-down imposition of what reformers see as "model" institutions, the CDF argues in favor of using our knowledge and experience to work to improve the bottom-up approach to transformation.[47]

CONCLUSION

I remarked at the beginning of this paper that the century coming to a close has been marked by two great economic experiments. The outcome of the first – the socialist/communist experiment that dominated much of the world scene during the century – is now virtually over, and the lessons from that experiment appear clear.

We are in the midst of the second great experiment – the transition from the socialist/communist economies to a market economy. That experiment has not proceeded in the way that many economists had predicted a short decade ago. To be sure, the process of transition is far from over. But it has not been an easy decade for most of the countries, and even China, with all of its successes, faces hard challenges ahead. Russia is a resource-rich country, with enormous potential. We know that for societies to function, the state must provide a certain basic minimal level of services, and that it takes resources to provide those services. In all societies, taxes are collected only because governments enforce tax laws, through the right to seize property in the event of a failure to comply. Russia, and the other countries, must show a resolve to enforce the tax laws and to provide the basic services of the state. With compliance, government revenue problems will be resolved – and in doing so, one of the main challenges facing the countries would be effectively addressed. Without compliance, having through bankruptcy and other legal means taken control of assets previously privatized, the governments would face a new opportunity to address some of the key issues, associated with privatization once again. Hopefully, this time, those issues would be faced with a better understanding of the broader principles of the market economy and the reform process. Hopefully, the countries – and their advisors – will have learned from the many bitter and disappointing failures – and the few successes – of the past decade.

NOTES

1. Gallup and Sachs, 1999, in the paper presented to last year's ABCDE Conference, has emphasized the importance of geography as a determinant of a country's economic prospects. See Figure 3 at the end of the text for a comparison of various countries' 1997 GDP relative to 1989.

2. To be sure, by some accounts, this is a slight overstatement of the decline, since some informal sector activity is not included, while by other accounts, this is a significant understatement of the decline, since market prices, not the shadow barter prices, are used to value output. Social indicators (which again must be taken with a grain of salt) do not show a rosier picture.

3. "Grand privatization plans are likely to be frustrated by: quarrelsome members of parliament, foot-dragging ministries, stubborn local politicians, cautious and/or confused law enforcement authorities, opportunistic managers, entrenched unions, rebellious workers, sullen and resentful citizens, bankrupt companies, illiquid banks, revolving-door governments, and the general chaotic nature of post-socialism, plus an occasional *deus ex machina*.... How robust is a privatization plan against such distortions? If the plan's implementation is distorted, will the plan lose only a small amount of effectiveness or will the plan dissolve into a mess? This design criterion of robustness-against-chaos is quite important in Eastern Europe, but it is even ore crucial in the former USSR." Ellerman 1993, p. 25–6.

4. The *Transition* newsletter sponsored by the World Bank and several other institutions has been one forum for this discussion, debate, and rethinking. *www.worldbank.org/html/prddr/trans/WEB/trans.htm.*

5. To be sure, in many cases, lip service was paid to these points, but the points were certainly not stressed — they were not, for instance, part of the key "conditionalities" — and, as always, actions spoke louder than words.

6. Yingi Qian, in the paper presented to this conference, argues forcefully that the closed capital accounts in China played a critical role in its success, not only enabling the financial system to provide a major source of income for the government (which it could not have done with full openness), but also in limiting the incentives and scope for asset stripping.

7. See Lieberman and Veimetra, 1996.

8. See Balcerowicz et al., 1998 for a discussion of the variety of exit procedures in the leading transition economies.

9. There is a long legal tradition that sees courts as evolving gradually and falteringly towards principles of (rough) efficiency, or at least "perceived" efficiency. In this perspective, then, one should expect independent courts in an economy with a large underutilization of resources to be sympathetic to "solutions" that provide for the continued utilization of resources. Supreme Court Justice William O. Douglas noted that: "Underlying all of our bankruptcy laws is the philosophy expressed by Henry Clay in 1840: 'I maintain that the public right of the State in all the faculties of its members, moral and physical, is paramount to any supposed rights which appertain to a private creditor.'" (1954, p. 289.)

10. See Spicer et al., 1998 for a discussion of the processes of creation and destruction in the Czech Republic.

11. On the other hand, one must guard against the fallacy that social institutions that arise to address the market failures from imperfections of information are *necessarily* welfare enhancing. The conditions under which decentralized social institutions lead to Pareto-efficient allocations (see Arnott and Stiglitz, 1991) are as restrictive as those under which decentralized economic institutions lead to Pareto efficiency (Greenwald and Stiglitz, 1986). For a non-technical discussion of these points in the context of privatization and the transition, see Stiglitz, 1993, 1994 (and for a more technical treatment, Sappington and Stiglitz, 1987).

12. One colleague quipped: "The institutional blitzkrieg destroyed without replacing

the old social norms—removing the last restraints against society-threatening levels of corruption. This is like using a flame-thrower to burn off an old coat of housepaint, and then lamenting that you couldn't finish the new paint job because the house burned down."

13. See, for instance, Knack and Keefer, 1997 for recent research; and for a review of the extensive literature on social capital, see Woolcock (forthcoming).

14. See Wolfensohn, 1997, 1998 and 1999 on the Comprehensive Development Framework (CDF).

15. See the township-village enterprises in China as in Weitzman and Xu, 1994, Lin et al. 1996, and Qian, 1999.

16. See Blanchard and Kremer, 1997 and Gaddy and Ickes, 1998 for current descriptions.

17. See Berle and Means, 1932 and the huge literature following it. See Roe, 1994, Kaufman et al., 1995, Stiglitz and Edlin, 1995, and Stiglitz, 1982, 1985 and 1994 for recent treatments.

18. An enormous literature has grown out of the early work such as Ross, 1973 and Stiglitz,1974. See Stiglitz, 1987 for an overview.

19. See Stiglitz, 1982.

20. For an early discussion of the theory of takeovers, see Stiglitz, 1972. Perhaps the most dramatic illustration of this was provided by Grossman and Hart's 1980 analysis of take-overs: take-overs by value-enhancing management teams would never be successful, since each shareholder has an incentive to retain his shares, so as to fully participate in the increased returns; while, if each shareholder believes that others will tender their shares, value-reducing, asset-stripping take-overs will be successful.

21. See Ellerman, 1998 for an institutional analysis and Weiss and Nikitin, 1998 for econometric analysis.

22. See Shleifer and Vishny, 1998 and Wedel, 1998.

23. In a recent book, one of the pioneers in employee stock ownership plans, Jeff Gates, has argued for a similar notion of "up-close capitalism". "As an example of the benefits of such 'up-close capitalism', Nobel laureate economist Myron Scholes touts the positive effect that employee stock ownership can have on corporate decision-making. In his view, such 'inside' ownership improves performance both directly (by encouraging insider challenges to poorly conceived management decisions) and indirectly—by influencing managers who know that the firm's owners are now working among them [1991]. Similarly, by including a component of *consumer* ownership [of utilities], the utility's managers (and their families) would live among shareholders who are also neighbors, schoolmates and teammates. Such a community-focused ownership stake could change the quality of business relationships across a broad spectrum because local, up-close capitalists have more at stake than do remote investors." (1998, pp. 13–4.)

24. Two examples of stakeholder privatization are the Polish privatization by liquidation (mostly leasing management and employee buyouts or MEBOs) and the Chinese township-village enterprises (TVEs). The fact that some would object to the TVEs being considered as "private" shows what a surreal fetish "privatization" has become. The Chinese managers and workers are immobilized in their TVE so these "barriers to exit" lead to a "logic of commitment" (see Kagono and Kobayashi, 1994) and "loyalty" (Hirschman, 1970) which together with a hard budget constraint yields a *de facto* private firm. In contrast, Polish firms held by the national investment funds (in effect, parastatal holding companies) are considered "private"

simply because the parastatal holding companies themselves floated their shares on the stock market and thus were "privatized".

25. This is reminiscent of the Japanese pattern of taking shareholding as symbolic of an underlying business relationship rather than being itself the relationship. "A high proportion of the holders of Japanese equity have more to gain from the other business they do with the company whose shares they hold than from profits or capital gains on the shares themselves. They are 'committed' in interest terms because they have a stake in the actual long-term growth of the company." (Dore, 1987, p. 113.) Thus "corporate governance" has a natural economic basis. See Blinder 1995 for a suggestion that the former socialist countries look towards Japan and East Asia for some ideas.

26. Perhaps the main stakeholder group is the workers and managers in an enterprise. In a perceptive paper early in the decade, Martin Weitzman (who, unlike the most prominent Western advisors, was a scholar of Soviet-style economies) gave the pragmatic argument for the worker ownership version of stakeholder privatization. "Under worker ownership, the workers themselves, or their agents, will have to control pay and negotiate plant shutdowns. The most acute 'us vs. them' stalemates may be avoided. Ownership is more concentrated relatively close to management decisions and can put more immediate pressure on performance. Regulatory capture may be avoided. Hard budget constraints may be more acceptable. There is less opportunity for financial manipulation." (1993, p. 267.) But it should be noted that concentrated ownership in the hands of an old manager may, in the FSU context, still lead to looting. With no eventual exit in sight to a strategic investor or a public market, the manager-owner's time horizon may collapse and lead, in the absence of constraint, to grabbing what he can rather than long-term wealth creation. Thus stakeholder ownership needs to be spread to a broad enough coalition that firm-threatening looting is prevented and each stakeholder is then constrained to "doing business" instead of "making a killing".

27. In other words, in large corporations, all stakeholders, not just shareholders, face public good-management problems: each feels powerless to affect outcomes, and to the extent that they can affect outcomes, most of the benefits accrue to others.

28. To be sure, all firms in a sector can face a financial crisis, if the sector has been receiving a subsidy from other sectors, or has accumulated liabilities (debts) on which interest is due, and such financial crises require financial adjustments.

29. This is doubly so in those cases where interest rates increased in ways that could not have been anticipated. By contrast, in some cases, firms were left with too little debt, so that the inefficiencies arising from excessive managerial discretion were given free reign. The role of debt as an incentive device has been emphasized in much of the literature on corporate governance of the past quarter century. See Jensen and Meckling, 1976.

30. See Michels, 1962 (1915).

31. See Stiglitz, 1994 for an extended discussion of decentralization in various contexts and for a discussion of the related principle of subsidiarity in government, see Begg et al., 1993, and in a company, see Handy, 1996 (next fn.).

32. See, for example, "Balancing Corporate Power: A New Federalist Paper" in Handy, 1996.

33. See "bootstrapping reforms" in Sabel, 1995 and "experimental decentralization" in Sabel and Prokop, 1996 for similar approaches. See Hirschman, 1958 for the original

discussion of low-fault-tolerance technologies (e.g., running an airline) as mechanisms to induce or pace social learning.

34. See McDermott, 1998 for a description of examples in Czech Republic, Stark, 1996 for Hungary, and Stark and Bruszt, 1998 for East Europe generally.

35. This process of "government by discussion" in the state and other social organizations has been emphasized by John Stuart Mill, Walter Bagehot, James Bryce, John Dewey, Frank Knight and Charles Lindblom (see Lindblom, 1990).

36. How the government can best do this is not always obvious. Devising appropriate "rules of the game" — bankruptcy laws which provide some clarity about what will happen if the firm does not restructure itself — are surely part of the overall incentive structure. Government-provided safety nets are important, since in most of the economies in transition, individuals depended on firms for many essential services; any corporate reorganization thus not only put at risk their jobs, but also these social services. Government assistance to spun-off units has to be carefully managed; providing such assistance only to firms going through bankruptcy gives an incentive to postpone reorganization, or at least to force the reorganization to occur through bankruptcy proceedings.

37. This problem went beyond sequencing to misunderstandings of market economics itself. Instead of seeing private property and competition as the "Siamese twins" of efficient wealth creation, privatization became a major fetish while competition policies and other market regulations were seen as minor afterthoughts. Policy advisors did note the need for competition policies but placed emphases on other issues such as the speed of privatization.

38. See Shleifer and Vishny, 1998.

39. Indeed Schleifer and Vishny note that the Russian privatization program "de-emphasized corporate governance precisely because the intent was to reduce the damage from government failure rather than from market failure". (1998, p. 11.) For a related discussion, see Dyck, 1999.

40. See Stiglitz, 1994 and the references there.

41. See Benziger, 1996.

42. See Elster et al., 1998 for the "rebuilding the ship at sea" metaphor and Morita, 1986 about *nemawashi*.

43. See Lin et al., 1996.

44. To be sure, cooperative equilibrium among "local" players does not assure a "national" Pareto-efficient outcome, if there are externalities extending beyond the players. But surely, these externality problems seem far smaller than the "free rider" corporate governance problems created under the alternative strategy.

45. See Frydman et al., 1993.

46. See Wolfensohn, 1997, 1998, and 1999.

47. For instance, in Yingi Qian's study of the Chinese reforms presented at this conference, "the main lesson from the Chinese experience is that considerable growth is possible with sensible but not perfect institutions, and that some 'transitional institutions' can be more effective than the best practice institutions for a period of time because of the second-best principle: removing one distortion may be counter-productive in the presence of another distortion." (1999, p. 6.)

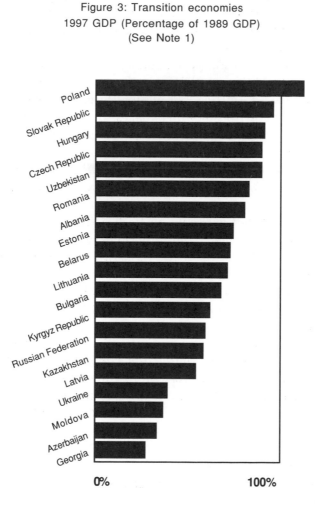

Figure 3: Transition economies
1997 GDP (Percentage of 1989 GDP)
(See Note 1)

REFERENCES

Arnott, R, and J. Stiglitz. 1991." Moral Hazard and Non-Market Institutions: Dysfunctional Crowding Out or Peer Monitoring." *American Economic Review* 81(1): 179–90.

Arrow, Kenneth. 1972. "Gifts and Exchanges." *Philosophy and Public Affairs* 1 (4): 343–62.

—— and G. Debreu. 1954. "Existence of an Equilibrium for a Competitive Economy." *Econometrica.* 22: 265–290.

Åslund, Anders. 1995. *How Russia Became a Market Economy.* Washington: Brookings.

——. 1999. *Why Has Russia's Economic Transformation Been So Arduous?* World Bank ABCDE Conference 1999, draft.

Balcerowicz, Leszek, Cheryl Gray and Iraj Hoshi, eds. 1998. *Enterprise Exit Processes in Transition Economies.* Budapest: CEU Press.

Baumol, W.J. 1959. *Business Behavior, Value and Growth.* New York: Harcourt Brace.

Begg, David et al. 1993. *Making Sense of Subsidiarity: How Much Centralization for Europe?* London: Centre for Economic Policy Research.

Benziger, V. 1996. "The Chinese Wisely Realized That They Did Not Know What They Were Doing." *Transition.* 7 (7–8 July–August): 6–7.

Berle, A., and G. Means. 1932. *The Modern Corporation and Private Property.* New York: MacMillan Company.

Blanchard, Olivier, and Michael Kremer. 1997. "Disorganization." *Quarterly Journal of Economics.* 112(4): 1091–126.

Blinder, Alan S. 1995. "Should the Formerly Socialist Economies Look East or West for a Model?" In *Economics in a Changing World: Economic Growth and Capital and Labour Markets.* Jean-Paul Fitoussi (ed). 5: 3–24.New York: St Martin's Press.

Burke, Edmund. 1937 (1790). "Reflections on the French Revolution." In *The Harvard Classics: Edmund Burke.* Charles Eliot (ed). New York: Collier: 143–378.

Coase, R.H. 1937. "The Nature of the Firm." *Economica.* IV (November 1937): 386–405.

——. 1960. "The Problem of Social Cost." *Journal of Law and Economics* 3: 1–44.

——. 1988. *The Firm, the Market and the Law.* Chicago: University of Chicago Press.

Dore, Ronald. 1987. *Taking Japan Seriously.* Stanford, CA: Stanford University Press.

Douglas, William O. 1954. *An Almanac of Liberty.* Garden City: Doubleday.

Dyck, Alexander. 1999. *Privatization and Corporate Governance: Principles, Evidence and Challenges for the Future.* Washington, DC: World Bank. Mimeo.

EBRD. 1998. *Transition Report: Financial Sector in Transition.* London: EBRD.

Ellerman, David. 1993." Management and Employee Buy-Outs in Central and Eastern Europe: Introduction." In *Management and Employee Buy-Outs as a Technique of Privatization.* D. Ellerman (ed). Ljubljana: Central and Eastern European Privatization Network: 13–30.

——. 1998. *Voucher Privatization with Investment Funds: An Institutional Analysis.* Washington DC, World Bank Policy Research Report 1924.

Elster, J. et al. 1998. *Institutional Design in Post-communist Societies: Rebuilding the Ship at Sea.* Cambridge: Cambridge University Press.

Frydman, R. et al. 1993. *The Privatization Process in Russia, Ukraine and the Baltic States.* Budapest: Central European University Press.

Fukuyama, Francis 1995. *Trust.* New York: Free Press.

Gaddy, C. and B. Ickes. 1998." Beyond the Bailout: Time to face reality about Russia's 'virtual economy'." *Foreign Affairs.* 77: 53–67.

Galbraith, Kenneth 1952. *American Capitalism.* Boston: Houghton Mifflin.

Gallup, J. L. and J. Sachs. 1999. "Geography and Economic Growth." *Proceedings of the 1998 Annual Bank Conference on Development Economics.* Pleskovic, B. and J. Stiglitz (eds). Washington, DC: The World Bank.

Gates, J. 1998. *The Ownership Solution.* Reading: Addison-Wesley.

Greenwald, B. and J. Stiglitz 1986. "Externalities in Economies with Imperfect Information and Incomplete Markets." *Quarterly Journal of Economics.* 101: 229–64.

Grossman, S.J. and O. Hart. 1980. "Takeover Bids, the Free Rider Problem and the Theory of the Corporation." *Bell Journal of Economics.* 11: 42–64.

Handy, Charles. 1996. *Beyond Certainty.* Boston: Harvard Business School Press.

Hayek, Friedrich 1979. *The Counter-Revolution of Science: Studies on the Abuse of Reason.* Indianapolis: Liberty Fund.

Hirschman, Albert O. 1958. *The Strategy of Economic Development.* New Haven: Yale University Press.

——. 1970. *Exit, Voice, and Loyalty: Responses to Decline in Firms, Organizations and States.* Cambridge: Harvard University Press.

——. 1973. *Journeys Toward Progress*. New York: Norton.

——. 1992. *Rival Views of Market Society*. Cambridge: Harvard University Press.

Hoff, K., A. Braverman and J. Stiglitz (eds). 1993. *The Economics of Rural Organization: Theory, Practice and Policy*. New York: Oxford University Press.

Jensen, Michael C., and William H. Meckling. 1976. "Theory of the Firm: Managerial Behavior, Agency Costs and Ownership Structure." *Journal of Financial Economics*. 3(4): 305–60.

Kagono, Tadao, and Takao Kobayashi.. 1994. The Provision of Resources and Barriers to Exit. In *Business Enterprise in Japan*, Kenichi Imai and Ryutaro Komiya (eds). Cambridge: MIT Press: 89–102.

Kaufman, A., L. Zacharias, and M. Karson. 1995. *Managers Vs. Owners*. New York: Oxford University Press.

Keynes, J.M. 1963. *Essays in Persuasion*. New York: Norton.

Knack, Stephen, and Philip Keefer. 1997. "Does Social Capital have an Economic Payoff? A Cross-Country Investigation." *Quarterly Journal of Economics*: 1251–88.

Lieberman, Ira, and Rogi Veimetra. 1996. "The Rush for State Shares in the 'Klondyke' of Wild East Capitalism: Loans-for-Shares Transactions in Russia." *George Washington Journal of International Law and Economics*. 29(3): 737–68.

Lilienthal, David. 1944. *TVA – Democracy on the March*. New York: Harper.

——. 1949. *This I Do Believe: An American Credo*. New York: Harper.

Lin, Justin Yifu, Fang Cai and Zhou Li. 1996. *The China Miracle: Development Strategy and Economic Reform*. Hong Kong: Chinese University Press.

Lindblom, Charles. 1990. *Inquiry and Change*. New Haven: Yale University Press.

March, J.G., and H.A. Simon. 1958. *Organizations*. New York: Wiley.

Marris, R.K. 1964. *The Economic Theory of Managerial Capitalism*. New York: Free Press.

Marshall, Alfred. 1897. "The Old Generation of Economists and the New." *Quarterly Journal of Economics* (January): 115–35.

McDermott, Gerald. 1998. *The Communist Aftermath: Industrial Networks and the Politics of Institution Building in the Czech*

Republic. Ph.D. dissertation in Political Science. Massachusetts Institute of Technology.

Michels, Robert. 1962 (1915). *Political Parties: A Sociological Study of the Oligarchical Tendencies of Modern Democracy.* New York: Collier.

Murrell, Peter. 1992. "Conservative Political Philosophy and the Strategy of Economic Transition." *Eastern European Politics and Societies.* 6(1): 3–16.

Piore, Michael, and Charles Sabel. 1984. *The Second Industrial Divide.* New York: Basic Books.

Plekhanov, Sergey. 1995. "The Road to Employee Ownership in Russia." In *Transforming Russian Enterprises.* John Logue, Sergey Plekhanov and John Simmons Eds. Westport CN: Greenwood Press: 35-70.

Popper, Karl R. 1962. *The Open Society and its Enemies: The High Tide of Prophecy: Hegel, Marx, and the Aftermath.* New York: Harper and Row.

Putnam, Robert. 1993. *Making Democracy Work.* Princeton: Princeton University Press.

Qian, Yingi. Forthcoming. *The Institutional Foundations of China's Market Transition.* Paper presented to 1999 Annual Bank Conference on Development Economics.

Roe, Mark J. 1994. *Strong Managers, Weak Owners: The Political Roots of American Corporate Finance.* Princeton: Princeton University Press.

Ross, Stephen. 1973. "The Economic Theory of Agency: The Principal's Problem." *American Economic Review.* 63 (May): 134–9.

Sabel, Charles, "1994. Learning by Monitoring: The Institutions of Economic Development." In *Rethinking the Development Experience: Essays Provoked by the Work of Albert O. Hirschman.* Lloyd Rodwin and Donald Schön (eds). Washington: Brookings: 231–74.

——. 1995. "Bootstrapping Reform: Rebuilding Firms, the Welfare State, and Unions." *Politics & Society* 23 (1 (March 1995): 5–48.

—— and Jane Prokop 1996. "Stabilization through Reorganization?: Some Preliminary Implications of Russia's Entry into World Markets in the Age of Discursive Quality Standards." In *Corporate Governance in Central Europe and Russia.* Roman Frydman,

Cheryl Gray and Andrzej Rapaczynski (eds). Budapest: CEU Press. 2: 151–91.

Sah, R. and J. Stiglitz. 1991. "Quality of Managers in Centralized and Decentralized Economic Systems." *Quarterly Journal of Economics.* 106: 289–96.

Sappington, S, and J. Stiglitz. 1987."Privatization, Information and Incentives." *Journal of Policy Analysis and Management.* 6(4): 567–82.

Scholes, Myron. 1991." Stock and Compensation." *Journal of Finance.* 46(July): 803–23.

Shleifer, Andrei, and Robert Vishny. 1998. *The Grabbing Hand: Government Pathologies and Their Cures.* Cambridge: Harvard University Press.

Spicer, A., G. McDermott, and B. Kogut. 1998. *Entrepreneurship and Privatization in Central Europe: The Tenuous Balance Between Destruction and Creation.* Working Paper 98-18, Philadelphia, Wharton School, U. of Penn.

Stark, David .1996. "Networks of Assets, Chains of Debt: Recombinant Property in Hungary." In *Corporate Governance in Central Europe and Russia.* Roman Frydman, Cheryl Gray and Andrzej Rapaczynski (eds). Budapest: CEU Press. 2: 109–50.

—— and Laszlo Bruszt. 1998. *Post-Socialist Pathways: Transforming Politics and Property in Eastern Europe.* New York: Cambridge University Press.

Stiglitz, Joseph 1972. "Some Aspects of the Pure Theory of Corporate Finance: Bankruptcies and Take-Overs." *Bell Journal of Economics.* 3 (2): 458–82.

——. 1974. "Incentives and Risk Sharing in Sharecropping". *Review of Economic Studies.* 41(April): 219–255.

——. 1982. "Ownership, Control and Efficient Markets: Some Paradoxes in the Theory of Capital Markets." In *Economic Regulation: Essays in Honor of James R. Nelson.* Kenneth D. Boyer and William G. Shepherd (eds). Ann Arbor: U. of Michigan Press: 311–41.

——. 1985. "Credit Markets and the Control of Capital." *Journal of Money, Banking and Credit.* 17(2 May): 133–52.

——. 1987. "Principal and Agent." In *The New Palgrave: Allocation, Information and Markets.* J. Eatwell, M. Milgate and P. Newman (eds). New York: Norton: 241–53.

——. 1993. "Some Theoretical Aspects of the Privatization: Applications to Eastern Europe." In *Privatization Processes in Eastern Europe*. Mario Baldassarri, Luigi Paganetto and Edmund S. Phelps (eds). New York: St Martin's Press: 179–204.

——. 1994. *Whither Socialism?* Cambridge, MA: MIT Press.

——. 1998. "More Instruments and Broader Goals: Moving Toward the Post-Washington Consensus." WIDER *Annual Lectures 2*, January 1998 [ch.1, this volume – Ed.].

—— and A. Edlin 1995. "Discouraging Rivals: Managerial Rent-Seeking and Economic Inefficiencies." *American Economic Review*. 85(5): 1301–12.

Wedel, Janine. 1998. *Collision and Collusion*. New York: St Martin's Press.

Weiss, Andrew, and Georgiy Nikitin. 1998. *Performance of Czech Companies by Ownership Structure*. Washington, DC, World Bank.

Weitzman, Martin. 1993. "How Not to Privatize." In *Privatization Processes in Eastern Europe*. Mario Baldassarri, Luigi Paganetto and Edmund S. Phelps (eds). New York: St Martin's Press: 249–269.

—— and Chenggang Xu. 1994. "Chinese Township-Village Enterprises as Vaguely Defined Cooperatives." *Journal of Comparative Economics*. 18: 121–145.

Wolfensohn, J. D. 1997. *Annual Meetings Address: The Challenge of Inclusion*. Hong Kong: World Bank. *www.worldbank.org/html/extdr/am97/jdw_sp/jwsp97e.htm*

——. 1998. *The Other Crisis: 1998 Annual Meetings Address*. Given at the 1998 World Bank/International Monetary Fund Annual Meetings. *www.worldbank.org/html/extdr/am98/jdw_sp/index.htm*

——. 1999. *A Proposal for a Comprehensive Development Framework* (A Discussion Draft). Washington, DC: World Bank.

Woolcock, Michael. Forthcoming. *Using Social Capital: Getting the Social Relations Right in the Theory and Practice of Economic Development*. Princeton, NJ: Princeton University Press.

Chapter 5

The Role of International Financial Institutions in the Current Global Economy

Address to the Chicago Council on Foreign Relations
Chicago, February 1998

The crisis in East Asia, an area that was previously viewed as the most successful developing region in the world, has had a profound effect on our thinking about development strategies, the international financial system and the role of international institutions. Many have seen in the crisis a confirmation of their favorite theories. Some have come away with the lesson that the crisis was the inevitable result of government interference in the economy, and that by destroying once and for all the so-called "East Asian model" the crisis has proved that free market capitalism is the only viable economic system. Others have seen the crisis as deliberately engineered by the West to restrain development in East Asian economies and pressure them to open their markets, a step these critics see as benefiting the West at the expense of East Asia.

I think that both of these views are wrong. It is hard, in particular, to reconcile the first view with the success of East Asia, the understanding of the lessons of that success, and the benefits that success has brought, not only to the people in the region but also to the world more generally. Government played an important role in the success of East Asia. But so did an outward orientation and trade policies, both promoted by the government itself.

Also, neither extreme is consistent with my, and most other people's, interpretation of the crisis. I will argue that although wc do not have, and are not likely to have, a complete theory of what precipitated the crisis, there are certain characteristics of the economy and certain government policies that increased these countries' vulnerability to a crisis and amplified the aftershocks. On the crucial question of the role of government in the crisis, I will argue that the crisis was caused in part by too little government regulation (or perverse or ineffective government regulation) in some areas and too many or too misguided government administrative controls in other areas.

But even with the best economic management, small open economies remain vulnerable. They are like small rowboats on a wild and open sea. Although we may not be able to predict it, the chances of eventually being broadsided by a large wave are significant no matter how well the boat is steered. Though to be sure, bad steering probably increases the chances of a disaster, and a leaky boat makes it inevitable, even on a relatively calm day.

EXPLAINING THE CRISIS IN EAST ASIA

The lessons we draw from the crisis depend to a large extent on our understanding of the causes of the crisis itself. Most explanations of the crisis begin with a long list of supposed problems of the East Asian countries. This leads many to the *post hoc ergo propter hoc* fallacy of believing that any problem that existed prior to the onset of the crisis is automatically a cause of the crisis. Instead, I would like to begin by briefly recounting some of the strengths and successes of the East Asian economies. This sets a higher threshold for our explanations: they need to be consistent both with this success and with the failure we have witnessed.

The successes of East Asia

For the last three decades, GDP per capita has consistently grown at five per cent or more annually in Indonesia, the Republic of Korea, Malaysia, and Thailand. These gains, it is important to remember, have brought with them extended lifespans, increased educational opportunity, and a dramatic reduction in poverty. Today two out of ten East Asians are living on less than $1 per day; in 1975 the number was six out of ten. Whatever else one says about so-called "crony capitalism," no one can draw a parallel between leaders like President Suharto, who oversaw a decline in the poverty rate from 64 per cent in 1975 to 11 per cent in 1995, and Mobutu Sese Seko, who looted Zaire, leaving its per capita income at the end of his reign at half of the level it was when he began.

One recent article claimed that the crisis would teach the East Asians the meaning of thrift. The lack of understanding of the East Asian miracle that this claim demonstrated is astounding. Indonesia, Korea, Malaysia and Thailand all save over one-third of their GDP, something from which the United States, with a national savings rate of 17 per cent of GDP, could well learn. The United States is justly proud that it managed last year to bring down its (federal) fiscal deficit to $22 billion, or 0.3 per cent of GDP. But compare that to Thailand, which had a (general government) surplus of 1.6 per cent of GDP last year, or Indonesia with its (general government) surplus of 1.4 per cent of GDP. Inflation, another warning sign that countries are trying to push beyond their capacity, was low and drifting still lower in the months before the crisis.

One particularly important aspect of the growth of the East Asian countries was the role played by the accumulation of what economists call human capital. One indication of this is the doubling of secondary school enrolment rates in East Asia in the last 25 years and the comparatively high level of tertiary education, especially for engineers and scientists. This human capital is not just good for growth; it is also helping East Asia cope with the crisis itself. When I visited Korea in December, in addition to my meetings with the government's economic team, I had the opportunity to meet with then presidential candidate Kim Dae Jung's economic advisers. I was extremely impressed with both the government's and the opposition's understanding of the Korean economy and the steps that needed to be taken to reform it. Korea had the human capital to field not just one but two first-rate teams.

East Asian vulnerability in an international context

This brief description should be enough to show that the models about crises that developed in response to the Latin American debt crisis in the 1980s are completely inadequate for understanding the causes or solutions of the East Asian crisis. The problems in East Asia revolve around private debt, not public debt. And the biggest worry has not been the overall indebtedness of the countries but the levels of short-term debt and portfolio outflows.

Most analysts agree about the sources of vulnerability in East Asia, including weak financial sectors, high levels of corporate debt, and inadequate levels of transparency. What is much less clear, however, is whether these factors can explain the scope, timing, and severity of the crisis. Looking beyond East Asia, there were numerous other countries with worse financial sectors and less transparency which did not experience a crisis.

An analysis of past crises also raises questions about whether the crisis could have occurred even without these weaknesses. As long as there were economic incentives to borrow from abroad, private corporations or non-bank financial institutions would have accessed international markets directly even if banks had been better regulated. This is, of course, what happened in Indonesia, where two-thirds of the external bank lending was to the non-bank private sector, among the highest fraction of any country in the world. No country can, does, or probably should regulate individual corporations at the level of detail that would be required to prevent the foreign exchange and maturity mismatches that arose.

The lack of transparency also undoubtedly contributed to the problems in East Asia, especially to the severity of the crisis. As the crisis began, markets realized that many firms in East Asia were much weaker than they had thought. Without reliable information for differentiating among firms, banks may have had difficulty distinguishing good firms from bad firms, leading them to constrict the supply of credit to all firms (or alternatively, to raise risk premiums for all firms).

But we should not forget that transparency is not enough to avoid crises. Some of the worst industrial country crises in the last decade occurred in Finland, Norway and Sweden, among the most transparent countries in the world. By contrast, Germany has not had a major banking crisis recently, despite the fact that German corporate governance is so complicated and information so scarce that most German firms cannot, or at least choose not to, satisfy the listing requirements for the New York Stock Exchange.

The contribution of government policies to the East Asian crisis

Crises or at least marked fluctuations in economic activity have been features of capitalist industrial economies for at least two hundred years.

The recognition that crises will occur even in well-managed economies should not lead us to abandon policy, but it suggests that we should try to explore ways to reduce the susceptibility of countries to crises, and to minimize the severity when they do occur.

A number of specific policies in East Asia shaped the incentives that led to the build up of vulnerability, especially in the form of short-term, dollar-denominated debt.

One policy was the *exchange rate peg*. Thailand had a *de facto* dollar peg for its exchange rate. As a result the exchange rate largely floated in a narrow band between 25 and 27 baht to the dollar from 1984, when the currency regime was adopted, to mid-1997. The belief that the exchange rate pegs would last convinced many investors to borrow in foreign currencies. One of the main rationales for an exchange rate peg is to maintain a nominal anchor that restrains inflation. But these were not countries that needed to restrain inflation. Prior to the adoption of pegged exchange rates, however, most of the countries in the region had relatively low inflation rates and the experience of the last decade suggests that the inflationary temptation is not a serious concern in East Asia. Experience also suggests that many countries, not just those in East Asia, have found it difficult navigating a smooth transition from an exchange rate peg.

A second policy that contributed to the crisis was the *sterilization of capital inflows*. In order to keep their nominal exchange rates from appreciating in response to the huge surge of capital inflows in the last few years, the East Asian economies sterilized the inflows by building up foreign reserves. International reserves in each of the four Southeast Asian economies increased from 1994 to 1996 by about $30 billion, or about a fifth of net capital inflows. The sterilization entailed high domestic interest rates, thus driving a large wedge between domestic and international interest rates, creating an additional incentive for companies to borrow from abroad.

A third policy was the *liberalization of capital accounts*, without which it is unlikely that the enormous inflows of capital could have occurred. It is worth observing that some of the countries with the weakest financial sectors, the greatest lack of transparency and the most corrupt political structures were hardly touched by the contagion from East Asia. These were countries with closed, or at least more closed, capital accounts.

Clearly, to the extent that the current crisis can be related to exposure in short-term foreign-denominated liabilities, countries that restricted those liabilities reduced their vulnerability. The question is, what did they give up? The ideological position is that free and unfettered markets generate higher growth. But the reality is that the East Asian countries, with their high savings rates, may have gotten relatively little additional growth from the surge in capital flows. When national savings rates are already above one-third of GDP, the additional investment that can be financed by capital inflows may contribute very little to the overall economy. Although there may have been a substantial short-run demand-side stimulus to the economies from this investment (a stimulus they hardly needed), in the long run it may contribute relatively little to the productivity growth of the economies.

And these gains may have been more than offset by the losses in growth as a result of the current turmoil. As important as the aggregate effects are the distributional implications: in the case of the poor and the most vulnerable, the consequences of the crisis could last a long time. They may well argue that, while they benefited relatively little from the capital flows, they have borne the brunt of the costs of adjustment.

This is not to say that steps that open up economies to larger capital flows are always unwise. Clearly, the gains from capital account liberalization would be considerably greater for economies that are far more capital-starved. One of the key issues to which I will turn later is how to achieve these benefits while mitigating the costs.

Finally, the crisis also seems to be partly the result of *inadequate financial regulation*, which allowed banks to make excessively risky loans without adequate monitoring. And part of that problem in turn was due to *excessively rapid financial liberalization* without commensurate strengthening of regulation and supervision. In the last decade Thailand has reduced reserve requirements, eased the rules governing non-bank financial institutions, expanded the scope of permissible capital market activities (such as allowing banks to finance equity purchases on margin), and increased access to off-shore borrowing. Beginning somewhat earlier, Korea eliminated many interest rate controls, removed restrictions on corporate debt financing and cross-border flows, and permitted intensified competition in financial services. While the advantages of these changes were lauded, the necessary increase in safeguards was not adequately emphasized.

(But here too, we have to keep our perspective. For every borrower, there is a lender. If domestic banks were foolish in lending to, say, Indonesian corporations, so too were the foreign banks. Indeed, the foreign lenders in many cases should be viewed as the marginal lenders. If they, presumably models of good banking practice, were willing to lend to these sometimes heavily indebted corporations, why should we be surprised that domestic banks were willing to lend as well?)

Again, the ideological position is that financial market liberalization is important because it also leads to faster economic growth, by reducing distortions in the market economy. But both empirical evidence and recent economic theory cast doubt on that proposition. There is evidence that economies that have engaged in mild financial restraints, such as moderate restrictions on interest rates – and that in doing so have increased the franchise value of their banks, enhancing the safety and soundness of the financial system – have, if anything, grown more quickly as a result. This evidence is consistent with theoretical studies that have shown that even increased capital requirements cannot efficiently offset the adverse incentives associated with diminished franchise values.

Excessively rapid financial liberalization can, in fact, undermine the strength of financial systems, thereby reducing growth. Many observers attribute the apparent increase in the frequency and severity of financial crises, especially in developing countries, to the way in which financial liberalization has been carried out.

One manifestation of inadequate financial regulation in East Asia was the overbuilding in commercial real estate that is so evident to any visitor to major cities in the region. This is a recent phenomenon. Thailand, for instance, used to restrict bank lending for real estate, both because it realized the danger of such lending and because it wanted to direct credit to what it viewed as more growth-enhancing investments. But again, partly under pressure from those who claimed that such restrictions interfered with economic efficiency, it liberalized, eliminating the restrictions with the predictable consequences we have seen. But even the overbuilding in East Asia needs to be put in perspective. The commercial vacancy rates in Bangkok and Jakarta have been around 15 per cent and are expected to rise to 20 per cent comparable to vacancy rates in Dallas and Houston today, and well below the rates of 30 per cent or higher seen in several major American cities in the 1980s. But to be sure, the exposure of banks and the systemic risk posed by these vacancies are much greater in East Asia.

We also must remind ourselves that it is very difficult to have good regulation. The United States, which has one of the best regulated financial systems in the world, is proud of the fact that it has gone nine years without a financial debacle. Also, in the 1980s many people claimed that because Sweden did not have deposit insurance, it would not be susceptible to banking crises. The banking crisis of 1991 laid that argument to rest.

Self-fulfilling panics and runs on currencies

Even if the East Asian countries had sound financial systems and good policies, the crises could still have occurred because of the runs on their currencies and the vicious cycles to which they gave rise. All you need is instability in beliefs. Of course, the shorter the maturity structure of debt, the higher the debt-equity ratio and the weaker the financial system, the greater are the instability of beliefs and the induced disturbance to the economy.

Whenever you have a small open economy, it will be vulnerable to sudden changes in sentiment. Writing during the Great Depression, John Maynard Keynes emphasized the volatile, psychological factors that affected investment and caused business cycles. Keynes thought that these factors were beyond rational explanation, and to emphasize this point he dubbed them "animal spirits". More recently, Alan Greenspan has brought the phrase "irrational exuberance" into our vocabulary. Unfortunately, in East Asia this irrational exuberance has recently given way to an irrational pessimism, a withdrawal of confidence and a run on economies with very open capital markets. Because expectations are volatile and, as I described in the rowboat metaphor in the introduction to this talk, even a well-managed economy can sometimes be overcome by changes in sentiment.

The irrational pessimism proved self-fulfilling as capital outflows, and the accompanying depreciating currencies and falling asset prices, exacerbated the strains on private sector balance sheets. The vicious circle has become even more vicious as financial problems have led to restricted credit, undermining the real economy and slowing growth. Given the region's financial fragility, the economic downturn may well feed on itself worsening bankruptcies and weakening confidence. Finally, the economic crisis has fostered political and social instability in some countries, further deepening the crisis.

The magnitude of the irrational exuberance/irrational pessimism can be seen in the spreads between East Asian debt and comparable, risk-free US Treasury securities. These spreads fell dramatically in early 1997, reaching a low of 90 basis points in Thailand and 110 basis points in Indonesia. They rose sharply at the onset of the crisis in July 1997, reaching roughly 500 basis points by the end of the year. Markets simply did not seem to notice, or reflect, what in retrospect many describe as the growing vulnerability of the East Asian economies.

Further evidence comes from the major rating agencies that did not downgrade their assessments of the East Asian countries until after the onset of the currency crisis. When these downgrades occurred, the result was another round of sell-offs of East Asian securities, driving the crisis still deeper.

I have indicated how many of the fundamental explanations of the crisis have done a poor job in explaining the scope or depth of the East Asian turmoil. Further evidence for the role of "animal spirits" comes from the timing of the crisis. Although conditions were deteriorating in some countries prior to the crisis, in other countries there was very little "news" that explains the onset of the crisis. The general facts of high debt-equity ratios, lack of transparency and weak financial systems were well known to investors during the periods when they were lending relatively cheaply to the East Asian countries. Much of the macroeconomic data, the "news", was actually turning more favorable in the run-up to the crisis. This is especially striking in Korea. Korean inflation rose to 5.5 per cent in mid-1996, but in the months before the crisis it had fallen to just over four per cent. Its trade deficit, one of the "culprits" in many explanations of the crisis because its counterpart was aggregate net borrowing from abroad, had fallen steadily throughout 1997, essentially reaching balance in the months before the crisis and moving into a small surplus in November.

LESSONS FOR ECONOMIC POLICY

The experience of East Asia, especially the vulnerability of small, open economies to the mercurial sentiments of investors, provides some important lessons about economic policy. Although economies may always be buffeted in the seas of changing expectations, good policies can make them less vulnerable.

The relationship between macroeconomic and microeconomic policy

One lesson is that we have become more sensitive to the relationship between what economists sometimes divide into the "macroeconomy" (output, the trade balance, interest rates, exchange rates) and the "microeconomy" (especially the financial system). One example is the question of how to restore confidence or, equivalently, how to persuade people to keep their capital in the country. At first blush, the obvious answer is to increase the rate of return, to increase the interest rate. But we need to ask the deeper question, why are people pulling their money out of the economy in the first place? Often it is because they do not believe that they will receive the promised rate of return; that is, they are worried about the possibility of default.

Higher interest rates increase the *promised* return, but in many circumstances they will also create financial strains, leading to bankruptcies and thus increasing the expectations of default. As a result, the *expected* return to lending to the country may actually fall with rising interest rates, making it less attractive to put money into the economy.

Moreover, even this expected return needs to be adjusted for risk. Policies that increase the likelihood of a major economic downturn inevitably increase the risk premium. Furthermore, while economists rightly focus on the economic consequences of their policies, they cannot ignore the political consequences. We know that there are systematic relationships between economic downturns and political disturbances, and we know that an enhanced likelihood of political disturbances will weaken confidence in the economy. This is not rocket science, even if it is not taught in standard economics courses.

In responding to crises, the goal of our policies is typically to restore market confidence. This raises a further question: just what or who is the "market"? Foreign investors, domestic investors and speculators may all respond to different policies in different ways. It is possible, for instance, that high interest rates might attract foreign capital, while leading domestic investors to move their money out of the economy in order to diversify against the greater likelihood of a domestic downturn. The overall effect of the policy on the exchange rate and capital flows would then depend on the magnitude of the reactions by these two groups.

Moreover, the crisis is another reminder of the complexity of the relationship between exchange rates and exports. Normally we assume that an exchange rate devaluation will make exporting more attractive. But if a crisis leads to corporate failures, which cascade into the bankruptcies of financial institutions and a generalized credit crunch, the responsiveness of exports may be much less than one would expect from normal experience. Addressing the problems in the financial sector, and trying to remedy the shortfalls in credit, may be as important a determinant of exports as the exchange rate.

Financial restructuring

Another set of lessons concerns financial restructuring, particularly the need to maintain the payments system and credit in the process of financial reform. This is very difficult. The standard approach used in dealing with the United States savings and loan crisis was to have the Resolution Trust Corporation (RTC) go into a failed thrift on a Friday evening, work through its books over the weekend, and reopen it under a new name and new management the following Monday. The depositors would see only a change in name and, if the process worked well, the only borrowers that would notice the effects would be the people who should not have had access to S&L funds in the first place, namely people with highly speculative investments. But even in this process, with all of its planning and the huge staff of the RTC, it is generally acknowledged that the US economy suffered a credit crunch that was partly responsible for the depth and persistence of the 1990–91 recession.

Restructuring the banking system is even more difficult in many developing countries, for several reasons. First, there is less technical, legal and institutional capacity for tasks like asset resolution. Second, the fraction of the banking system with bad assets and insolvencies is often far larger; there are fewer healthy banks to take over the weak banks. Third, the banking systems may be more complex, with a mixture of state and private banks. The state banks may carry with them an implicit guarantee for depositors. A government announcement that it will not guarantee the private banks can easily generate a run on the private banks, especially if the government shuts down some banks but leaves doubts about the health of some of the remaining banks.

Restructuring done the wrong way can create havoc. It can lead to credit crunches, contributing to the insolvency of firms that otherwise would have survived. And given the financial and production interconnections among firms in the economy, the problems in some firms can cascade down into insolvency and illiquidity among other firms throughout the economy. These problems quickly get translated to the financial sector as a whole, and even production and real output.

Of course, a key issue in strengthening the financial sector is to do so in ways that enable it to more effectively fulfil its role in promoting economic growth. One can obtain complete security by having narrow banks and forbidding them to make loans to new enterprises, but doing so would inhibit their role in promoting investment, entrepreneurship and growth.

Corporate governance

As important as strengthening the financial sector is, that alone will not suffice. As I have already noted, the corporate sector can borrow from abroad, exposing a country to similar vulnerabilities. High debt-equity ratios, lack of transparency and inadequate accounting standards, lack of protections for minority shareholders, and other aspects of corporate governance clearly played a role in causing and magnifying the East Asian crisis. Some of these issues may be readily addressed; others, such as the high debt-equity ratios, may require more time. At the onset, governments should correct the tax, regulatory and banking practices that encouraged the high debt-equity ratios. For instance, capital requirements associated with loans to firms with high debt-equity ratios should be increased commensurate with the risk associated with these loans. Given the externalities the systemic risk associated with these high debt-equity ratios a good case can be made for going further: that is, actually introducing tax and regulatory policies to discourage high debt-equity ratios. Encouraging pension programs and employee stock option programs (ESOPs) might simultaneously strengthen the social safety net, improve social cohesion and provide a strong equity base for the corporate sector.

PREVENTING CRISES BY CONTROLLING
CAPITAL FLOWS

We cannot expect to eliminate all fluctuations or all crises. Even if we could eliminate all of the "problems" and "mistakes" in economic policy, it is unlikely that we could fully insulate economies against shocks, including events such as the OPEC oil price increases in the 1970s or changes in market sentiment, such as occurred in the current East Asian crisis. Furthermore, although there is much more scope for policy reforms in developing countries, we should not delude ourselves into thinking that this can take place overnight. Building robust financial systems is a long and difficult process. In the meantime, we need to be realistic and recognize that developing countries have less capacity for financial regulation and greater vulnerability to shocks. We need to take this into account in policy recommendations in all areas, especially in the timing and sequencing of opening up capital markets to the outside world and in the liberalization of the financial sector.

We must bear in mind too in designing policy regimes (such as opening up capital markets) that we cannot assume that other aspects of economic policy, such as macroeconomic policy or exchange rates, will be flawlessly carried out. The policy regimes we adopt must be robust against at least a modicum of human fallibility. Airplanes are not designed to be flown just by ace pilots, and nuclear power plants have built into them a huge margin of safety for human error.

One feature of a robust policy regime is that it minimizes the long-term consequences of the inevitable fluctuations in economic activity, including preventing crises and setting up mechanisms for orderly workouts when they do occur. This means designing financial systems that buffer the economy against shocks rather than magnify the shocks. At the same time, we want to ensure that adequate savings are mobilized and allocated to productive investments. Again, a robust financial system is essential.

Although domestic economic reforms can go a long way toward achieving these goals, some international effort may be required. I think that the time is ripe for an open debate and discussion on the advantages and limitations of a variety of approaches, including some form of taxes, regulations, or restraints on international capital flows.

The importance and limitations of information

Before discussing these measures, I would like to discuss one important part of the strategy: the need for greater transparency and more information. Both the Mexican and the East Asian crises were partly triggered and propagated as a result of investors learning that reserves were smaller than they had thought and that short-term debt was higher. The result was not just a withdrawal of short-term credit, but portfolio outflows as well.

Perhaps even more important than the dissemination of misleading information, at least in some countries, was the general lack of information which, as I said, makes it difficult for investors to distinguish between firms and financial institutions that are healthy and those that are not. In response, investors shied away from all. With more credible information systems, firms that remain healthy would be able to retain access to credit.

The standard macroeconomic data would not have been very helpful in predicting the East Asian crisis, which depended on the composition and allocation of private-to-private capital flows. Unfortunately, getting information about private sector spending and borrowing is much more difficult than obtaining comparable information about public finances. This is especially the case when transparency is limited. In a world where private-to-private capital flows are increasingly important, we will need to recognize that monitoring and surveillance are going to be especially challenging. The growing use of derivatives is increasingly making the full disclosure of relevant information, or at least the full interpretation of the disclosed information, even more difficult.

We should remember, too, that the great merit of a market economy is that dispersed information is aggregated through prices and the incentives they create for behavior, without the need for any centralized collection of information or planning. There is a certain irony about praising a market economy for this decentralization of information, and at the same time complaining about the lack of aggregate data necessary to assess systemic risks.

Moreover, we should not be under the illusion that having improved data is sufficient for financial markets to function well. In East Asia much of the important information was available, but it had not been integrated into the assessment of the market. Furthermore, it is impossible to eliminate all uncertainty and asymmetries of information. Entrepreneurs will always know more about their investments than will the banks that lend to them, and managers will always know more about their actions than shareholders will. Without the correct incentives, even perfect aggregate information would not be sufficient for the efficient, or stable, functioning of markets.

Although our information about private capital flows is imperfect, and although even with vastly improved information I am not sanguine that we or the market would be able to predict or forestall all crises, I do think that the returns from improving our statistical bases are significant. My caution is only that we should not be misled into thinking that this will solve our problems. Better information, seemingly the most important improvement in the international financial architecture to come out of the last crisis, should not lull us into complacency.

The economic justification for "intervening" in the market

After the Mexican crisis many said that this was the last time any crisis like that would occur. The East Asian crisis, just two years after the problems in Mexico, should serve to remind us that we will have more crises in the future. The question we need to ask is what actions can be undertaken, by lending countries, borrowing countries or the international community, to reduce the frequency or magnitude of these crises.

I do not think that a blanket objection to the government intervening in international capital markets would be a very good way to begin this discussion. The roughly $110 billion package for East Asia is clearly a major intervention in the workings of the free market. The international community justifies this support because it is worried about the potential for systemic risk in these types of crises.

In the case of East Asia there is much less risk to the banks in developed countries than they faced in the Latin American debt crisis in the 1980s: in June 1997 BIS-reporting banks had only 19 per cent of their capital in loans to East Asia, compared with 58 per cent to the Latin American countries with debt difficulties in 1982. The risk that worried policymakers in the current circumstances was that the crisis would spread to other developing countries.

There is no consensus in the economics profession about the

significance of contagion and systemic risk. Neither the theory nor the evidence seems decisive. There is a controversy in part because we simply have not run the "experiment" to see what would have happened to the international financial system without the international bailouts for Latin America in the 1980s or Mexico in 1995. In both of these cases, as with East Asia, policymakers have been understandably reluctant to simply stand by while the dice were being thrown. But what there can be little argument about is that *if* you believe in systemic risk, or even if you believe that governments are likely *ex post* to engage in bailouts because they believe in systemic risk, then you must also believe that *ex ante* government interventions including prudential regulation may be warranted.

There are two possible economic justifications for this intervention. The first is that the social risk is not equal to the private risk so that, left to themselves, markets will accumulate more risk than is socially efficient. This is analogous to pollution, which imposes greater costs on society than are borne by the polluter alone. In this case, we typically tax or regulate the pollution. The same logic would suggest some type of tax or regulation on international capital flows. We should recognize that most countries have various forms of taxes or regulation on the domestic financial system, including measures like reserve requirements or deposit insurance. These are justified by the systemic risk to which financial decisions give rise and by the interventions (e.g., bailouts) which so frequently arise. Although these may or may not be feasible or desirable at the international level, I do not think it would be consistent with our other policies to rule these steps out on *a priori* grounds.

Another possible economic justification for intervening in the market with the rescue package is that the market is not even pricing private risk efficiently: that is, that the market is irrational. One form of irrationality that is sometimes discussed is the claim that market participants can be overly focused on the immediate term, particularly in figuring out what other market participants are going to do. This is what Keynes referred to as a "beauty contest" in which contestants are trying to guess who the other judges think is most beautiful, not who actually is the most beautiful. As a result, markets can diverge from long-run fundamentals which, according to this view, are more stable than the actual market outcomes.

There is an extensive economics literature documenting what is called the market's "excess volatility". If it is correct, then, some measure like a Tobin tax (a tax on exchanging currency) could increase the cost of short-term speculation by raising the cost of round-tripping, while still allowing markets to respond to changes in the long-run fundamentals. Again, I am just raising the Tobin tax as an illustration; in practice, there are serious questions about its feasibility, especially in a world of rapid financial innovation, where it could be easy to circumvent.

(The argument sometimes put forward that the bailouts do not cost anybody anything can, similarly, be looked at in two different ways. If markets are "rational" then the fact that the interest rate charged is below the market interest rate for these loans is evidence that there is, in an *ex ante* sense, a real subsidy to the borrower, even if *ex post* we have been repaid for the loans made in previous bailouts. Alternatively, markets may be "irrational", charging an excessively high risk premium one that cannot be justified by the real risk. Then the intervention in the market may be costless; but this argument certainly undermines confidence that markets by themselves are likely to yield efficient outcomes.)

The "intermediate targets" of international financial regulation

If we accept the argument that some form of intervention, a term that includes prudential financial regulation, is justified to bring the private risks into line with the social risk, the next question is what "intermediate targets" should we focus on to achieve this broad goal? Two objectives come to mind.

One of our objectives should be to try to influence the *pattern of capital flows*. Currently, 75 per cent of private capital flows to only a dozen countries, and most low-income countries have little access to private capital relative to the size of their economies. Procyclicality is another undesirable feature of the international capital flows. Countries seem to get the most private capital when they are growing strongly and need it least and have a relatively harder time accessing capital in hard times when they need it most. As a result capital flows do relatively little to smooth the business cycle and may even amplify it. Accomplishing this objective, however, may be very difficult.

Another objective concerns the *composition of capital flows*. There is now broad agreement about the value of foreign direct investment, which brings not just capital but also technology and training. Preliminary evidence from East Asia also shows that consistent with past experience, foreign direct investment is relatively stable, and certainly far more stable than other forms of capital flows.

Unlike foreign direct investment, short-term capital does not bring with it ancillary benefits. In the form of trade credits it provides an important, and relatively inexpensive, source of international liquidity without which no economy, especially an export-oriented economy, could run. In addition to providing liquidity, short-term capital, along with other forms of flows, allows a country to invest more than it saves. When this money is invested productively, the benefits to the economy are large. But when the saving rate is already high, and when the money is misallocated, the additional capital flows just increase the vulnerability of the economy. Moreover, given their volatility, what well-managed economy would risk basing long-term investments on short-term flows? Hence, short-term capital's value in increasing GDP is at most limited.

The large benefits of foreign direct investment, and the costs and benefits of short-term capital flows, have led many people to investigate ways to encourage long-term investments while discouraging rapid round trips of short-term money. There are many components of such a strategy. First, we need to eliminate the tax, regulatory and policy distortions that may, in the past, have stimulated short-term capital flows. Examples of such distortions are evident in the case of Thailand where the tax advantages for the Bangkok International Banking Facilities encouraged short-term external borrowing, but subtle examples exist almost every-where. Without risk-based capital requirements for banks, for instance, incentives for holding certain assets and liabilities will be distorted. Second, several countries have imposed prudential bank regulations to limit the currency exposure of their institutions. Colombia's regulations seem to have served it well during the recent crises.

But these measures may not go far enough, especially once it is recalled that corporate exposure may itself give rise to vulnerabilities. And the systemic risks to which such exposure can give rise provide ample justification for taking further measures, as I have already suggested. Among the ideas currently under discussion are inhibitions on capital inflows. In thinking about how to accomplish this, we should look to the lessons of the Chilean experience. Chile has imposed a reserve requirement on all short-term capital inflows, essentially a tax on short-maturity loans. The overall efficacy of these controls is the subject of much discussion, but

189

even most critics of the Chilean system acknowledge that the reserve requirement has significantly lengthened the maturity composition of capital inflows to Chile. This may be part of the reason that Chile was one of the few countries in the region that was relatively unaffected by the Tequila crisis in 1994–5 and the current East Asian crisis.

Still other measures employ tax policies, for example, limiting the extent of tax deductability for interest in debt denominated or linked to foreign currencies. The problems of implementing these policies may in fact be less than those associated with the Chilean system.

RESPONDING TO CRISES: THE CHALLENGE OF ORDERLY WORKOUTS

A keystone in the development of modern capitalism has been limited liability and bankruptcy laws. Modern bankruptcy laws attempt to balance two considerations: promoting orderly workouts so that business values can be retained and production losses can be kept to a minimum, and providing appropriate incentives so that those engaged in risky behavior bear the consequences of their actions.

In the absence of orderly workout procedures, countries may worry that unless they issue guarantees or assume private debts, the disruption to the economy will be unbearable.

Similarly, the international community has long complained about the problem of moral hazard, the fact that lenders have been at least partially bailed out. To be sure, in many cases the bailout has been far from complete and lenders have lost money. Still, to the extent that there is any bailout, they have not been forced to bear the full risks associated with their investment, and the belief that in the future that might be the case can give rise to the moral hazard. Again, the international community faces a dilemma: it often sees no alternative to a bailout; the risks of not undertaking an action seem unacceptable. After each crisis, we bemoan the extent of the bailout and make strong speeches saying that never again will lenders be let off the hook to the same extent. But, if anything, the "moral hazard problem" has increased, not decreased, with each successive crisis.

While the experiences of the last twenty years suggest that lenders can be forced to bear more of the costs than they have in at least some of the more recent crises, it is also clear that the middle of the crisis is not the right time to deal with these issues.

We can, however, prepare for the next crisis. I believe that there is more that we can do to facilitate orderly workouts, to reduce moral hazard, to make those investors who are most likely to reap the benefits of a bailout pay part of the costs and, more broadly, to reduce the discrepancy between social and private returns to certain forms of risky international lending. But we should not underestimate the difficulties involved. In the aftermath of the Mexican crisis, there was a resolve to do all of this. In the aftermath of yet another crisis, we now need to revisit all of these issues.

THE ROLE OF THE WORLD BANK

Before concluding, I would like to discuss the role of the World Bank, both in this crisis and more broadly. The World Bank is a development institution, not a crisis fighter. We focus on project lending and structural reforms that enhance long-run development and poverty alleviation. In East Asia, however, the roots of the crisis have been at least as much in the structural features of the economies, like the systems of financial regulation, as they have been in the macroeconomic dimensions. As a result, structural reforms, and the World Bank's support and technical assistance, have been an important part of the short-run stabilization strategy in East Asia.

Addressing pressing issues such as weak financial sectors, lack of transparency and poor governance in the corporate sectors and weaknesses in external liability management will help restore confidence among foreign and domestic investors. This is an important part of the strategy to reactivate the East Asian economies and thus to protect and extend the region's enormous social and economic achievements.

In supporting these goals, the World Bank has pledged roughly $16 billion to the region, the equivalent of almost an entire year's lending program. These pledges comprise $1.5 billion to Thailand, $4.5 billion to Indonesia, and up to $10 billion to Korea. We have already disbursed substantial sums. In Korea, for instance, the Bank's $3 billion economic reconstruction loan was approved by the Board only three weeks after the crisis and was disbursed the very same day.

At the same time the World Bank, together with our partners, has the responsibility for ensuring that the poor and vulnerable suffer as little as possible in the process of adjustment. Financial crises typically bring with them large increases in unemployment, which often linger well after the initial crisis has passed. The devastating consequences for the poor can persist long after capital flows and economic growth resume.

The immediate need is for the government in these countries to step in and fill the income-security gap that will be left by companies closing and workers losing their jobs. Over the longer term, the World Bank will be working with the countries in the region to help them design modern, durable social safety nets that complement their other structural reforms. We should be mindful, however, that it will not be possible to create an effective social safety net overnight, especially in the rural sector, and the pace and content of reforms should take this into account.

Looking forward, there is potentially a broader role for the World Bank. The changing world will need to be matched by changes in the international financial architecture. Because of their global perspective, international institutions, including the World Bank, will have an important role to play in this international dialogue.

CONCLUDING THOUGHTS

It has become a cliche to refer to the new globalized economy. Yet the fact is, reductions in transport and communication costs have been accompanied by reductions in government-created impediments to the free flow of ideas, goods, and capital. We do live in a more integrated international economic community.

Somewhat more than a century ago, when nation-states were being formed, there was a recognition that the new nation-states needed a new set of economic institutions to realize their full potential. In the United States in 1863, in the midst of the Civil War, as Congress grappled with the challenge of providing the foundations of a new, stronger, unified country, it established the world's first financial sector regulatory body, the Office of the Comptroller of the Currency. It has taken more than a century before the country began to feel comfortable with a system of national banking, and even today there are misgivings in many parts of the country.

Today, we stand on the edge of a new world economy. But we do not have international institutions to play the role that the nation-states did in promoting and regulating trade and finance, competition and bankruptcy, corporate governance and accounting practices, taxation and standards within their borders. Navigating these uncharted shoals will be a great challenge. But just as much of the prosperity of the past hundred and fifty years can be related to the expansion of markets that those transformations afforded, so too the prosperity of the next century will depend in no small measure on our seizing the opportunities afforded by globalization.

In approaching the challenges of globalization, we must eschew ideology and over-simplified models. We must not let the perfect be the enemy of the good. As one of my friends put it, in a downpour, it is better to have a leaky umbrella than no umbrella at all. I believe that there are reforms to the international economic architecture that can bring the advantages of globalization, including global capital markets, while mitigating their risks. Arriving at a consensus about those reforms will not be easy. But it is time for us to intensify the international dialogue on these issues.

Chapter 6

Scan Globally, Reinvent Locally: Knowledge Infrastructure and the Localization of Knowledge

Keynote Address to the First Global Development
Network Conference, Bonn, December 1999

"Every alleged example of local implementation of central policy, if
it results in significant social transformation, is in fact a process of
local social discovery." (Donald Schön)

It is a great pleasure for me to be here to help inaugurate the Global
Development Network. In my remarks this evening, I want to do two
things: first, to explain why I think the Global Development Network is
so important, and why it is that the World Bank has taken such an active
role in acting as a catalytic agent in promoting it; and second, to develop
some of the underlying epistemology that lies behind the creation of this
new institution.

I. THE IMPORTANCE OF THE GLOBAL DEVELOPMENT NETWORK

Towards a new relationship between the developing and developed countries

It has been just over fifty years since the beginning of the end of colonialism, and just a decade after the end of the Cold War. Yet old ways of
interacting persist, and it takes time for the evolution of new modes of
behavior, new bases for relationships based on equality and respect.

I realize that it has become unfashionable to refer back to the dark days
of colonialism, and yet, as we end this century and attempt to develop
institutions to meet the challenges of the next, our success in doing so

will depend, I believe, in understanding the histories, how we – both the developed and developing countries and the economies in transition – came to where we are today. Colonialism served to eviscerate existing institutions in the affected countries which embraced almost all of the developing world. It tried to graft on to existing cultures foreign institutions and ideas, but in a process of imposition, in which control and authority lay outside and not within, it is not surprising that the graft did not take hold. What was left in its place was a void – the old was destroyed, but nothing really viable had been created in its stead. Worse still, in all too many countries, they were left without the human capital required to create an alternative, let alone to adapt to the rapid changes that have marked the latter half of the twentieth century. And too many countries were robbed of the dignity and self-confidence with which to address these imposing challenges that would have put strains on societies even in a far better position.

The colonial mentality has evolved. While no one today speaks, like Kipling, of the White Man's Burden, I have too often sensed a paternalism that is but a close cousin. Gone are the days of gunboat diplomacy, forced signing of unfair trade treaties, the Opium Wars, forcing Egypt into being a protectorate because of bad debts. But no one would claim that the playing field in the international trade negotiations, debt restructuring and any of the other multitude of arenas in which the developed and developing countries interact is a level one. Economic power relationships play out with potentially no less disastrous consequences for the developing countries. This point was brought home forcefully by the terms and conditions imposed on the countries receiving bail-outs in the East Asia crisis, which, as Martin Feldstein pointed out, went far beyond what was required for addressing the concerns of the crisis. Democratic processes were undermined, as countries were forced to sign agreements changing the basic mandates of central banks and previously negotiated trade agreements were overturned, as new founded bargaining powers based on the weakened positions of the affected countries were exploited.

So long as the Cold War persisted, there was neither time nor opportunity to address these fundamental issues. That conflict, a battle of competing ideologies, values, economic systems, was all-consuming. And the impact of that conflict on the developing countries was profound. Too often, they took the view the enemy of their colonial enemy was their friend, and embraced their socialist ideology. They saw some of the successes of Russia, its rapid emergence from feudalism to a world superpower, and underestimated the costs it had imposed and overestimated the underlying strengths. The end of the Cold War, the failure of the communist system, thus forced the developing world to re-examine fundamental beliefs.

In the meanwhile, the world was changing rapidly. A new generation of leaders was emerging in the developing world, partially freed from the scars of colonialism, highly trained, with a new sense of self-confidence. Globalization brought prospects of integration into the world economy with access to technology, markets and capital. Global competition offered the prospect of a new relationship between developing countries and multinationals, with more of the surplus accruing to the developing world. But many of the ways of interacting between the developed and developing world did not take full cognizance of these changes. Conditionality – while ostensibly based on freely negotiated terms of agreement – went far beyond what could be justified by fiduciary responsibility and democratic accountability on the part of the developed countries and the international financial institutions. With the end of the all-consuming Cold War, there ensued a new emphasis on democracy and democratic processes, and it came to be recognized that the way conditionality in practice worked often undermined these democratic processes and institutions. New perspectives on development focused on development as a transformation of society, a change in minds and mindsets, and it came to be recognized that such transformations could not be imposed, and indeed, the attempt to do so could often be counterproductive. Thus, the subsequent econometric results suggesting that conditionality was ineffective in promoting development came as no surprise.[1] In response to these changes, the World Bank evolved a new framework for thinking about development, which was both more comprehensive in its approach and more inclusive in its involvement. At its center was, as President Wolfensohn expressed it, "putting the country in the driver's seat".[2]

This brings me to why I think the Global Development Network is so important. If the developing countries are really to be "in the driver's seat" they have to have the capacity to analyze the often difficult economic issues which they face. Local researchers, combining the knowledge of local conditions – including knowledge of local political and social structures – with the learning derived from global experiences, provides the best prospects for deriving policies which are both effective and engender broad-based support. That is why locally-based research institutions are so important.

I have, on several occasions, also spoken of the importance of democratic institutions for successful development. To be sure, we should value democratic institutions as an end in themselves, not just as a means to more successful development. But the lessons of this century have been clear: authoritarian regimes have caused untold human suffering. Amartya Sen has argued forcefully that famines themselves can be checked by democratic processes; it is not the shortage of food but its maldistribution, and democratic processes would simply not tolerate such outcomes. Think tanks, policy institutes, play a vital role in promoting the informed public discussion that is absolutely essential for meaningful democratic processes and the generation of a political consensus. These institutions, and the associated institutions of a free and vibrant press and independent universities, provide an important check on the abuse of power including abuses of majorities against minorities and the widespread corruption which has been shown to have not only a corrosive effect on society, but to undermine development efforts themselves.[3]

This century has seen the battle between two ideologies; but the end of the Cold War does not mark the end of ideology. Ideological battles continue to be fought, sometimes on a grand scale, more often on a minor scale. Recent discussions of capital market liberalization is illustrative of the former. Many strongly advocated this, in spite of the absence of evidence suggesting that, for most developing countries, it would promote their growth or investment; indeed there was some evidence suggesting that it would not do so, and that it would in fact increase the risks which they faced, risks which they were ill-prepared to undertake and which would inevitably increase the extent of poverty in their countries. Unfortunately, the predictions of the critics of capital market liberalization have been more than borne out. How can we explain the strong advocacy of a major change in the international economic architecture other than by ideology, and/or capture by certain special interests? But the strongest antidote to both is science theory and evidence. "Science" – at least the word – can of course be abused; as the word has undertaken positive overtones, ideologies claimed to find justification for their tenets in "science". Yet the foundations of the scientific methodology have managed to withstand such abuses, whatever form they take.

We in the ideas business should never forget the power of ideas.

Keynes put this forcefully when he said that: "Practical men, who believe themselves to be quite exempt from any intellectual influences, are usually the slaves of some defunct economist. Madmen in authority, who hear voices in the air, are distilling their frenzy from some academic scribbler of a few years back."[4] The scribblers of America's Declaration of Independence themselves surely did not know either the power or the reach of their ideas when they wrote, "All men are created equal." They may have had in mind, "All property-owning white males are created equal." But the force of the idea came from its appeal to deep principles, and once articulated, they took on a life of their own a life which brought within its embrace first blacks, then women. And that same force lives on: it does not stop at America's border. The same force of argument that led the American colonialists to declare their independence from Britain doomed the end of colonialism more generally. And today its reach is broadened, to attack neo-colonialist mentalities and economic imperialism. Indeed, as an economist, I find it remarkable how often the force of the arguments can overcome the logic of self-interest and become an important agent for reform and change.

Recent discussions of transparency arising from the East Asia crisis help illustrate what is at issue. Originally, Western bankers and their governments contended that the underlying problem giving rise to the crisis was a lack of transparency, in a thinly veiled attempt to explain how the Western banks could have engaged in such bad lending practices themselves (every loan needs both a borrower and a lender, and the lender is fully as much at fault for a bad loan as the borrower) and, for the international institutions and Western governments which had pushed premature financial and capital market liberalization, to evade responsibility for their misguided policy advice. But the concept of transparency took on a life of its own, spreading its potentially disinfecting sunlight to areas that were far from the original intentions – a demand for transparency on the part of the hedge funds and the off-shore banks, and ultimately on governments, central banks and the international financial institutions themselves. This demand for transparency is now joining forces with basic concepts of equality, in demands for a re-examination of the very process of governance of the international institutions.

I have lauded the virtues of the kind of think tanks and research institutions which are gathered here today. It is my hope, and the World

Bank's hope, that by bringing these institutions together into a global development network, they will add strength to each other, not only through the exchange of knowledge, but through a common understanding of the importance that they play in promoting sustainable, democratic and equitable development. Let me be clear: in many parts of the world, there are substantial obstacles confronting these institutions, from the ubiquitous financial constraints to the shortage of those with the requisite skills, both in research and in articulating key ideas in ways which allow their widespread dissemination and facilitates public debate. But in too many countries there are further, artificially created barriers – hostile governments, trying to suppress democratic debate, worried about the consequences of public scrutiny of their actions. And here, I believe, is one arena where, standing together, we can exert international social pressure: there are basic core standards which all countries need to adhere to, institutional principles that constitute the *sine qua non* of meaningful democratic debate. The basic human rights of a free press and free speech can be undermined by the exertion of economic pressures, which is why these institutions need to be independent of the government with assured independent sources of funding, and why the individuals within the institutions need to be protected by academic freedom.

We should not be surprised at either the vehemence or the subtlety with which these institutions and the individuals within them may be attacked, or at attempts to undermine their credibility, especially so by governments whose political legitimacy is questioned. And the same holds true at the international level, and perhaps more so. For we must recognize that, while international institutions can take or promote actions which have huge effects on the economic fortunes of millions and the political fortunes of many, their governance has a certain lack of representativeness along numerous dimensions – the developing countries and their billions of people are underrepresented; and while the voice of financial interests is heard loudly and with clarity, it is not clear that other voices – the workers, who risk losing their jobs or seeing real wages plummet as a result of misguided policies, or the small businesses forced into bankruptcy by what in any other context would be viewed as usurious interest rates – are heard at all.

Within nation states, there are some governments who derive their legitimacy not only by the electoral process but also by their ability to build a national consensus – a consensus based on trying to find a shared sense of values, a broad sense of equity, and a common understanding of the underlying economic processes. In such cases, the success of the policies adopted – including the sense of equitable sharing of the fruits of growth or the pain of contraction – is often a prerequisite for the maintenance of that legitimacy. By contrast, policies based on ideologies not widely shared, especially when those ideologies are seen to serve the self-interests of special interests and to result in inequitable burden sharing, undermine the credibility of the institution, and when the institution's effectiveness in part depends on its credibility, then there is a downward vicious spiral. No wonder then that such institutions find open discussion and public debate about the appropriateness of policies even months or years later an anathema.

Today, no one is upset at the debate over whether Roosevelt's New Deal policies had much impact in bringing the US economy out of its depression; such understanding is essential if we are to craft policies designed to address economic downturns in the future. But within the international community today, there are still many who are greatly upset at revisiting the question of the appropriate response in the global financial crises of 1997 and 1998. The argument seems to be: The emperor may have no clothes but mentioning that fact risks global economic instability! I, at least, have greater faith in our global economic architecture than that.

But this does raise some fundamental issues: when the governance process of any public institution is subject to questioning, when there is a lack of representativeness, a failure to establish consensus, a reliance on ideology rather than science; (especially an ideology closely linked to the interests which are disproportionately represented in its governance), a clear evidence of lack of equitable burden sharing and a record of failure, it is time to rethink basic premises. Many institutions are learning to become learning institutions, adapting to changing circumstances. At the World Bank, this is precisely the course that President Wolfensohn set five years ago. I raise these issues here, not because this is necessarily the appropriate forum for their discussion, but because I believe that you and your institutions have a vital role in raising these questions and demanding answers that are responsive to the perspectives and concerns of the developing world.

More generally, the world is embarking on an experiment – a closely integrated global economy which is striving for global governance without global government. If this experiment is to be successful, it will be based on a process of global consensus building, in which institutions and individuals that are coming here this week for the first time, in the Global Development Network, will be pivotal.

II. EPISTEMOLOGICAL FOUNDATIONS

Knowledge infrastructure and the GDN

Let me now move to the second topic of my talk this evening, concerning the nature of knowledge and the role of knowledge in development. The World Bank's initiative in fostering the Global Development Network is part of the idea of the Bank as a "Knowledge Bank". We have come to appreciate the transformative power of knowledge in development (World Bank 1998). Yet we must be wary of simple analogies between a "knowledge bank" and a "money bank".

Disembodied knowledge has the characteristics of a public good (non-rivalrous and, once public, non-excludable)[5] while money is the quintessential private good. Thomas Jefferson, the third President of the United States, described knowledge in the following way: "He who receives an idea from me, receives instruction himself without lessening mine; as he who lights his taper at mine, receives light without darkening me."[6] In doing so, Jefferson anticipated the modern concept of a public good.[7] Thus disembodied knowledge for development is indeed a global public good and, like other public goods, it would be undersupplied if left entirely to private initiative.

The internet has in practice brought knowledge access closer to the ideal of a global public good. The communication revolution has made great strides in facilitating communication within countries and has also enhanced the ability of developing and transitional countries to tap into the global pool of (codified) knowledge. The internet should prove to be a tool of immense power in sharing knowledge within our network of GDN institutes.

Today, developing countries face both great risks and great opportunities. Internet growth has been most rapid in the United States, and not, surprisingly, slowest in the less developed countries. The enhanced ability to share and acquire knowledge in the advanced industrialized countries may increase the knowledge gap, resulting in the less developed countries becoming even more disadvantaged.

At the same time, they can tap into a larger knowledge pool than they ever had access to before. Today, a child anywhere in the world who has access to the internet has a modern "Alexandria Library" at her fingertips. It is too soon to see how these opportunities and forces for convergence or divergence will play out, whether the knowledge gap between developed and developing countries will be widened or narrowed. But it is clear that it is incumbent upon the developing and transitional countries to do everything they can to enhance their ability to tap into the reservoir of global knowledge. The GDN partners are local nodes in that emerging global knowledge infrastructure.

Knowledge has a number of characteristics which differentiate it from ordinary goods. We have already noted several of these including the global public goods nature of knowledge. The peculiar characteristics of knowledge makes it incumbent on us to think anew about how we can effectively promote the transformative power of knowledge. In particular, what is the role of local knowledge institutions such as the policy and research institutes of the GDN in the broad process of democratic social learning?

I see a role far more subtle than just the technology-driven visions of "downloading" global knowledge as useful as that may be. I want to argue three main theses:

i.   The overwhelming variety and complexity of human societies requires the *localization of knowledge*;
ii. Practical know-how is largely *tacit knowledge* that needs to be learned by horizontal methods of twinning, apprenticeship and seconding;
iii. Each society, through its knowledge institutions, should take the *active role* ("in the driver's seat") in the local learning process.

That is, one size of "clothing" does not fit all societies, a society learns to be a "tailor" partly by apprenticeship (it is hard to write down all that needs to be known about tailoring in a book, and even were it possible to do so, it may not be the most efficient way by which information can be transmitted from one individual to another), and a society should be its own "tailor" to find the best fit.

Types of development knowledge

General versus local knowledge

We will analyze knowledge along two dimensions, the general-local dimension and the explicit-implicit dimension. Global public knowledge exemplifies knowledge that is general and explicit. As we move along these dimensions, we will see the different roles of central as well as local knowledge institutions. We start with the general-local dimension.

Money "travels" better than knowledge. General knowledge is knowledge that holds across countries, cultures, and times; local knowledge takes account of the specifics of place, people and time. "Every man is mortal" is general knowledge, while "Drive on the left" is a best practice in London but not in New York. A "best practice" might work well in some countries but fail miserably when recommended in other contexts.

In questions of institutional development, it is very difficult to know a priori just how general is a "best practice". Robert Cole studied the diffusion in industry of quality circles and Japanese-style quality methods. The process of local adaptation was so extensive and creative that it amounted to a local reinvention of the "global best practice".

> The significance of this point of view is that contrary to the simplistic use of the term by many economists, there is, in principle, no such thing as diffusion of best practice. At best, there is only the diffusion of best practices, practices that evolve in the course of their diffusion. Contrary to popular wisdom, there are times when it pays to reinvent the wheel! (Cole, 1989, p.117.)

Donald Schön in a study of social learning concluded that "every alleged example of local implementation of central policy, if it results in significant social transformation, is in fact a process of local social discovery" (1971, p. 161). Prudent counsel is to scan globally for best practices but to test them locally since local adaptation often amounts to reinventing the "best practice" in the new context. The Knowledge Bank can "scan globally"; the GDN partners have to "reinvent locally".

Many "visiting economists"[8] have painfully discovered that the "devil is in the (local) details". It is the local component of knowledge that requires adaptation which in turn requires the active participation of those who know and understand the institutional environment. Local adaptation cannot be done by the passive recipients of "development knowledge"; it must be done by the "doers of development"[9] in the course of their activities.

There are two points here: the necessity that knowledge be made locally applicable and that the adaptation be done by the local "doers of development" (not given as a gift or imposed as a conditionality from the outside). It is by the local selection, assimilation and adaptation of knowledge that local doers "make it their own." Even by taking a machine or device apart and putting it back together again, one can more "make it one's own" even if there is little adaptation or redesign. Those of us who have been teachers are familiar with this principle: successful teaching requires active learning.

In the context of development, where what is involved is "social learning" and adaptation, more is entailed: it is not just a matter of being "open" or "closed" to outside knowledge; it is a matter of being open to outside knowledge in a way that reaffirms one's autonomy. For Gandhi, this was intellectual *swaraj* (self-rule or autonomy)

> I do not want my house to be walled in on all sides and my windows to be stuffed. I want the cultures of all lands to be blown about my house as freely as possible. But I refuse to be blown off my feet. (Gandhi, quoted in Datta 1961, p. 120.)

Only by remaining "on one's feet" from an intellectual standpoint can the local doers have the self-confidence to select, assimilate and adapt the external knowledge instead of being overwhelmed and rendered intellectually dependent and subservient.

Considerable effort is required to adapt development knowledge to local conditions and culture. The research institutes and policy institutes ("think tanks") of the GDN are examples of local knowledge institutions that can play that important role. In the developed countries and increasingly in developing countries, think tanks have proliferated and have become important agents to introduce and adapt new policy initiatives.[10] Think tanks or research institutions are no less needed to transplant social innovations to new contexts. The Japanese use a metaphor based on the gardening technique called *nemawashi* of slowly preparing and wrapping each root of a tree in order to transplant it.[11] The chances of a successful transplant are much great than if the tree is simply pulled up in one place and planted in another.

Development institutions have sometimes tried a "quicker" transplant method. After a quick trip to a country, the standard wisdom (in earlier days, typically the Washington consensus), is conveyed, often with little attempt even to nuance it to the economic, political and social situations of the country. The policy advice would frequently be backed up by conditionalities on policy-based lending to motivate the country to implement the best-practice recipes – indeed given the lack of broad-based buy-in, and often the unsuitability of the advice to the country's situation, conditionality was the only way of having the advice followed. Occasionally, in an attempt to achieve broader based support, experts might come in to give a longer senior policy seminar to local government officials; the experts then return home hoping that their sound advice will take root. Yet this policy reform process is designed to promote neither active learning nor lasting institutional change. As these reforms were externally imposed, rather than actively appropriated by the country, there was often little "ownership" of the reforms. Compliance might be only perfunctory; the "quick" transplant might soon wither and die.

Here is an illustration. Foreign advisors would never have the power of an occupying army. Yet the American Army in post-war Japan showed the limitations of trying to change institutions by imposing new laws and statutes.

> When SCAP [Supreme Commander for the Allied Powers] broke up the Mitsui and Mitsubishi trading companies into hundreds of fragments, 213 successor companies in all... the employees loyally rallied round the new fragments formed by their old section or subsection chiefs... who in turn adhered to the companies organized by their old division chiefs...and directors, and all of them recombined as soon as they could. Within five years, like droplets of mercury coalescing into ever bigger drops on contact with each other, both the Mitsubishi and the Mitsui trading companies were substantially reconstituted as before. Two hundred thirteen became two again. Their staffs had been held together by personal relations in the meantime. (Cohen 1987, p. 358.)

Those personal relationship and social habits are part of the "invisible root structure" – the social embeddedness of institutions – that requires more subtle methods of transformation than just issuing decrees or passing new laws.

By the same token, Japan was "given" anti-trust laws that were similar to those that have worked so effectively in the United States; yet these laws never really took root, with an evolving competitive structure far different from that of the US

Local policy and research institutes can be seen as *nemawashi* organizations who carefully adapt and prepare a transplanted policy initiative to survive and perhaps thrive in the local environment. It takes longer, but the roots are better prepared for the local soil. The political process of changing policies and implementing new ideas is usually rather messy and in need of "high maintenance" support. The officials or parliamentarians constantly need more information and advice – more "backup", more thinking about how best to adapt the policies to local circumstances – in order to carry out the policy reforms. As a result of this process of adaptation, which often involves virtually reinventing the idea perhaps by finding and emphasizing local antecedents, the government officials see the policy reform not as a foreign imposition but as a local product which addresses their needs and which they can sponsor.

Advisors from developed countries or international organizations may not always fully appreciate these problems. The "knowledge business" has its own political economy. Those who are legitimated in their expertise, prestige and privileges by the "universality" of their messages are disinclined to recognize limitations or subtleties in the local applicability of their technical expertise.[12] Novel complexity, genuine uncertainty, conflict of values, unique circumstances and structural instabilities are all downplayed or ignored since they might diminish the perceived potency of the expertise and undercut the client's faith in that potency. On the other side, the client may want the security and comfort of being in the hands of the professional expert who will solve the perplexing problems.[13] These are some of the strong institutional forces to under-appreciate the subtleties of local knowledge, to hamper the growth of autonomous client ownership, and to stymie the development of indigenous local knowledge institutions.

Codified versus tacit knowledge

Now we move to the explicit-implicit or codified-tacit dimension of knowledge. Explicit or codified knowledge is knowledge that can be spoken, written, and codified to be saved on a computer disk or transmitted over a telephone line. But we know more than we can say. We know how to ride a bike, to recognize a face or to tell a grammatical sentence in our native language, but we would be hard put to turn this knowledge into explicit or codified knowledge to archive in a database for dissemination over the internet. Michael Polanyi (1962) pioneered the distinction between tacit (or personal) and explicit knowledge in the philosophy of science, and the distinction has since proven important to understand problems in the transfer of technologies, not to mention the "transfer" of institutions.[14] A technology is sometimes identified with blueprints and instruction books.

> But in fact technology consists of complex "bundles" of information both codified and tacit – as well as physical capital. Because tacit information is not readily transferable among firms and countries, technological blueprints do not contain inherent performance characteristics (such as set productivity levels). Instead, these blueprints have to be translated into specifications and procedures that are specific to particular applications – an uncertain creative process that can result in highly variable levels of performance. (Bell and Pavitt 1995, p. 74).

The same holds a fortiori for "social technologies" or institutions. In a codified description of a "best practice" case study, the uncodified tacit knowledge is often "the rest of the iceberg".[15] Some tacit knowledge might be transformed into codified knowledge (see Nonaka and Takeuchi 1995) so that it could be transferred by conventional methods. But the remaining tacit knowledge needs to be transmitted by special methods such as apprenticeship, secondments, imitation, study tours, cross-training, twinning relations, and guided learning-by-doing. These methods of transferring tacit knowledge will be called "horizontal" methods of knowledge transfer in contrast to "vertical" methods where knowledge can be codified, transmitted to a central repository or library, and then accessed by interested parties.

We have seen two reasons why the theory of "downloading the best practice" fails: the best practice needs to be localized and much of the best practice may be in the form of practical know-how that cannot be "downloaded". But there is still an important role for international development agencies (global knowledge): even concerning that tacit dimension of the best practice, the central agency may know who knows X without knowing X itself. It is "second-order" knowledge of where the

207

practical knowledge is; it is a "pointer" to the practical knowledge. A central agency can fruitfully play a match-making, facilitating and brokering role in horizontal learning – not a direct training role. In particular, the Knowledge Bank is in a good position to "scan globally" to identify good practices, and then it can play a *brokerage role* to facilitate a horizontal learning process between the developing countries facing certain problems and the countries with successful practices.[16] It can perform another role: certifying the quality of the messengers and messages; in a noisy world, with many alternative theories vying for center stage, there needs to be some ways of sorting through the cacophony, establishing credibility.

The various methods of horizontal learning differ substantially from those employed in traditional classroom settings, where what goes on is "vertical" teaching and training in explicit codified knowledge.

- Study tours arranged by local knowledge institutes allow people to "see how it is done" in nearby societies. The Marshall Plan for the postwar reconstruction of Europe involved many horizontal techniques such as study tours of business leaders ("business to business") and government officials.

- Cross-training is being "shown how to do it" by those who have already "done it", particularly in nearby societies. It is the implicit knowledge alternative to being explicitly "told how to do it" by an international expert.

- Twinning or secondments pair together similar organizations or institutions for a horizontal transfer of know-how.

- Foreign direct investment might also be viewed as a method of horizontal learning. For instance, a major source of learning about lean production methods and their adaptation to American culture was Japanese direct investment in production facilities in the United States.

Due to the tacit component in the practical development knowledge, few of the real reasons for the success might be captured in the codified knowledge of the "best practice" case study. In addition there would be much variation due to *Rashomon* effects, academic predilections, and ideological precepts in the best-practice case studies.[17]

The architect of social change can never have a reliable blueprint. Not only is each house he builds different from any other that was built before, but it necessarily uses new construction materials and even experiments with untested principles of stress and structure. Therefore what can be most usefully conveyed by the builders of one house is an understanding of the experience that made it at all possible to build under these trying circumstances. (Hirschman 1970, 243; quoted in Scott, 1998, p. 328.)

For instance in one World Bank Institute program, local institutes arranged for government officials, law-makers and business people from an African country to learn directly and horizontally from a nearby East Asian country which faced similar economic and ethnic problems not too long ago, all of which was undoubtedly more effective than seminars based on codified case studies taken as blueprints.

Summary of knowledge dimensions

The general versus local dimension and the codified versus tacit dimension can be used to generate a 2 x 2 table.

	Codified Knowledge	Tacit Knowledge
General Knowledge	Global public goods. Generally applicable and "downloadable", i.e. can be transferred by conventional vertical teaching methods – but "rediscovery" improves ownership.	General tacit knowledge (e.g., implicit grammatical rules of English) could be learned by horizontal methods (e.g., natural language learning) or might be partly) codified and taught.
Local Knowledge	Localized explicit knowledge. Even if hypothetically available from center, should be locally "reinvented" to have ownership.	"The hard stuff". Combines horizontal learning and local reinvention.

III. ACTIVE SOCIAL LEARNING

Negative effects of passive learning

My third thesis is that the knowledge institutes and policy-makers of developing countries should play an active role in reappropriating and adapting knowledge for development (even if the center could through some sort of "flexible specialization" make a local adaptation and transmit it to the locality).

The contrasting "standard view" (usually held implicitly rather than espoused explicitly) sees a central authority transmitting universal messages and best practices formulas along a transmission belt to passive clients who are encouraged by aid and constrained by conditionalities to "get the message". Rather than encouraging clients to develop their analytical and research capacities, the process of imposing conditionalities undermines both the incentives to acquire those capacities and clients, confidence in their ability to use them. Rather than involving large segments of society in a process of discussing change – thereby changing their ways of thinking – excessive conditionality reinforces traditional hierarchical relationships. Rather than empowering those who could serve as catalysts for change within these society, it demonstrates their impotence. Rather than promoting the kind of open dialogue that is central to democracy, it argues at best that such dialogue is unnecessary, at worst that it is counterproductive.

That standard view of delivering knowledge for development leads to an impairment in the self-confidence, self-esteem and self-efficacy of the clients.[18] The message behind the "main messages" is that the clients are unable to take charge of their own learning process and to find out these things in their own way. They need to be "helped", to be shown the way. New forms of intellectual colonialism are masked as "quality control". But these ways in which the standard methodology "shows them the way" only reinforces the clients' passivity and perceived lack of self-efficacy.

In addition to lacking self-confidence about the efficacy of their actions, parties might lack self-confidence in their own intelligence, judgment, and other cognitive skills. In an extreme state of dependency, they might be like a marionette not only in their "actions" but also in their opinions, views, and "knowledge". This cognitive aspect of dependence is clearly very relevant to understanding the detrimental effects of passive learning and tutelage.

The cognitively dependent recipients of the main messages will also often play a role in perpetuating the dynamics of stifling critical reason in favor of bureaucratic "reason" in the development agencies. As such countries have become cognitively dependent, they might be distressed if they should hear the "authorities" arguing among themselves about "development knowledge" and development strategies. They are accustomed to being told the "best practices" to follow, so it weakens their faith in the prestigious authorities if there is any public disagreement. How can the patient have faith in "warring doctors"? Thus the complaints (real or imagined) of the cognitively dependent clients are used as arguments within the international agencies to keep any real debate about development strategies well behind the closed doors of the major development organizations. (To be sure, there may be other reasons for the international agencies wishing to stifle open discussion: public scrutiny of failed policies within the developed countries could not only undermine the support for these agencies, but induce more accountability and improved governance, weakening their current sense of autonomy. And there is a real risk that such public scrutiny could force changes in their policies and practices.)

The obvious corollary of the traditional mode of operation is that there will be very little learning in the sense of correcting mistakes at the level of the development agency. Once there is a public commitment of the agency to a certain view, then the agency's prestige and "brand name" is on the line. Any untoward consequences of the policies must be due to flawed implementation on the part of the clients. Criticism from outside the agency can usually be ignored, and criticism from within the agency must be suppressed because it would weaken the franchise value of the brand name and "confuse" the clients. But note that in defending their own autonomy, they undermine the autonomy of the very countries they are supposed to help; even the language they use to defend the "no debate" position is one which connotes an aura of benevolent paternalism but one which demonstrates a complete lack of faith in the country to make its own decisions.

IV. SOCIAL LEARNING, CONSENSUS-BUILDING, AND OTHER DEMOCRATIC PROCESSES

Learning how to learn

We now turn to the positive virtues of active learning, and to the broader vision of democratic processes as active social learning writ large.

George Bernard Shaw insightfully quipped: "If you teach a man anything he will never learn it." (1962, p. 174.) Ortega y Gasset wisely

211

suggested: "He who wants to teach a truth should place us in the position to discover it ourselves." (1961, p. 67.) Thus if a global knowledge-based institution wants a country to learn a "truth" about development, then it should help the local knowledge institutes and policy-makers to carry out the requisite research, experimentation and social dialogue to learn it themselves to make it a "local social discovery". Creating this local knowledge infrastructure and practice entails "learning how to learn",[19] that is, creating the capacity to close the knowledge gap, an essential part of a successful development strategy. This process of autonomous social learning is not a "feel-good frill"; it is a key part of developing local democracy.

Social learning and effective change cannot be imposed from outside. Indeed, the attempt to impose change from the outside is as likely to engender resistance and barriers to change as it is to facilitate change. At the heart of development is a transformation in ways of thinking, and individuals cannot be forced to change how they think. They can be induced to take certain actions, or even to utter certain words; but they cannot be forced to change their hearts and minds. To impose a model without a self-directed local learning process would be to "short circuit" and bypass the active learning capacity of the local policy-makers and to promote a state of passivity, dependence, and tutelage.

This process of encouraging autonomous local social learning is closely connected with the whole process of promoting democracy. Some social thinkers – with John Dewey perhaps foremost among them – have emphasized that active social learning writ large provides a social philosophy for democracy as government by discussion and consensus-building.

> To foster conditions that widen the horizon of others and give them command of their own powers, so that they can find their own happiness in their own fashion, is the way of "social" action. (Dewey, 1957, p. 270.)

For all alike, in short, the chief thing is the discovery and promotion of those activities and active relationships in which the capacity of all concerned are effectively evoked, exercised, and put to the test. ... This cooperation must be the root principle of the morals of democracy. (Dewey and Tufts, 1908, p. 303–4.)

212

Beyond technocratic development models

Predominant currents of development thinking in the past have usually been more narrowly technical, at least in economics. It has been almost an article of faith that if certain technical allocation issues were solved, economic development would inevitably follow. The problem of development was seen as a technocratic problem of increasing capital investment and allocating resources more efficiently – not as a process of democratic social learning.

As an illustration, consider two of my predecessors as Chief Economist: Hollis Chenery in the 1970s and Anne Krueger in the 1980s. The two came at the development problem from very different perspectives: Chenery from the planning perspective, Krueger emphasizing the need to "get prices right" and to leave markets to work their magic. But both approaches saw development as a technical problem requiring technical solutions: better planning algorithms, better trade and pricing policies, better macroeconomic frameworks. Neither approach reached deep down into society, nor did either one emphasize the participatory nature of the development transformation.

Poland has in recent years implemented particularly effective policies for its post-socialist transition, and India has likewise found an effective development path. In spite of many changes in government, those countries have stayed their course. The reason for their effectiveness is not just some technical "correctness" of the policies but the ownership the countries have for policies arrived at through their own participative processes of democratic discussion, consensus-building and *swaraj*. Outside agents, including donors, can encourage ownership through persuasion – that is, through presenting evidence, both theoretical and empirical, that particular strategies and policies are more likely to bring success than other approaches. But the degree of ownership is likely to be even greater when the strategies and policies are developed by those within the country itself, when the country itself is in the driver`s seat.

Consensus-building and democracy

Inside a country, the ability to resolve disputes in a "democracy-friendly"[20] manner is an important part of social and organizational capital. Reforms often bring advantage to some groups while disadvantaging others. There is likely to be greater acceptance of reforms – a greater participation in the transformation process – if there is a sense of equity, of fairness, about the development process, a sense of ownership derived from participation, and if there has been an effort at consensus formation. Numerous examples (such as Ghana) have showed the importance, for instance, of consensus formation in achieving macroeconomic stability. By contrast, a decision to, say, eliminate food subsidies that is imposed from the outside, through an agreement between the ruling elite and an international agency, is not likely to be helpful in achieving a consensus and thus in promoting a successful transformation.

Charles Lindblom (1990) contrasts the technocratic model for governing society with the alternative model of a self-guiding democratic society based on the use of "reflective intelligence" (Dewey), the competition of ideas, and government by discussion. To quickly see the distinction, Lindblom suggests to "compare Marx with Franklin Roosevelt or Jan Tinbergen with Saul Alinsky" (p. 216). In the technocratic (Marx-Tinbergen) model, the "correct solutions" are already defined but may be unknown. If "scientific" techniques could uncover those answers – even localized answers independent of any political process – then the answers could be whispered into the ear of the Prince and disseminated from the central authority to passive citizens. After severely criticizing technocratic development paradigms, Hirschman counsels "a little more reverence for life, a little less strait-jacketing of the future, a little more allowance for the unexpected – and a little less wishful thinking".[21]

In the model of a self-guiding democratic society, preferences and self-determined actions are endogenously transformed in the social/political process. Social "democracy-friendly" dialogue – led by local knowledge institutions as in the GDN – builds consensus; it does not "discover" or "impose" consensus. Those who participate in the consensus-building process then have an "ownership" of the resulting policies, and thus that policy knowledge will be transformative.

CONCLUDING REMARKS

We are embarking here on an enterprise of potentially immense importance creating a new global institution, the Global Development

Network, devoted to enhancing democratic governance at the local, national, regional and global levels, to promoting dialogue, and to strengthening the processes of consensus-building. Underlying all of these efforts is the pursuit of knowledge – global knowledge about general principles, local knowledge about how those general principles play out in the multitude of local contexts over our vast globe, knowledge based on well-constructed theories and meticulous analysis of the empirical evidence. I believe it is only through such open discussion and active research that we shall break free from the chains of ignorance, the traps of poverty, the grip of elites and the blinders of ideology and self-interest – in our quest for a more democratic, equitable and sustainable transformation of societies.

NOTES

1. See World Bank 1998b.
2. The "country in the driver's seat" theme is one of the central themes in the Comprehensive Development Framework (CDF) outlined in Wolfensohn, 1997, 1998, and 1999a, b and in Stiglitz, 1998.
3. See World Bank, 1997 or Transparency International and IBRD, 1998.
4. Keynes, 1936, p. 383. In the same vein, the early nineteenth century poet Heinrich Heine (1797–1856) pointedly remarked: "Mark this, ye proud men of action: ye are nothing but unconscious hodmen of the men of thought who, often in humblest stillness, have appointed you your inevitable work." (Heine, 1959, p. 106) (A "hodman" carries bricks or mortar for a mason.)
5. See Stiglitz (1995) and *Economic Report of the President* (1997). While the public good properties of knowledge had long been noted (Arrow, 1962), early articulations of knowledge as a public good (in the sense defined by Samuelson, 1954) include that of Stiglitz, 1977 and Romer, 1986. For an early textbook discussion, see Stiglitz, 1986.
6. See Jefferson, 1984 (1813).
7. As did Augustine (pp. 354–430) who said in one of his sermons: "The words I am uttering penetrate your senses, so that every hearer holds them, yet withholds them from no other... All of you hear all of it, though each takes all individually. I have no worry that, by giving all to one, the others are deprived. I hope, instead, that everyone will consume everything; so that, denying no other ear or mind, you take all to yourselves, yet leave all to all others." (Augustine quoted in Wills, 1999, p. 145).
8. See the classic article by Dudley Seers, 1962.
9. Quoted from President Mkapa of Tanzania in Wolfensohn, 1999.
10. See Smith, 1991, Langford and Brownsey, 1991, Ostry, 1991, Telgarsky and Ueno 1996, Stone et al., 1998, and Struyk, 1999.
11. "It is a time-honored Japanese gardening technique to prepare a tree for transplanting by slowly and carefully binding the roots over a period of time, bit by bit, to prepare the tree for the shock of the change it is about to experience. This process,

called *nemawashi*, takes time and patience, but it rewards you, if it is done properly, with a healthy transplanted tree." (Morita, 1986, p. 158)

12. James Scott (1998, p. 339] quotes an illustrative passage from Sinclair Lewis Arrowsmith: "They said... that he was so devoted to Pure Science... that he would rather have people die by the right therapy than be cured by the wrong."

13. See Schön's treatment (1983) of the technical expert in contrast with reflective practitioner.

14. See Ryle, 1945–6 for the earlier distinction between knowing how and knowing that, Oakeshott, 1991 for a treatment of practical knowledge versus technical knowledge, Schön, 1983 for a related treatment of professional versus instrumental knowledge, and Scott, 1998 on metis versus episteme/techne. The tacit/codified distinction looms large in Nonaka and Takeuchi, 1995, and they note that Larry Squire, 1987 gives a dozen labels for similar distinctions.

15. Even the codified part may suffer from the "*Rashomon* effect" (different people giving very different descriptions).

16. That is the brokerage model of the Knowledge Bank (see Sundquist 1978) which is sometimes juxtaposed to the storehouse or library model. Since explicit knowledge of the best practices (and of the pointers to tacit know-how) can be "downloaded", each model has some applicability. It is a question of emphasis.

17. For instance, if the chief policy-maker of the IMF and I each wrote up a case study of the Malaysian capital controls, the cases would probably look rather different.

18. See Lane, 1991 and Bandura, 1995.

19. I developed the concept of "learning to learn" and its implications for economic growth in Stiglitz, 1987.

20. See Hirschman, 1991, p. 168, for a contrast of consensus-building dialogue with the adversarial "rhetorics of intransigence."

21. See Hirschman, 1970, p. 239; quoted in Scott, 1998, p. 345.

REFERENCES

Arrow, K. 1962. "The Implications of Learning by Doing". *Review of Economic Studies*, 29: 155–73.

Bandura, Albert (ed.) 1995. *Self-Efficacy in Changing Societies,* Cambridge: Cambridge University Press.

Bell, M. and K. Pavitt. 1995. "The Development of Technological Capabilities". In *Trade, Technology, and International Competitiveness*. I. ul Haque (ed.) Washington, World Bank, 69–101.

Cohen, Theodore, 1987. *Remaking Japan: The American Occupation as New Deal*, New York: Free Press.

Cole, Robert E. 1989. *Strategies for Learning*, Berkeley: University of California Press.

Datta, Dhirendra Mohan. 1961. *The Philosophy of Mahatma Gandhi.* Madison: University of Wisconsin Press.

Dewey, John. 1957. *Human Nature and Conduct: An Introduction to Social Psychology*, New York: Modern Library.

Dewey, John and James Tufts. 1908. *Ethics*, New York: Henry Holt.

Economic Report of the President. 1997. Washington: United States Government Printing Office.

Heine, Heinrich. 1959. *Religion and Philosophy in Germany*. J. Snodgrass 'tr.'. Boston: Beacon Press.

Hirschman, Albert O. 1970. "The Search for Paradigms as a Hindrance to Understanding." *World Politics*. 22 (April).

——. 1991. *The Rhetoric of Reaction: Perversity, Futility, Jeopardy*. Cambridge: The Belknap Press.

Jefferson, T. 1984 (1813). "No Patent on Ideas." Letter to Isaac McPherson, August 13, 1813. In *Writings*. New York, Library of America: 1286–94.

Keynes, J.M. 1936. *The General Theory of Employment, Interest and Money*. New York: Harcourt, Brace & World.

Lane, Robert E. 1991. *The Market Experience*. New York: Cambridge University Press.

Langford, John W. and K. Lorne Brownsey (eds.). 1991. *Think Tanks and Governance in the Asia-Pacific Region*. Canada: Institute for Research on Public Policy.

Lindblom, Charles. 1990. *Inquiry and Change*. New Haven: Yale University Press.

Morita, A. 1986. *Made in Japan*. New York: E.P. Dutton.

Nonaka, I., and H. Takeuchi. 1995. *The Knowledge-Creating Company*. New York: Oxford.

Oakeshott, Michael. 1991. *Rationalism in Politics and Other Essays*. Indianapolis: Liberty Fund.

Ortega y Gasset, Jose. 1961. *Meditations on Quixote*. New York: Norton.

Ostry, Sylvia (ed.). 1991. *Authority and Academic Scribblers: The Role of Research in East Asian Policy Reform*. San Francisco: ICS Press.

Polanyi, Michael. 1962. *Personal Knowledge: Towards a Post-Critical Philosophy*. Chicago: University of Chicago Press.

Romer, P.M. 1986. "Increasing Returns and Long-Run Growth." *Journal of Political Economy*. 94:5. 1002–37.

Ryle, Gilbert. 1945–6. "Knowing How and Knowing That." *Proceedings of the Aristotelian Society*. XLVI: 1–16.

Samuelson, P. 1954. "The Pure Theory of Public Expenditure." *Review of Economics and Statistics*, 36, 387–9.

Schön, Donald A. 1971. *Beyond the Stable State*. New York: Norton.

———. 1983. *The Reflective Practitioner: How Professionals Think in Action*. New York: Basic Books.

Scott, James C. 1998. *Seeing Like a State: How Certain Schemes to Improve the Human Condition Have Failed*. New Haven: Yale University Press.

Seers, Dudley. 1962. "Why Visiting Economists Fail." *Journal of Political Economy*. 70 (4, August).

Shaw, George Bernard. 1962. *The Wit and Wisdom of Bernard Shaw*. Stephen Winsten (ed.). New York: Collier.

Smith, James A. 1991. *The Idea Brokers: Think Tanks and the Rise of the New Policy Elite*. New York: Free Press.

Squire, L.R. 1987. *Memory and Brain*. New York: Oxford University Press.

Stiglitz, Joseph E. 1977. "Theory of Local Public Goods." In *The Economics of Public Services*, M.S. Feldstein and R.P. Inman (eds.). Macmillan Publishing. 274–333.

———. 1986. *Economics of the Public Sector*. New York: W.W. Norton.

———. 1987. "Learning to Learn, Localized Learning and Technological Progress." In *Economic Policy and Technological Performance*. Dasgupta and Stoneman (eds.). Cambridge University Press. 125–53.

———. 1995. "The Theory of International Public Goods and the Architecture of International Organizations" United Nations Background Paper 7. Department for Economic and Social Information and Policy Analysis. July.

———. 1998. "Towards a New Paradigm for Development: Strategies, Policies" and Processes. Raul Prebisch Lecture at United Nations Conference on Trade and Development (UNCTAD). Geneva. 19 October. [ch. 2, this volume – *Ed.*]

Stone, Diane, Andrew Denham and Mark Garnett (eds.) 1998. *Think Tanks Across Nations: A Comparative Approach,* Manchester University Press.

Struyk, Raymond. 1999. *Reconstructive Critics: Think Tanks in Post-Soviet Bloc Democracies*. Washington DC: Urban Institute Press.

Sundquist, James. 1978. "Research Brokerage: The Weak Link." In *Knowledge and Policy: The Uncertain Connection*. Laurence Lynn (ed.). Washington DC: National Academy of Sciences. 126–44.

Telgarsky, Jeffrey, and Makiko Ueno. 1996. *Think Tanks in a Democratic Society: An Alternative Voice*. Washington DC: Urban Institute.

Transparency International and IBRD. 1998. *New Perspectives on Combating Corruption*. Washington DC: World Bank Institute.

Wills, Garry. 1999. *Saint Augustine*. New York: Viking.

Wolfensohn, J.D. 1997. Annual Meetings Address: The Challenge of Inclusion. Hong Kong: World Bank. *www.worldbank.org/html/extdr/am97/jdw_sp/jwsp97e.htm*.

——. 1998. The Other Crisis: 1998 Annual Meetings Address. Given at the 1998 World Bank/International Monetary Fund Annual Meetings. *www.worldbank.org/html/extdr/am98/jdw-sp/index.htm*.

——. 1999a. "A Proposal for a Comprehensive Development Framework." Washington DC: World Bank.

——. 1999b. Annual Meetings Address: Coalitions for Change. Given in Washington DC, 28 September 1999.

World Bank, 1997. *World Development Report: The State in a Changing World*. New York: Oxford University Press.

World Bank 1998a. *World Development Report: Knowledge for Development*. New York: Oxford University Press.

World Bank 1998b. *Assessing Aid: What Works, What Doesn't, and Why*. Washington: World Bank.

Chapter 7

Participation and Development: Perspectives from the Comprehensive Development Paradigm

Remarks at the International Conference on Democracy,
Market Economy and Development
Seoul, February 1999

INTRODUCTION

The relationship between democracy and development has long been debated. In the years immediately following World War II, there was a belief (articulated, for instance, in Paul Samuelson's classic textbook) in a tradeoff between democracy and growth. The Soviet Union, it was argued, had grown faster than the countries of the West, but in order to do so had jettisoned basic democratic rights. Later, with the enormous success of the East Asian economies in the 1960s and 1970s, the lack of full participatory democracy in many of the most successful countries was once again seen as reflecting these tradeoffs.

A subject of this importance has not escaped the statisticians' close scrutiny, with the kind of ambiguity that we have come to expect from such cross-sectional and time series analyses – compounded by severe measurement problems.[1] The host of factors that affect growth and that interact with each other make it difficult to identify with clarity the precise role of any particular factor. Even if we could establish a positive correlation, it would be necessary to ascertain a causality: does democracy promote growth or does growth promote democracy? If democracy is a "luxury" good, then those with higher incomes, or who see their incomes rising faster, will want more of this "luxury".

While the data may leave open the question of the precise relationship between the variables, the data – and the Soviet experiences – have made it clear that there is not the strong kind of tradeoff once envisioned. Countries can strive for openness and participation without fear that it will hamper development. Furthermore, research at both the macro-economic and micro-economic level has provided considerable insight into some of the ingredients that contribute to successful long-term growth. I will argue that broadly participatory processes (such as "voice", openness and transparency) promote truly successful long-term development. This is not to suggest that those processes guarantee success, or that there are no risks inherent in these processes. Some societies that are highly participatory, at least in formal structure, have failed to achieve development success. But it does mean that an understanding of the centrality of open, transparent, participatory processes in sustainable development helps us to design policies – strategies and processes – that are more likely to lead to long-term economic growth and that reinforce the strengths of the processes themselves.

I shall relate these lessons to the comprehensive development paradigm that is emerging[2] and, more broadly, to the transformation of the world's economy from an industrial economy to a knowledge economy.[3]

I. PARTICIPATION AND THE TRANSFORMATION OF SOCIETY

The comprehensive development paradigm sees development as a transformative movement. As I put it in my Prebisch Lecture [1998a; ch. 2, this volume – *Ed.*] last fall:

> Development represents a transformation of society, a movement from traditional relations, traditional ways of thinking, traditional ways of dealing with health and education, traditional methods of production, to more "modern" ways. For instance, a characteristic of traditional societies is the acceptance of the world as it is; the modern perspective recognizes change, it recognizes that we, as individuals and societies, can take actions that, for instance, reduce infant mortality, increase lifespans and increase productivity.

The comprehensive development paradigm contrasts with the dominant paradigm of the past half-century, which focused more narrowly on certain economic or, even more narrowly, allocative issues. It was argued that if only one could increase the supply of capital and the efficiency of resource allocations, development would occur. There is, in this sense, a close proximity in perspective between my predecessors as chief economist of the World Bank – Hollis Chenery, say, on the one hand, representing the modern evolution of the planning approach, and Anne Krueger, say, on the other hand, focusing on the reliance of market mechanisms. They disagreed on how best to improve the efficiency of resource allocations and to increase the level of investment, but they agreed that these were the central aspects of a growth strategy.

Since then we have come to see these perspectives as too narrow: they may be necessary conditions (and even that has been questioned), but they are far from sufficient. We now realize that "a dual economy is not a developed economy". [4] That is, it may be possible to raise productivity and even change mindsets within an enclave of the economy without achieving a true development transformation of the society as a whole.

The inadequacy of the traditional, narrowly economic approach has been highlighted by the experience in Russia and many of the other economies in transition. According to the standard model, the former socialist regime, with its central planning (which by necessity was informationally inefficient), distorted prices and attenuated incentives, led to outputs that were markedly below the economy's potential output. Reforms – privatization, free market prices, decentralization – even if not perfectly implemented, should have moved the economy far closer to its potential, and output should have risen. Since at the same time defense expenditures were cut back drastically, consumption should have increased markedly (unless savings increased – which did not happen). But in fact, output and consumption in most of the former socialist countries remains markedly below their levels of a decade ago, when the transition began. Part of the explanation lies in the destruction of organizational capital; part lies in the fact that far more than privatization is required to make an effective market economy; but yet another part of the explanation lies in the destruction of the already weak social capital, manifested in the growth of the so-called mafia.

If a change in mindset is at the center of development, then it is clear that attention needs to be shifted to how to affect such changes in mindset. [5] Such changes cannot be "ordered" or forced from the outside, however well-intentioned the outsiders may be. [6] Change has to come from within. The kinds of open and extensive discussions that are central to participatory processes are, I suspect, the most effective way of ensuring that the change in mindset occurs not only within a small elite, but reaches deep down in society. Indeed, there is a whole tradition that identifies "government by discussion" as key.[7]

The broad range of participation

In this paper, I will use the term "participation" in the broadest sense, to encompass transparency, openness and voice in both public and corporate settings. There are a variety of institutional arrangements that are consistent with "participation" in this sense. And the term "participatory processes" refers not just to those processes by which decisions are made in national governments, but also to processes used at local and provincial levels, at the workplace and in capital markets.

This brings me to an important point: from this comprehensive development perspective, I would argue that participation does not refer simply to voting.[8] Participatory processes must entail open dialogue and broadly active civic engagement, and it requires that individuals have a voice in the decisions that affect them.[9]

Processes, not just outcomes, are key to this broader interpretation of participation. The stress on processes is a natural outgrowth not only of the increasing emphasis on equity, but also of our greater recognition of agency problems. That is to say, we now recognize the great importance of potential discrepancies between the actions taken by a party (the government, for example) and the interests of those that the party is supposed to serve.[10] A government that engages in secrecy, making it impossible for citizens to have informed opinions about policies that are critical to their lives and the well-being of their country, weakens accountability and the quality of decision-making.[11] A government that controls TV stations – often the way that a majority of the population becomes informed – or one that allows a small oligarchy to control the media also undermines accountability. Over the short term, a country may be able to engage in a meaningful national dialogue on its future evolution without free elections; but in the long run, the dissonance may become too great. The legitimacy of those in decision-making positions will depend not only on their actions being in accord with these "democratic sentiments", but also on those positions being attained through

open electoral processes. While "buying elections" is almost everywhere
a source of opprobrium – votes cannot or at least should not be traded in
the market place as if they were a commodity[12] – it has been argued that
the way electoral campaigns are run in many Western countries amounts
to little more than "buying votes". Campaign contributions are required to
"persuade" voters (via 30-second sound bites), and those providing the
funds have undue influence in policy formulation.[13]

In many countries, an absence of rule of law and a lack of transparency
both weaken the economy and undermine participatory processes. In some
countries, for instance, while there are "rules" designed to ensure fair treatment of all, the rich and powerful have special access to the seats of
political power and use that influence to obtain for themselves special favors
and exemptions from the rules. They may also "buy" special access to the
legislative and executive branches of government, thereby obtaining rules
and regulations that are of benefit to them.

The adverse impacts of these policies on economic growth have been
well documented. There is evidence, for example, that secure property
rights and the rule of law – which tend to go hand in hand with a system
of effective checks and balances – are associated with higher levels of
investment and growth.[14] In addition, recent research has shown that
countries earn multiple benefits when they adopt good policies – which
include open, transparent governance – and avoid the kinds of distorted
policies that are associated with preferential treatment of special interests. Not only is growth faster, but foreign aid is also more effective in
such contexts.[15]

Concentrations of economic power and wealth will almost inevitably be
translated into attempts at political influence. The question is, what can be
done about this? Part of any strategy is to limit these concentrations of
wealth and economic power. This provides part of the justification for
redistributive taxation, and especially inheritance taxation. It also provides
part of the motivation for the anti-trust laws enacted in the United States at
the end of the last century. More broadly, Thomas Jefferson, the third
President of the United States, the author of the American Declaration of
Independence, and a great believer in democratic institutions, argued for
the importance of smallholder agriculture if the newly founded American
democracy was to flourish. Today, this view translates into active government support for small and medium-size enterprises. Part of the intent of
the corporate restructuring currently going on in Korea is to limit the reach

of this economic power; but there are concerns that in the process of rationalization of industry, concentrations of power in certain industries may actually increase. The temporary gains in efficiency may, I suggest, be more than offset by the inefficiencies introduced by excessive market power – and even if that were not the case, one should raise questions about the potential adverse effects on participation and openness.

There is a second prong to the strategy: strengthening the "checks" on abuses of this power and influence. This prescription encompasses at least three elements. The first is to strengthen civil society, as a source of countervailing power – from political parties, to unions, to consumer groups, to think tanks, and to a variety of other NGOs. In the parlance of modern economics, ensuring participatory processes, and promoting the public good more broadly, is itself a public good. As with other public goods, there will be too little provision of such participatory processes in the absence of public support. A strong civil society is an important element in a strategy of implementing meaningful democratic reforms.

Second, governments should not only increase transparency, but also recognize that there exists what I have termed the basic "right to know". [See ch. 8, this volume – *Ed.*] Citizens have a right to know what the government is doing and why. They have a right to know if "exceptions" are made to certain rules and regulations. Again, to refer to the legal structure with which I am most familiar, the Freedom of Information Act has provided a way of enforcing at least a modicum of the citizens' right to know. Third, societies should extend citizens' rights to legal recourse, to sue. The United States recognized that political pressures might be brought to bear to induce governments not to act to break up monopolies and prevent anti-competitive practices, and as a result, the anti-trust laws provided that any injured party could sue for triple damages. Though the law has been interpreted too narrowly and occasionally abused in the United States, such civil remedies seem particularly desirable in economies burdened by a history of large enterprises exercising excessive political influence. These are minimal steps in ensuring government accountability and the rule of law.

Corporate governance and economic efficiency

Many of the issues I have just discussed are relevant not only to governments, but also to the governance of corporations. Corporations are public institutions: they collect funds from the "public" and invest them in productive assets. Workers too are stakeholders in corporations; given imperfections in labor mobility, a worker who is mistreated or fired cannot costlessly turn to other options (as he or she might in idealized neoclassical models). The managers of a corporation are in a fiduciary position of trust. Even if they are large shareholders, their actions affect others, from minority shareholders to bondholders to workers. While contractual arrangements between the corporations and each of these parties may delimit the scope of action of managers, the managers still have considerable room for action.

Laws affecting governance (and their implementation) have implications for both equity and efficiency. If minority shareholders or bondholders cannot be ensured fair treatment, they will not be willing to turn funds over to the corporation, and its growth will be limited, or else the firm will have to turn to banks as a source of finance. But even this recourse to bank finance has its limits: as leverage increases, the risk of bankruptcy increases. And if many firms in the economy have high leverage, then the economy as a whole may be threatened with a financial crisis, the costs of which may be borne by taxpayers and workers, not just the firm and its lenders. A strong legal system providing for corporate governance is essential to an effective capital market. And a strong bank regulatory system is essential if banks are not to provide the high levels of leverage that put the entire economy at risk.

Let me be clear: these are issues that involve both economics and participatory processes. For if businesses are allowed to delay the building of the necessary legal and regulatory framework or to subvert their effective implementation – because of insufficient participation by average citizens in decision-making – then those citizens will face adverse consequences that clearly are not of their own making.

While the legal system must, for instance, entail both strong protection of minority shareholders and the kinds of "fair trading" provisions incorporated in typical securities and exchange regulations, it must go beyond that, to ensure transparency and accountability. There need to be both civil and criminal actions, for instance, associated with fraud. Civil action, and the threat of it, can help make up for weaknesses or corruption in state supervision and enforcement: where civil action is possible, there are far more actors in the economy who have an incentive and a right to ensure enforcement of laws.

Today, the issues that I have discussed in this and the preceding section are recognized to be central to the success of an economy even under the narrower objective of maximizing economic growth. As the 1997 *World Development Report* showed forcefully, if governments are not transparent, countries will fail to attract investment and growth will slow. Our recent report on aid effectiveness[16] reinforced the conclusions about public governance as a contributor to growth. Recent events have suggested that corporate governance is also quite important; without a modicum of transparency and accountability in the corporate sector, investment and growth may lag. As Jim Wolfensohn has recently remarked, "free markets cannot work behind closed doors".

Making change acceptable, and the acceptance of change

As I emphasized in my Prebisch Lecture (1998a), development requires a change in mindset, and in particular, an acceptance of (and indeed a seeking out of productivity-enhancing) change. Change is often threatening – and sufficiently risk-averse individuals are willing to pass up opportunities for expected gain to avoid the downside risks.

Participatory processes ensure that these concerns are not only heard, but also addressed; as a result, these processes dissipate much of the resistance to change. Consider an example that is particularly relevant in a time of globalization. As one who supports lowering trade barriers, I am nonetheless dismayed to note that all too often ardent free-trade advocates cavalierly dismiss the opponents, including those who stand to lose by free trade, and refer to them as "special interests" trying to protect their existing "rents". But among those hurt by trade reforms will be many who will lose their jobs; if the economy is suffering under an unemployment rate of ten per cent or more, there is a great risk of extended unemployment. And if the society lacks an adequate safety net, the unemployed worker risks true impoverishment, with disastrous effects on the lives of all family members. What is of concern to the worker is not just his loss of "rents", but the loss of his family's livelihood. Those experts who are not disciplined by having to be accountable to the citizenry too often ignore this. Inclusive processes make it more likely that these legitimate concerns will be addressed. In this way, they can ensure greater equality, and even allow more efficient outcomes – given that the loss in output from extended periods of unemployment may far outweigh the losses associated with the inefficient use of resources.

Participation is thus essential to effect the systemic change in mindset associated with the development transformation, and to engender policies that make change – which is at the center of development – more acceptable. And because individuals have had a voice in shaping the changes, in making them more acceptable, change is likely to be accepted or even embraced, rather than reversed at the first opportunity.

Participation and project effectiveness

I have argued that participation is necessary for a fully effective, society-wide development transformation. Recent research has also begun to provide evidence for this point at the grass-roots level, demonstrating the benefits of participation in development projects.[17] It is not only that such participation brings to the project relevant information that outside development agencies (or even governments) are not likely to have. Participation also brings with it commitment, and commitment brings with it greater effort – the kind of effort that is required to make the project successful.[18] For example, schools in which parents have a voice may be more successful partly because such participation engenders parental involvement in the school – and in their children's work. Water projects in which there has been more community participation are more likely to be successful, because participation will help support the kind of long-term maintenance that is required to keep them effective.

The knowledge economy and participation

One of the major changes facing the developed and less developed world is the growth of the "knowledge economy". Elsewhere, I and others have argued that the knowledge economy will lead to a change in the ways of organizing production (and society more generally), changes which give rein to greater participation of individuals in decision-making. Indeed, success in the knowledge economy – whether at the firm level or at the level of the society – will require such change. Tayloristic vertical structures were designed to enforce and coordinate certain physical behaviors while knowledge-based work organization involves greater recognition of the autonomy and self-direction of the mind. Knowledge is best acquired not by passive rote memorization but by the active involvement of the learner. Learning is by doing, not by watching or memorizing. These activist principles were embodied, for example, in John Dewey's pragmatic philosophy of education.[19]

To foster the active involvement of the learner, the motivation should ideally be intrinsic to the activity, not a super-added carrot or stick. While external incentives can modify short-term behavior, they usually will only temporarily override rather than change the internal system of motivation. When the extrinsic incentives are removed, behavior reverts to the previous motives. All of these principles are fundamental for the knowledge-based transformation of a developing country. "Best practices" or reforms that are imposed on a country through conditionality ("carrots and sticks") may very well fail to produce lasting change. They will tend to undermine people's incentives to develop their own capacities and weaken their confidence in using their own intelligence. There is a real danger that an external development agency, instead of acting as a catalyst or midwife to empower change, will only short-circuit people's learning activities and reinforce their feelings of impotence. The external incentives may temporarily overpower the springs of action that are native to the institutional matrix of the country, but that will probably not induce any lasting institutional reforms.

Broad participation in the vital activities of a developing society, like shop-floor participation in a company, is at least helpful, and perhaps even necessary, to foster a lasting transformation. Active involvement brings commitment to the lessons being learned and ownership of the results. Participation and involvement is not just a matter for government officials or managers; it needs to reach deeper to include those who are often excluded and who are key to the strengthening of social and organizational capital.[20] Outside experts can encourage "ownership" of "best policies" through persuasion, but the degree of ownership is likely to be much greater if those who must carry out the policies are actively involved in the process of shaping and adapting, if not reinventing, these policies in the country itself.

Success in a knowledge-based economy will also require a highly educated citizenry, with strong higher-level cognitive skills, and it will require an effective and decentralized communications network, like the Internet. Both of these enhance the possibilities of more effective participation, and make it more difficult to suppress it.

Participatory processes and the effectiveness of decisions

I began this paper by referring to the debates earlier in this century concerning the tradeoff between democracy and development. Underlying that debate was the hypothesis that participatory processes inhibited the kind of quick decision-making required for rapid economic growth. Supporters of this view sometimes make an analogy to the military, a highly hierarchical organization in which prices play little role. Few have suggested the use of market mechanisms for the allocation of scarce military resources in the middle of a war. Presumably, there is a belief that over short periods of time and for well-defined objectives, centralized control may be a more effective organizational form.[21]

Earlier in this century, rapid industrialization was viewed very much in the same terms: resources had to be marshalled quickly, which made the military model an attractive one to many societies. The Soviet Union, for example, saw time as of the essence. With the state and society threatened by hostile outside forces, its leaders felt that delay would be highly costly, and therefore development had to be imposed from above at rapid speed – and, as it turned out, at great cost.

There has been regrettably little work defining clearly the circumstances under which hierarchical decision making is more effective than decentralized market mechanisms. (See Stiglitz, 1975, and Sah and Stiglitz, 1986.) It appears that while markets may work far more efficiently in the long run, there may be short-run circumstances – often entailing dramatic changes in the direction of resource allocation, such as when a country goes to war – in which market mechanisms are either too slow or too unreliable. Certainly, the experience of extended periods of unemployment and under-utilization of capacity – as illustrated by the Great Depression, and perhaps by the frequent financial crises which have plagued the world's economies over the past quarter century[22] – suggests that market mechanisms do not always work quickly to allocate resources efficiently.

Open, participatory processes may result in delay. Take an example from my own country, the United States. It has been more than two decades since changes in demography and in the pace of productivity increase made it apparent that the US social insurance system was not financially viable. And yet until recently, the political processes have not found it possible to begin to address the underlying problems – even in the case of solutions that appear to be supported by almost all experts, such as correcting the bias in the cost of living adjustment.

But as maddeningly slow as open political processes sometimes seem to be, it is not clear that less participation yields results any more quickly on average. Consider how different types of governments might react when faced with an insolvent banking system. An autocratic government may indeed move quickly and effectively to address the problem, if it chooses to pursue the best interests of society. But if instead it is beholden to financial-sector leaders and fears losing their support, the government may well use public funds to keep a sinking system afloat for as long as possible, before finally being forced into real reform. Compared with the latter case, a participatory political system – one that represents the interests of depositors and taxpayers as well as moneyed interests – might well mobilize more quickly to confront the problem.[23]

In any event, offsetting any potential costs of openness and participation are, I believe, their overwhelming advantages. Most of the literature has focused on the advantages of decentralizing decision-making, which – if done right – can give more people a chance to participate in those decisions.[24] I do not want to review here all the arguments – the lower variability of decision quality that comes with decentralized decisions[25]; the fact that rejected projects get a "second chance", which implies that fewer good projects (ideas) are rejected;[26] or the opportunity for experimentation and learning that comes with decentralization.

Participation and political sustainability

But I do want to dwell for a moment on an argument for participatory processes that has perhaps received too little attention. Earlier, I argued that such processes make change more acceptable and more accepted. When democratic processes work well (that is, when the majority does not simply impose its wishes on the minority, or conversely), they entail a process of consensus-building. This means that once a new policy has been adopted, it can better weather the vicissitudes of the political process.[27] For example, India's economic reforms of the past decade were not imposed from the outside, but were adopted from within, and in a way that has engendered broad support on the basic tenets. As a result, most of the key reforms have been sustained, even as governments have changed. More generally, when a society adopts reforms after a process of consensus-building, the political debate can move on to other issues – such as the next steps in reform – without feeling a continuous need to revisit prior decisions. By contrast, when there is a perception that the reforms were imposed from outside, the reforms themselves become the subject of political debate, lessening their sustainability.

II. ECONOMIC AND SOCIAL DEVELOPMENT

Too often, development is interpreted as being synonymous with economic development, the increase in per capita GDP. To be sure, one of the key factors differentiating more from less developed countries is per capita income. And increases in per capita income are clearly helpful for improving health and education, and for making it possible to pursue a host of other objectives that require resources. Figure 1 (p. 233) shows that, by and large, countries with higher per capita incomes also have higher "social indicators". But while the two tend to move together, there is far from perfect correlation: certain countries and provinces (like Sri Lanka, Costa Rica and Kerala [province of India – *Ed.*]) that have pursued active pro-poor social policies have managed to achieve social indicators that are far better than the norm for those at their per capita income. Korea has long shown similar trends, educating its children at far higher rates than we would have naïvely predicted based on income levels. Conversely, other countries that have failed to mind these social concerns have health and education levels far below what would be expected for a country at their level of income.

As I argued in my WIDER Lecture (1998c) [ch. 1, this volume – *Ed.*], we need to broaden our objectives, beyond an increase in per capita GDP, for instance, to sustainable and equitable development. Here, I want to emphasize another aspect, one that both has intrinsic value and is necessary for the attainment of many of these other objectives. I will call this aspect "social development", by which I mean the ability of a society to peacefully resolve conflicts and to address amicably sources of common concern when interests differ. Societies in which there is a high level of violence,

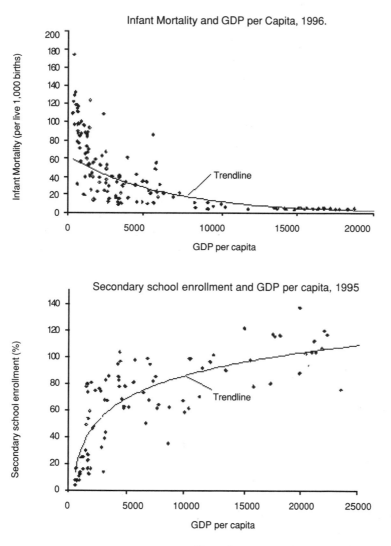

Figure 1

either within the family or the community, would in these terms be marked by a low level of social development. Similarly, societies that suffer an extended "gridlock" – where important issues cannot be addressed over long periods of time because conflicting positions cannot be resolved – would, in these terms, be marked by a low level of social development More broadly, social development entails a greater sense of trust and responsibility – such as a credit culture, in which those who borrow "expect" to pay back the lender – a higher level of social capital, and a greater "internalization" of some of the important externalities (such as those associated with the environment).[28]

Little need be said about the direct value of "social development" – in holding down crime, for example. The costs of violence in socially less developed societies go well beyond expenditures directed at protecting oneself against it; the threat of violence also gives rise to considerable anxiety and uncertainty, even if neither can adequately be assigned a price tag. But here, I want to focus not on this direct value, but on the relationship between social and economic development, as well as the impact of open, participatory and transparent processes on that relationship.

Social development promotes economic development

Social development enhances economic development. Typically, "social" enforcement (reputation) mechanisms are more efficient than are "explicit" legal enforcement mechanisms. That is, it is more cost-effective if transactions take place in an environment in which businesspeople have some confidence that they will not need to sue each time to have a contract enforced. Recent growth research has seemed to bear out this contention at the economy-wide level, showing that trust and shared civic norms are associated with better economic performance.[29] Now that the development of financial institutions is widely recognized as an essential ingredient in a development strategy, a credit culture – that is, a socially developed culture that expects the repayment of debts, whether or not legal enforcement is imminent – is increasingly being recognized as contributing to financial depth. Similarly, both foreign and domestic business people will shy away from investing in an economy with a high level of crime, corruption and violence,[30] all symptoms of low levels of social development.

234

But economic development often undermines social development

The problem is that in the process of economic development, countries often regress in terms of social development. Social sanctions that previously worked well to internalize externalities within a community lose their potency when labor becomes highly mobile and when communities themselves become fragile. Social capital may deteriorate, before the country is able to establish the kinds of less personalized social capital associated with more advanced industrialized countries.

Economic policies that fail to pay attention to the social dimension may make matters worse

Often, poor policy design has exacerbated this tendency for economic growth and change to fray the social fabric. I view with particular concern the increases in unemployment that are often associated with "adjustment". When workers are deprived of the opportunity to be meaningful participants in the community by working – when, through no fault of their own, they simply cannot find work – they lose self-esteem. Welfare is no substitute for work; and in any case, many developing countries lack even an adequate social safety net, so that the adverse consequences of unemployment are truly dire.

Other than impoverishment, unemployment can give rise to other social ills. As the Nobel Prize-winning economist Gary Becker has pointed out, crime stems at least in part from the expectation of economic gains.[31] Those prospective gains loom larger, and the threat of punishment provokes less fear, when a person's other options for earning a living vanish. This is not to say that the typical unemployed worker turns to a life of crime, but only to note that despair and blocked opportunity can tear at the social fabric and reduce willingness to abide by laws. Since the resulting rise in crime levels is likely to exact significant economic and psychic costs, as I noted before, policymakers must take these costs into account when weighing the advantages of contractionary adjustment policies.

Participatory processes and the restoration of social capital

Open, transparent, and participatory processes can play an important role in preserving or, if necessary, reestablishing social capital. Participation itself can help create a sense of community, a *sine qua non* for a high level of social capital. If individuals believe that they have had meaningful participation in the decisions that are affecting them, they will be more willing to accept changes, even if they are adversely affected. But if they believe that those changes have been imposed on them, either by outsiders or by illegitimate governments who have not taken their concerns into account, then resentment is more likely to mount and to lead to socially destructive outcomes.

A minimal sense of community entails making sure those that are most disadvantaged – particularly those who face starvation or severe medical problems – are taken care of, in at least a minimal way. This year's Nobel Prize-winning economist, Amartya Sen (whom many of you heard speak yesterday), has stressed that democratic societies simply do not allow famines to occur.[32] Perhaps this is a low bar for a community to hurdle, but it is a crucial one nonetheless. Communities that do not allow such severe impoverishment are more likely to be trusted by a worker who faces potentially disruptive change because she will feel that her concerns are taken at least somewhat into account.

Open dialogue with a free and vigorous press, with a diversified ownership of media (including TV) is, I would argue, essential for the development of this sense of community. With secrecy, and without such open dialogue, there will always be the suspicion that decisions were made not on the basis of "community" interests, but on the basis of "special interests" (and often these suspicions are justified).

Let me elaborate briefly on this point. The problem is that with secrecy, individuals cannot tell from the outcomes alone whether their interests have received due attention. They observe outcomes that are clearly disadvantageous to them. They are told, for instance, that matters would have been even worse had not the given policies been pursued, or that in future things will be better. They may suspect that the interests of others – whether well-placed domestic business leaders or foreign lenders – may have been placed above the interests of less well-connected domestic actors, such as workers. In such circumstances, ensuring fair processes is essential; but if decisions are made in secret – or if there is not even full disclosure of the terms of an agreement – there will be little confidence that the processes were themselves fair.

Economic development can promote social development

While economic development in the past has often undermined social development, economic development today can serve to reinforce social development and participatory processes. For an essential ingredient of economic development is improved education and better communications. The latter enables individuals to be better informed about issues in a timely way, and the former puts individuals in a better position to use that information to form intelligent views concerning the merits of alternatives.

Well-designed education systems, which can both contribute to and be financed by economic development, have also served an important role in building social cohesion. Korea's education system is an excellent example. Although Korea has recognized the need to reform certain features of that system in the 1990s, over the past several decades the system has done much to reinforce social cohesion, in my view. The availability of mass education and the meritocratic principles underlying the system have strengthened confidence in the equity of social outcomes, in the process deflating any tendency toward social envy and dissent. On the flip side, poorly-designed education systems that reinforce social stratification may well undermine a broad sense of social cohesion and impede social development.

III. SOCIAL COHESION, ECONOMIC POLICY, AND THE COMPREHENSIVE DEVELOPMENT PARADIGM

The central argument of this paper has been that open, transparent, and participatory processes are important ingredients in the development trans-formation – important both for sustainable economic development and for social development that should be viewed as an end in itself and as a means to more rapid economic growth.

Nowhere are such processes more important than in economic policymaking. While, to be sure, there are certain policies that make everybody worse off or everybody better off, in the real world many of the most important policy decisions entail choices among policies that cannot be so easily rejected or embraced. That is to say, there are real tradeoffs among policies: not only do some people gain more than others, but some actually lose.

Many have remarked at the increase in social tensions that followed upon the Latin American crisis of the 1980s. In many cases, education expenditures were cut back, and inequality and unemployment increased. We need not engage here in the debate whether adjustment policies exacerbated these problems, or whether they would have been worse, but for the adjustment assistance and the policies that accompanied that assistance. But what is clear is that all too often the process by which the decisions were made did not comport well with open, transparent and participatory principles: not only were negotiations that led to adjustment typically conducted in secret, but even the outcomes sometimes were not fully disclosed.

My concern here is not only reality but also perception. Indeed, perceptions are sufficiently widespread at least to suggest that there may be some reality in them, and in any case, the perceptions themselves become part of the reality with which we have to deal. The widespread perception that I encounter is that adjustment packages of the 1980s often did not take into account as fully as they might have the social and economic consequences of the policies on the poor. In the East Asian crisis, these concerns have been compounded by another perception: that the adjustment packages went beyond actions that were necessary to deal with the crises. (Whether correct or not, this view has drawn enormous attention. Martin Feldstein, for instance, in his highly influential *Foreign Affairs* article last year, argued that the conditions on adjustment packages went not only beyond matters of direct concern to the crisis, but even into concerns that were more properly political than economic. In his view, these questions clearly should have been decided through participatory political processes.[33])

This perception – that economic decision-making on certain key questions has been less than fully participatory – has been reinforced by the secrecy in which negotiations often occur. Without prejudging whether secrecy is essential for market stability and for the successful conduct of negotiations (but see my Oxford Amnesty Lecture (1999c) [ch. 8, this volume – *Ed.*] for my reservations on these arguments for secrecy), the adverse consequences should be clear: as I have already noted, there will always be a suspicion that moneyed and vested interests, not common welfare, have dictated solutions. This problem is exacerbated when top decision-makers do not even go through the motions of weighing choices among various plausible alternatives. Instead, when decision-making is shielded from the public view, the recommended action is often adopted as if it were the only appropriate and feasible action – though it is perfectly transparent to most citizens that that is not the case.[34]

Whether we like it or not, whether it is justified or not, there is now in much of the world a legacy of suspicion and doubt. Opponents see in development conditionality an echo of the colonial bonds that their countries threw off only one or two generations ago. And while conditionality is at least widely perceived to have undermined transparency and participation, there is little evidence that it has achieved much in terms of better policies.[35] The results should perhaps not be that surprising, given that policies imposed through conditionality are seldom politically sustainable. Indeed, in many cases, as we have noted, the policies are at least perceived to have contributed to the country's problems, undermined meaningful participation and led to further breakdown of social cohesion. For example, privatization in Russia has not resulted in an effective market economy, and it increased inequality without any compensating increase in productivity or growth. Rather than providing incentives for wealth creation, it provided incentives for asset-stripping – with huge movements of "private" capital abroad. Moreover, the way that privatization was carried out resulted in media concentrations that undermined the viability of broad, informed public participation. Of course, none of these "failures" were themselves explicitly part of the recommendations, but conditionality may have done little to forestall them. While privatization was often a condition that was both explicit and highly visible, far less stress was placed on the institutional arrangements that might have mitigated these problems. Had a more broadly participatory process arrived at a homegrown privatization scheme which was then carried out on a schedule determined by domestic concerns, perhaps the combined wisdom and knowledge of the citizenry could have headed off the most egregious failures of privatization.

Those who provide funds – including those of us at the World Bank – must recognize that we have a fiduciary and moral responsibility to make sure that the funds are well spent. Future generations in the borrowing country will be obligated to pay back the loans, and unless the returns are sufficient, borrowing today will impoverish future generations, rather than enriching them. If funds end up financing capital flight at overvalued exchange rates, for example, it is hard to see how this enriches future generations! (Thus, it may be argued, it is not so much whether conditions are attached to making funds available that matters, but what those conditions are, and how they are arrived at.)

These are among the concerns that have motivated the World Bank to seek new ways of working with developing countries. In the Comprehensive Development Framework that President Wolfensohn outlined in his annual speech, he proposed a new approach to development assistance. Not only did it emphasize the holistic nature of the development process, but it strove to create a new process, one that would entail a new set of relationships, not only between the Bank and the country, but within the country itself and between the country and all donor agencies. Central is the notion that the "country (not just the government) must be in the driver's seat".

One of the important results emerging from recent research on aid is not only that conditionality is ineffective, but that aid is highly effective in good policy environments. Moreover, we need to recognize that funds are fungible: in effect, money goes to overall budgetary support. It makes sense therefore to give assistance to countries that have adopted good policies; a comprehensive development framework enhances the likelihood that the country will adopt such policies and sustain them. The emphasis on fungibility does not mean an end to project lending: budgetary assistance needs to be complemented with "knowledge" and "technical assistance," and project lending is often the most effective way to combine the two. But we do have to take into account the overall framework for that lending. In developing their strategies, countries may not approach matters exactly as we international bureaucrats – unfettered by political constraints – would. I am not sure on whose judgment I would more often rely, particularly if my objective is the long-run political sustainability of reforms. Those within a country may be in a better position to make the difficult judgments on how best to create a sustainable consensus behind reforms. No decisions are more important than those that affect the economy. Clearly, the citizens need to be informed of the consequences of those choices – and on this there is often debate, even among so-called experts. No institution, whether domestic or international, has a monopoly on wisdom, and it is imperative that there be a full articulation of the evidence concerning the consequences of alternative policies.

CONCLUDING REMARKS

I have here discussed mainly general principles. But these principles translate into concrete actions. I illustrated this with one example in the previous section: how these principles necessitate a change in the way external assistance interacts with developing countries. I have also stressed the importance of the processes by which decisions are made – how consensus-building, open dialogue, and the promotion of an active civil society are more likely to result in politically sustainable economic policies and to spur the development transformation.[36]

There are many other examples of how these principles can guide development action. In some cases, the perspectives put forth here reinforce arguments central to development policy in recent years: the importance of education, and, in particular, the education of women; the need for better communications, which can best be promoted by encouraging a competitive telecommunications sector; the central role of "good government" (inducing a lack of corruption); and the importance of the rule of law and of reducing scope for discretionary actions in a strategy to reduce corruption.

The view that I have offered here – with its emphasis on the simultaneous pursuit of social and economic development – places renewed emphasis on the need for governments to pursue policies that maintain full employment. There are many dimensions to this: avoiding crises – which necessitates strong governmental regulation of financial institutions and the pursuit of sound macro-economic policies – and responding to crises in ways that minimize the length and depth of unemployment.

It also places a renewed emphasis on the importance of competition policy. The origins of competition policy, it will be recalled, lie not only in the concern for promoting efficiency, but also the desire to avoid the concentrations of economic power that can corrode transparency and participatory processes. Nowhere are these concerns more important than in the media.

The comprehensive approach to development also raises new concerns: the structure of education systems, for instance, may lead to or perpetuate social stratification, undermining social cohesion, or it can be a key ingredient in nation building. More than just "efficiency in the delivery of services" is at stake. Given the importance of consensus formation, capacity building – creating the capacity for those within a country to forge their own development strategies and to have an active debate about the central tenets – needs to move more towards the center.

Though democracy has a long tradition – in the West, it dates back at least to the Greek city-states – it has been slow to evolve and remains highly fragile. It was only in the century now coming to a close that universal suffrage became the norm. Many countries have been slow to grant those basic rights that I believe to be so necessary for an effective participatory system – the right to a free press, free speech, the right to organize to pursue common objectives (both in general, and for workers in particular). Many governments continue not to recognize the people's fundamental "right to know", pursuing secrecy well beyond the domain where national security requires it.

Democracy, and participatory processes more generally, is also fragile. Repeatedly, we have seen high levels of social disorder lead to calls for "strong" (read "anti-democratic") government to restore the basic foundations of law and order without which individuals cannot live and work together. We have seen how economic policies, and the manner in which they are adopted, can either contribute to social cohesion or to social disorder. Countries that have experienced hyperinflation are well aware of the economic, and thus social, disruption to which the failure of the basic market mechanisms can give rise. But too often the wrong lesson has been read from these experiences: hyperinflation is seen as the underlying problem, and therefore it has to be avoided at all costs. But the real cause is the huge disruptions in the social and economic order that result from hyperinflation; therefore if policies designed to prevent inflation at the same time contribute directly to social and economic disorder, the consequences will be equally disastrous. (Indeed, Keynes, in his *The Economic Consequences of the Peace* (1920), predicted the adverse consequences of the terms of the Versailles Treaty, well before the particular way in which those consequences would manifest themselves became clear.)

The world has experienced financial and currency crises of increasing frequency and severity,[37] with widespread economic and social repercussions. There is a growing consensus about the causes of the crises, and about the policies that must be adopted to reduce their frequency and severity and to mitigate the consequences (developing stronger safety nets, for example).[38] But no safety net can fully replace the security provided by an economy running at full employment. No welfare system will ever restore the dignity that comes from work. It is imperative that countries not only implement policies that prevent crises and minimize their depth and adverse consequences, but also that they respond to these crises in ways that maintain as high a level of employment as possible.

But while globalization and economic change provide new challenges for sustainable comprehensive development, they also offer new opportunities and have made open, participatory, transparent processes essential for long-run success. This is as true for the private sector as for the public. As we stand at the threshold of the twenty-first century, there is much to be learned from the failures of the century coming to a close. We cannot shut our eyes to the disasters brought on by totalitarian regimes: similar disasters must be avoided at all costs. Nor can we ignore the link between these failures and the economic and social disorder that preceded them.

We now know more about how to manage an economy than we did seventy-five years ago. We can hope that in the coming decades, we will make use of this knowledge, our broad understanding of the development process, and the new opportunities afforded by the changing economy to strengthen and extend development through comprehensive strategies. In this vision, these development strategies will incorporate social as well as economic development, arrived at through open, transparent and participatory processes, that extend the fruits of development in a sustainable way to all the citizens of the developing world.

NOTES

1. For an earlier review, see "Symposia: Democracy and Development" (1993) in the *Journal of Economic Perspectives*, including the article by Przeworski and Limongi.
2. See Wolfensohn (1998, 1999) and Stiglitz (1998a).
3. See Department of Trade and Industry (1998a, 1998b) and Stiglitz (1999b).
4. Stiglitz (1998a).
5. "All [vicious development] circles result from the two-way dependence between development and some other factor, be it capital or entrepreneurship, education, public administration, etc. But the circle to which our analysis has led us may perhaps lay claim to a privileged place in the hierarchy of these circles inasmuch as it alone places the difficulties of development back where all difficulties of human action begin and belong: in the mind." (Hirschman, 1958, p. 11.)
6. In the West, the clear recognition of the inability to externally force a change in mindset dates from the Reformation. "As little as another can go to hell or heaven for me, so little can he believe or disbelieve for me; and as little as he can open or shut heaven or hell for me, so little can he drive me to faith or unbelief." See Luther, 1942

(1523). This insight was basic to the liberty of conscience and the attitudes of religious tolerance fostered in Europe after the Reformation.

7. See, for example, John Stuart Mill (1972 [1859]), Walter Bagehot (1948 [1869]), James Bryce (1959 [1888]), John Dewey (1927, 1939), Ernest Barker (1967 [1942]), Frank Knight (1947), and Charles Lindblom (1990).

8. "In theory, the democratic method is persuasion through public discussion carried on not only in legislative halls but in the press, private conversations and public assemblies. The substitution of ballots for bullets, of the right to vote for the lash, is an expression of the will to substitute the method of discussion for the method of coercion." (Dewey, 1939, p. 128.)

9. See Hirschman (1970) for a discussion of "voice".

10. Agency theory is one of the principal strands in the modern theory of the economics of information. See, for example, Ross (1973), Stiglitz (1974), and the huge literature that followed. The essential point is that because of imperfections of information, actions of agents are not perfectly observable, and one cannot infer whether the agent took the "appropriate" action from observing outputs alone.

11. See Stiglitz (1999c).

12. Some free marketeers would disagree with this proposition. For an excellent discussion of the rationale for why voting should not be so treated, see Tobin (1970).

13. Lindblom makes this point in a particularly challenging way: "Among the defects of the existing competition of ideas, none seems more impairing and more easily remedied, given the will, than that well-financed communications, whether well-financed by the state, by private organizations, or by wealthy elites, overpower poorly financed ones. Many societies have accepted, at least as a principle, that children should deserve an education whether their parents can afford it or not, and that everyone deserves some forms of life-protecting medical services regardless of ability to pay. But no society has yet grasped the importance of separating rights of communication from ability to pay." (Lindblom, 1990, p. 296.)

14. Knack and Keefer (1995), Clague et al. (1996).

15. World Bank (1998).

16. World Bank (1998).

17. See Isham, Narayan and Pritchett (1995) and Isham, Kaufmann, and Pritchett (1997).

18. "But, over time, development experience has shown that when external experts *alone* acquire, analyze and process information and then present this information in reports, social change usually does not take place; whereas the kind of 'social learning' that stakeholders generate and internalize during the participatory planning and/or implementation of a development activity *does* enable social change." (World Bank, 1996, p. 5.)

19. Dewey recognized as well the connection between political and economic conditions. "If you wish to establish and maintain political self-government, you must see to it that conditions in industry and finance are not such as to militate automatically against your political aim." (1939, p. 53.)

20. See Wolfensohn (1997) for a discussion of the importance of inclusion in the development process.

21. The time-limited effectiveness of "military" methods was conveyed by Talleyrand's quip that one can "do anything with a bayonet except sit on it".

22. While such crises have marked capitalism from its origins, crises appear to be more frequent and deeper. See Caprio and Klingebiel (1996) and Lindgren, Garcia and Saal (1996).

23. I am indebted to Phil Keefer for this example.
24. By "decentralization", I refer here not just to governmental decentralization, but to any process (including market processes) that allows larger numbers of people to have inputs into decisions.
25. The extreme failures of the twentieth century from Stalin to Hitler to Pol Pot have all arisen in totalitarian regimes. This observation is consistent with the theoretical predictions of Sah and Stiglitz (1991).
26. See, for example, Sah and Stiglitz (1986).
27. In Japanese management practice, the slower but more effective process of participatory decision-making is likened to careful transplantation. "It is a time-honored Japanese gardening technique to prepare a tree for transplanting by slowly and carefully binding the roots over a period of time, bit by bit, to prepare the tree for the shock of the change it is about to experience. This process, called *nemawashi*, takes time and patience, but it rewards you, if it is done properly, with a healthy transplanted tree." (Morita, 1986, p. 158.)
28. See for example, Coleman (1988), Dasgupta (1997), Putnam (1993), Fukuyama (1995) and Stiglitz (1997a).
29. Knack and Keefer (1997).
30. See, for example, World Bank (1997).
31. See Becker (1968).
32. See Sen and Drèze (1990).
33. See Feldstein (1998).
34. Even if it were, a dialogue behind closed doors would certainly not convince them otherwise.
35. See Chibber, Dailami, de Melo and Thomas (1995). Much of the conditionality concerns "timing" – certain actions (for example, the privatization of a particular company) are required to occur within a particular time horizon. Even if conditionality increased the speed of privatization slightly, the benefits of doing so may well not be worth the cost: the economic losses from a slight delay may be small compared to the gain from allowing the process of democratic decision-making to work its course. And indeed, in many cases, by encouraging excessive speed, the manner in which privatization has been conducted has been far from ideal. Governments have received far less than they would have in a more orderly process, and the magnitude of economic restructuring associated with privatization (and therefore the gains in efficiency) has been far smaller than it might have been. In several countries, the privatization process has resulted in undermining, rather than strengthening, confidence in market processes.
36. My immediate predecessor at the World Bank, Michael Bruno (1993), also argued that such processes have been effective means of addressing issues of macro stability.
37. Caprio and Klingebiel (1996).
38. See, for example, Stiglitz (1998b).

REFERENCES

Bagehot, W. 1948 (1869). *Physics and Politics*. New York: Knopf.

Barker, E. 1967 (1942). *Reflections on Government*. London: Oxford University Press.

Becker, G.S. 1968. "Crime and Punishment: An Economic Approach." *The Journal of Political Economy* 76 (2), 169–217.

Bruno, M. 1993. *Crisis, Stabilization, and Economic Reform: Therapy by Consensus*. Oxford: Clarendon Press.

Bryce, J. 1959 (1888). *The American Commonwealth*. New York: G.P. Putnam & Sons.

Coleman, J. 1988. "Social Capital and the Creation of Human Capital." *American Journal of Sociology* 94 (Suppl.), S95–S120.

Caprio, G., and D. Klingebiel. 1996. "Bank Insolvencies: Cross-Country Experience." Policy Research Working Paper 1620. Washington, DC, World Bank:

Chibber, A., M. Dailami, J. de Melo and V. Thomas. 1995. *Restructuring Economies in Distress: Policy Reform and the World Bank*. World Bank and Oxford University Press.

Clague, C., P. Keefer, S. Knack and M. Olson. 1996. "Property and Contract Rights in Autocracies and Democracies." *Journal of Economic Growth* 1(2), 243–76.

Dasgupta, P. 1997. "Social Capital and Economic Performance." Paper presented at the World Bank Conference, Social Capital: Integrating the Economist's and the Sociologist's Perspective. April.

Dewey, J. 1927. *The Public and Its Problems*. Chicago: Swallow Press.

———. 1939. *Freedom and Culture*. New York: Capricorn.

Department for Trade and Industry. 1998a. *Our Competitive Future: Building the Knowledge-Driven Economy*. London: Cm 4176.

Department for Trade and Industry. 1998b. *Our Competitive Future: Building the Knowledge-Driven Economy: Analytical Background*. *www.dti.gov.uk/comp/competitive/an_reprt.htm*.

Feldstein, M. 1998. "Refocusing the IMF." *Foreign Affairs*. 77, 20–33, March–April.

Fukuyama, F. 1995. *Trust: The Social Virtues and the Creation of Prosperity*. New York: Free Press.

Hirschman, A.O. 1958. *The Strategy of Economic Development*. New Haven: Yale University Press.

——. 1970. *Exit, Voice and Loyalty: Responses to Decline in Firms, Organizations and States.* Cambridge, Mass: Harvard University Press.

Isham, J., D. Narayan and L. Pritchett. 1995. "Does Participation Improve Performance? Establishing Causality with Subjective Data." *World Bank Economic Review* 9 (2).

Isham, J., D. Kaufmann, and L. Pritchett. 1997. "Civil Liberties, Democracy, and the Performance of Government Projects." *World Bank Economic Review* 11 (2), 219–42.

Keynes, J.M. 1920. *The Economic Consequences of the Peace.* New York: Harcourt, Brace and Howe.

Knack, S., and P. Keefer. 1995. "Institutions and Economic Performance: Cross-Country Tests Using Alternative Institutional Measures." *Economics and Politics* 7 (3), 207–27.

——. 1997. "Does Social Capital Have an Economic Payoff?: A Cross-Country Investigation." *Quarterly Journal of Economics* 112 (4), 1251–88.

Knight, F. 1947. *Freedom and Reform.* New York: Harper & Row.

Lindblom, C. 1990. *Inquiry and Change.* New Haven: Yale University Press.

Lindgren, C.-J., G. Garcia, and M. Saal. 1996. *Banking Soundness and Macroeconomic Policy.* Washington: International Monetary Fund.

Luther, M. 1942 (1523). "Concerning Secular Authority." In F. W. Coker (ed.), *Readings in Political Philosophy.* New York: Macmillan 306–29.

Mill, J.S. 1972 (1859). *On Liberty.* In H. B. Acton (ed.), *J.S. Mill: Utilitarianism, On Liberty, and Considerations on Representative Government.* London: J.M. Dent & Sons.

Morita, A. 1986. *Made in Japan.* New York: E.P. Dutton.

Przeworski, A., and F. Limongi. 1993. "Political Regimes and Economic Growth." *Journal of Economic Perspectives* 7 (3), 51–69.

Putnam, R. 1993. "The Prosperous Community: Social Capital and Economic Growth." *Current.* October.

Ross, S. 1973. "The Economic Theory of Agency: The Principal's Problem." *American Economic Review.* 63, 134–9.

Sah, R., and Stiglitz, J.E. 1986. "The Architecture of Economic Systems: Hierarchies and Polyarchies." *The American Economic Review* 76 (4), 716–27.

——. 1991. "The Quality of Managers in Centralized Versus

Decentralized Organizations." *Quarterly Journal of Economics* 106 (1), 289–25.

Sen, A. and J. Drèze. 1990. *The Political Economy of Hunger.* Oxford: Clarendon Press.

Stiglitz, J.E. 1975. "Incentives, Risk and Information: Notes Towards a Theory of Hierarchy." *Bell Journal of Economics*, 6 (2), 552–79.

——. 1997a. "Remarks on Social Capital: Integrating the Economist's and the Sociologist's Perspectives." World Bank Conference, 28 April.

——. 1997b. "The Economic Recovery of the 1990s: Restoring Sustainable Growth." Paper presented to the Macroeconomics Seminar at Georgetown University, Washington, DC, 4 September 1997.

——. 1997c. "The Long Boom?: Business Cycles in the 1980s and 1990s." Paper presented to the Center for Economic Policy Research, Stanford University, California, 5 September 1997.

——. 1998a. "Towards a New Paradigm for Development: Strategies, Policies and Processes." Paper given as Prebisch Lecture at UNCTAD, Geneva. October 19. [ch. 2, this volume – *Ed.*]

——. 1998b. "Must Financial Crises Be This Frequent and This Painful?" Given as 1998 University of Pittsburgh McKay lecture. *www.worldbank.org/html/extdr/extme/js-092398/index.htm.*

——. 1998c. "More Instruments and Broader Goals: Moving Toward the Post-Washington Consensus." WIDER Annual Lectures 2, January 1998. [ch. 1, this volume – *Ed.*]

——. 1999b. "Public Policy for a Knowledge Economy." Remarks at the Department for Trade and Industry and Center for Economic Policy Research. London, UK 27 January 1999.

——. 1999c. "On Liberty, the Right to Know and Public Discourse: The Role of Transparency in Public Life." Paper presented as 1999 Oxford Amnesty Lecture. [ch. 8, this volume – *Ed.*].

——. "Symposia: Democracy and Development." 1993. *Journal of Economic Perspectives* 7(3).

Tobin, J. 1970. "On Limiting the Domain of Inequality." *Journal of Law and Economics* 13 (October).

Wolfensohn, J.D. 1997. "Annual Meetings Address: The Challenge of Inclusion." Washington: World Bank. *www.worldbank.org/html/extdr/am97/jdw_sp/jwsp97e.htm.*

——. 1998. "The Other Crisis: 1998 Annual Meetings Address." Given at the 1998 World Bank/International Monetary Fund Annual

Meetings.   *www.worldbank.org/html/extdr/am98/jdw-sp/
index.htm.*

——. 1999. "A Proposal for a Comprehensive Development Framework
(A Discussion Draft)." Washington: World Bank.

World Bank. 1996. *The World Bank Participation Sourcebook.*
Washington: World Bank.

——. 1997. "Crime and Violence as Development Issues in Latin America
and the Caribbean." Mimeographed. Office of the Chief Economist,
Latin America and the Caribbean. Washington: World Bank.

——. 1998. "Assessing Aid: What Works, What Doesn't, and Why."
Washington: World Bank.

Chapter 8

On Liberty, the Right to Know and Public Discourse: The Role of Transparency in Public Life

Oxford Amnesty Lecture
Oxford, January 1999

INTRODUCTION

Amnesty International has long been an effective champion of free speech, one of the basic human rights. Free speech is both an end in itself – an inalienable right that governments cannot strip away from the citizenry – and a means to other equally fundamental goals. Free speech provides a necessary check on government: a free press not only makes abuses of governmental powers less likely, it also enhances the likelihood that basic social needs will be met. Amartya Sen, the winner of this year's Nobel Prize in economics, has argued forcefully that famines do not occur in societies in which there is a free press.[1] It is not the lack of food in the aggregate that gives rise to famines, but the lack of access to food by the poor in famine regions. A free press exposes these problems; once exposed, the failure to act is absolutely intolerable.

I want to push the argument one step further, and argue that there is, in democratic societies, a basic right to know, to be informed about what the government is doing and why. To put it baldly, I will argue that there should be a strong presumption in favor of transparency and openness in government. The scourges of secrecy during the past 70 years are well known – in country after country, it is the secret police that has engaged in the most egregious violations of human rights. I want to talk today about the kind of secrecy that is pervasive today in many democratic societies. Let me be clear: this secrecy is a far cry from that pursued by

250

Joseph Stiglitz

the totalitarian states that have marred the century that is drawing to a close. Yet this secrecy is corrosive: it is antithetical to democratic values, and it undermines democratic processes. It is based on a mistrust between those governing and those governed; and at the same time, it exacerbates that mistrust.

Francis Bacon pointed out long ago that "knowledge itself is power". Secrecy gives those in government exclusive control over certain areas of knowledge, and thereby increases their power, making it more difficult for even a free press to check that power. In short, a free press is necessary for a democratic society to work effectively, but without access to information, its ability to perform its central role is eviscerated.

The consequences of secrecy can be grave. Consider one example that loomed over much of this century. In his recent book, Senator Moynihan has argued powerfully that the Cold War and many of its manifestations, such as the arms race, were greatly exacerbated by the secrecy imposed by the military establishment.[2] A more open discussion of the evidence would have shown what is now all too apparent – Russia was not the formidable opponent, the industrial giant, which it was depicted as for almost half a century.

In this lecture, I want to set forth the case for greater openness and transparency in government. It may seem ironic that I, an American, should be delivering this lecture here, in the United Kingdom: after all, the United States and the United Kingdom are two of the most open and transparent societies in the world. And indeed, they set an example for much of the rest of the world. Yet we should not take comfort in that relative virtue: our countries are still bedevilled by far too much secrecy, far too little transparency. If we are truly to set an example for the rest of the world, we must confront our own issues of transparency and openness head on.

SECRECY AND TRANSPARENCY IN RECENT PUBLIC POLICY DEBATES

Before turning to the analytics of the subject – to the causes and consequences of secrecy – I want to begin with a few more personal words. My interest in openness has been long-standing. As with so many others of my generation, for me the Vietnam War brought home forcefully

251

this and other fundamental issues facing our society. I remember vividly conversations we had back in Cambridge, Massachusetts, in the mid-1960s concerning the dilemma facing the members of the Council of Economic Advisers, which advises the US President. One of the Council's duties was to make economic forecasts. It was apparent to many of us that the government was spending far more on the Vietnam War that it was admitting. One of the problems was that not only did we not know for sure how much it was spending, but we did not even know who knew, and so we did not know the true extent of culpability of President Johnson's economic advisers. You will recall the context. Johnson was trying to avoid the proverbial guns vs. butter trade-off; he wanted both his War on Poverty and his War on Vietnam. The major consequence of his attempt to deceive the American people through secrecy was inflation – the inflationary episode that was subsequently reinforced by the oil shock, and that wreaked such havoc during the subsequent decade. We, the young assistant professors at Harvard and MIT, debated among ourselves the responsibility of the President's economic advisers. How open should they have been about the situation? Should they have resigned in protest if the Administration refused to put forward an honest forecast? How would we act in a similar situation? During my tenure as Chairman of the Council of Economic Advisers, I would repeatedly confront similar – though fortunately, far less dramatic – issues and find myself reflecting back on those conversations of three decades ago.

A few years later, while I was the Drummond Professor of Political Economy here at Oxford, I was approached to do some consulting for the British government. In that capacity, I was asked to sign the Official Secrets Act. This troubled me. Britain was not at war, and nothing that I might do would even remotely touch upon matters of national security. What rationale could there be for such secrecy? It was, in my case, mainly a formality – but a formality that raised important questions that I promised myself I would revisit someday. It is thus fitting that I use this opportunity, here at Oxford, to return to the broader issues of openness.

As an economist of the public sector, I have long argued for the virtues of transparency and openness. In one of my earlier textbooks, I contrasted two views of taxation: one view described the art of taxation as akin to plucking a goose in a manner that ensures that it does not squawk.[3] The value-added tax is consistent with this mindset; one of its alleged virtues is that individuals pay the tax in drips and drabs, so that they are never fully conscious of how much they pay for public services. I had taken the contrasting view of taxation, arguing that one of the major attributes of a good tax system was transparency.[4] One of my major criticisms of the corporate tax, for example, was that the burden of that tax was not transparent.

Later, when I turned my attention to monetary economics in the aftermath of the US savings and loan crisis, I had been one of the many who had argued for more transparent accounting systems in the United States.[5] Specifically, I argued for moving to mark-to-market accounting – that is, requiring banks to record all assets at their current market value.[6] I had pointed out the huge distortions associated with current practices.[7] To be sure, since it will be difficult to mark to market non-marketed assets, not all assets will be treated the same; the realization of this may affect how we use the more accurate information that marking-to-market provides. But how could one really argue that it is better to have an accounting system that is less accurate? Similar issues of transparency arose in establishing risk-based capital-adequacy standards. The question was how to gauge the risk of long-term bonds. What is relevant is the risk of a change in market value; given their substantial market volatility, long-term bonds can hardly be considered perfectly safe.

These are but two examples – in public finance and monetary economics – illustrating the importance of transparency in public life. Indeed, for the past 30 years, I have spent a large fraction of my professional life on the "economics of information", on the consequences of imperfections of information and on the incentives for gathering – and hiding – information. It is thus, perhaps, natural, that, as the issue of transparency has moved front and center in the public debate, I should turn to the question, of what have we learned – both from theory and practice – concerning the role of information in public decision making.

THE RATIONALE FOR OPENNESS

With these remarks as prelude, let me turn now to the case for openness. I shall divide my remarks into seven sections. In the first, I shall give the most basic rationale for openness. In the second, I shall describe the incentives of those within government for secrecy. In the third, I shall trace through some of the adverse consequences of secrecy, as it is often pursued by public officials. In the fourth, I shall comment on how it is in fact that secrecy is enforced. In the fifth, I shall discuss the variety of circumstances that represent the exceptions to the presumption for openness, reviewing the arguments put forward for secrecy by the advocates of secrecy. In the sixth, I shall discuss some of the elements required for implementing a regime of greater openness in public discourse. In the final section, I shall try to pull together the arguments, summarizing my case for greater openness in democratic societies.

It is, perhaps, worth noting that the issue of secrecy in matters of public affairs has been long a source of public concern.[8] The arguments against secrecy cohabitate with the arguments against censorship and in favor of free speech.[9] The classic case was made in John Milton's *Areopagitica* (1644),[10] but James Madison, the architect of the First Amendment of the US Constitution guaranteeing the right of free speech, captured the crux of the argument.

> A people who mean to be their own governors must arm themselves with the power that knowledge gives. A popular government without popular information or the means of acquiring it is but a prologue to a farce or a tragedy or perhaps both.[11]

Jeremy Bentham based his constitutional system on the motive of "personal interest corrected by the widest publicity" and took publicity as the principal check against misrule.[12] John Stuart Mill, in his famous essay, "On Liberty" (1859), held that subjecting arguments to public scrutiny was unconditionally beneficial and provided the most assured way of sorting out good from bad arguments.[13] In "Considerations on Representative Government" (1861), Mill extended the argument for "publicity and liberty of discussion" to emphasize the virtues of popular participation.[14]

Walter Bagehot developed a strong case for "government by discussion" and played an important role in fostering those ideas during his editorship of *The Economist*. The modern economics of information emphasizes that once knowledge is made public, then it becomes a public good that cannot be made private again. Bagehot makes the same point in his inimitable way pointing out at the same time the role of information in free choice.

> "Democracy", it has been said in modern times, "is like the grave: it takes, but it does not give". The same is true of "discussion".

> Once effectually submit a subject to that ordeal and you can never withdraw it again; you can never again clothe it with mystery, or fence it by consecration; it remains for ever open to free choice, and exposed to profane deliberation. (Bagehot, 1948 (1869), p. 167.)

To me, the most compelling argument for openness is the positive Madisonian one: meaningful participation in democratic processes requires informed participants. Secrecy reduces the information available to the citizenry, hobbling their ability to participate *meaningfully.* Any of us who has participated in a board of directors knows that the power of a board to exercise direction and discipline is limited by the information at its disposal. Management knows this, and often attempts to control the flow of information.[15] We often speak of government being accountable, accountable to the people. But if effective democratic oversight is to be achieved, then the voters have to be informed: they have to know what alternative actions were available, and what the results might have been. Those in government typically have far more information relevant to the decisions being made than do those outside government, just as management of a firm typically has far more information about the firm's markets, prospects, and technology than do shareholders, let alone other outsiders. Indeed, managers are paid to gather this information.

The question is, given that the public has paid for the gathering of government information, who *owns* the information? Is it the private province of the government official, or does it belong to the public at large? I would argue that information gathered by public officials at public expense is owned by the public – just as the chairs and buildings and other physical assets used by government belong to the public. We have come to emphasize the importance of intellectual property. The information produced, gathered and processed by public officials is intellectual property, no less than a patentable innovation would be. To use that intellectual property for private purposes is just as serious an offense against the public as any other appropriation of public property for private purposes. There are, to be sure, circumstances in which fully sharing that information may not be appropriate – the important "exceptions" to the presumption for openness that I will discuss later in this talk.

One might argue that, in a society with a free press and free institutions, little is lost by having secrecy in government; after all, there are other sources of relevant information. Indeed, modern democratic societies, recognizing the importance of information for effective governance, try to protect the freedom and independence of the press and endeavor to promote independent think-tanks and universities, all to provide an effective check on government in many areas. The problem is that often government officials represent the only or major timely source of relevant and timely information. If officials are subjected to a gag order, then the public has no real effective substitute.

To reiterate, openness is an essential part of public governance. Albert Hirschman[16] described exit and voice as instruments for discipline in organizations. For public organizations, exit is typically not an option, and therefore greater reliance is placed on voice. In the private marketplace, how a firm organizes itself – whether it keeps secrets or not – makes little difference. Customers care about the products and prices; and regardless of how the firm organizes production, if it produces good products at low prices it will succeed. There are transparency issues, of course: firms often lack the incentive to disclose fully the attributes of their products, and government, accordingly, enforces a variety of disclosure requirements,[17] including truth in advertising, disclosure requirements on loans, disclosure requirements on firms seeking to raise capital publicly and fraud laws. But by and large, market mechanisms (including reputation) provide essential governance to firms.

But public organizations are not subjected to the same kind of discipline. It is only through voice – through informed discussion of the policies being pursued – that effective governance can be exercised. Because in many of the areas in which public agencies operate they have an effective monopoly, exit is not an option. Consider the difference between a doctor in a community in which there are many physicians and a doctor who is the only source of advice in the community. The doctor might be tempted to blame the patient when his prescription fails to work: the patient did not do exactly what was asked. But *if there is competition,* if the prescriptions of the doctor do not work – possibly because no patient can follow them precisely – the doctor will eventually lose his practice, his reputation will be tarnished, and his patients will exercise "exit". If there is monopoly however – if there were a single doctor dispensing treatment – the doctor might well try to control information. He might well argue that doing so is necessary to maintain confidence in his cures (and, because of the placebo effect, there may even be a grain of truth in the argument); and he knows that competitive pressure will not force him to disclose information and that exit is not an effective option.

In all organizations, imperfections of information give rise to what economists call *agency* problems. As a result, there may be important disparities between, say, the actions of managers and the interests of shareholders. Similarly, in the public sector agency problems may give rise to a disparity between, say, the actions of those governing and those that they are supposed to serve. In modern parlance, the lack of an exit option may exacerbate the consequences of these agency problems. Quite obviously, improvements in information – decreases in secrecy – can reduce the magnitude and consequences of these agency problems.

THE INCENTIVES FOR SECRECY

The arguments presented in the preceding section provide, I think, a compelling case for openness. Yet even seemingly public-spirited public servants often engage in secrecy. In some cases, it is because they worry about demagoguery, fearing that openness allows demagogues to enter the fray and to sway innocent voters. Anyone who has ever lost a public debate is convinced of the importance of demagoguery, especially as used by special-interest groups to advance their own interests. Yet this is the fundamental quandary of democracy: although we recognize its pit-falls, there is no real alternative to public debate.[18] In the end, we are committed to having voters make decisions at least about the decision-makers. Shouldn't we prefer that they be better informed – that is, in a better position to evaluate the quality of decision-making?

But compelling as these public interest arguments for openness may be, they run up against powerful private incentives, the private incentives of government bureaucrats, elected officials and the special interest groups which try to influence them. Public Choice theory has emphasized the importance of these incentives.[19] In this section, I shall take a closer look at these private incentives.

Two such incentives have received extensive attention. The first is that secrecy provides some insulation against being accused of making a mistake. If a policy fails to produce desired results, government officials can always claim that matters would have been even worse but for the government policy. While we all recognize human fallibility, government officials seem particularly loath to own up to it, and for good reason: the public judges mistakes harshly. But there is a vicious circle: given that so little information is disclosed, the public must rely on results in judging government officials. The officials receive credit for good results, whether they deserve the credit or not; and they are condemned for bad results, whether they are the result of government action or inaction. With more information, the public might be able to discern more accurately the *value added* of public action.

Conversely, secrecy breeds more of itself.[20] Given that so little information is disclosed, any disclosure of a policy failure is taken as a far more important piece of news. There are thus even greater pressures not to disclose. If more information were disclosed, then the adverse consequences of disclosing a failure would be smaller, and the adverse consequences of not disclosing (of hiding) a failure might be far greater. Given that secrecy is the norm, however, the public does not attach great opprobrium to those who engage in the practice. It is what they have come to expect of public officials, who, after all, they suspect of not really serving in the public interest.

While those engaged in making the policy may well have an incentive to suppress such a discussion, the question is, from the framework of the architecture of public policy, shouldn't there be a presumption in favor of, and an insistence on, openness?

The second incentive that public officials have for pursuing secrecy is that secrecy provides the opportunity for special interests to have greater sway. In some societies, this takes the naked form of corruption and bribery. But even in societies where this is viewed as unacceptable, politicians need campaign funds to get elected and re-elected. The special interest groups who provide the funds do not do so for the greater public good, but because they believe that by doing so they can influence policy in ways that enhance their profits and profitability. But if these actions in support of special interest groups are subject to public scrutiny, the scope for favoritism is greatly circumscribed. It is in the midnight meetings of the tax committees that the special provisions benefiting one firm or another are introduced. In the words of Justice Brandeis, "sunlight is the most powerful of all disinfectants". Secrecy is the bedrock of this persistent form of corruption, which undermines confidence in democratic governments in so much of the world.

These, as I have said, are the traditional arguments for openness. There are three others that I want to discuss today. The first is that lack of information, like any form of artificially created scarcity, gives rise to rents. The adverse consequences of rent-seeking have long been of concern. There is an unhealthy dynamic: the public official has an incentive to create secrets, which earns him rents. The existence of secrets give rise to a press determined to ferret out the secrets. One of the ways in which public officials reap the rents is to disclose "secrets" to those members of the press that treat them well. Thus, not only is the public deprived of timely information – which I have argued is theirs by right – but government officials use their control of information to distort information in their favor. It is not just the puff pieces of which public officials are so fond. Rather, it is the very characterization of events and circumstances. Woe be to the reporter who breaks the implicit contract! Ostracism – being cut off from the source of news – is the consequence; and even a liberal-minded editor has no choice but to reassign the reporter. One reporter from a reputable newspaper, having offended the powers that be that he depended upon for his stories, went from covering prominent national issues out of Washington to reporting from and on Detroit. This symbiotic relationship between the press and officialdom undermines confidence in both, and interferes with the ability of a free press to carry on its essential functions. Can a reporter be an effective critic, if his access to the information he requires to be informed can be curtailed upon the submission of an excessively critical article?

There is another, even more corrosive, effect of secrecy and an incentive for secrecy by public officials. I referred earlier to management's attempt to control information in limiting the ability of shareholders and their elected directors to exercise discipline. Elsewhere, I have also shown how by *creating* information asymmetries, managers can create barriers to the entry of outside managers, to takeovers, and by doing so, can increase their managerial rents (at the expense of shareholders).[21] The same is true of public managers – elected officials. If outsiders have less information, voters may feel less confident that they will be able to take over management effectively. Indeed, the lack of information of outsiders does increase the costs of transition, and makes it more expensive (for society) to change management teams. The fact that the alternative management teams have less information means that there is a higher probability that any proposals that they put forward will be ill-suited to the situation. By increasing the mean cost of transition and increasing the subjective variance, secrecy puts incumbents at a distinct advantage over rivals.[22]

By the same token, secrecy undermines participation in democratic processes even by voters. Voters are more likely to exercise independent judgments – both to vote, and to vote independently of party – if they feel confident about their views. And this in turn requires that they be informed. There is a cost to becoming informed. While most voters are not perfectly selfish – if they were, it would be hard to rationalize participation in the political process at all (after all, the public good is a public good) – they have a threshold, a limit to the amount of their time and energy they are willing to invest in the pursuit of the public interest. Secrecy raises the price of information – in effect, it induces more voters who do not have special interests not to participate actively, leaving the field more to those with special interests. Thus, it is not only that special interests exercise their nefarious activities under the cloak of secrecy, but that the secrecy itself discourages others from providing an effective check on the special interests through informed voting. This highlights the importance of "public information institutions" designed to ferret out information for the benefit of the public: a free and if-need-be adversarial press (as opposed to a captive or lapdog press), the legitimate opposition always playing a probing and possibly devil's advocate role (buttressed by practices like the Opposition's questioning of Government in Parliament), and a myriad of public interest organizations (such as Amnesty International) to blow the whistle on the cloaked activities of the special interest groups. In addition, secrecy may discourage potential competitors, not only because their prospects of success in the voting process are (rationally) reduced, but because it increases their own subjective uncertainty about whether they can improve matters. How often have officials become elected on a platform, only to discover that the budgetary situation is far worse than had been envisioned, forcing them to abanon all their previously designed plans and engage in a budget balancing act (for which they may have neither a comparative advantage nor a passion)?

THE ADVERSE EFFECTS OF SECRECY

In the previous section, I set forth some of the reasons that public officials so ardently pursue secrecy, even when openness is so apparently an essential part of democratic processes. One of the reasons for devoting so much time to understanding the incentives for secrecy is that unless we understand the drive for it, we cannot succeed in uprooting it. But another reason is that it provides deeper insights into the adverse effects of secret.

I have already called attention to several of these adverse effects. Secrecy provides the fertile ground on which special interests work; secrecy serves to entrench incumbents, discourages public participation in democratic processes and undermines the ability of the press to provide an effective check against the abuses of government.

But the adverse effects are more pervasive. To maintain secrecy, often the circle of those involved in decision-making is greatly circumscribed; those who are able to provide valuable insights are cut out of the discussion. The quality of decision-making is thereby weakened. There is, again, a vicious circle. With more mistakes, public officials become more defensive; to protect themselves, they seek even more secrecy, narrowing in the circle still further, eroding still further the quality of decision-making.

Public programs may be designed not on the basis of the impact that they have, but on (government officials' beliefs about) the perceptions of those impacts. Those perceptions will be affected by the information that is publicly available; program design may be as sensitive to those perceptions (and the extent to which they can be controlled) as to their real impact.

There is still one more, related effect: as the space of informed discourse about a host of important issues gets circumscribed, attention gets focused more and more on *value* issues. It takes an enormous amount of information to make judgments concerning complex economic issues. It takes far less (or a far different kind of) information to come to a view concerning abortion or family values. Thus, secrecy has distorted the arena of politics. The adverse effects of secrecy are multiple: not only are important areas of public policy not dealt with effectively, but also debate focuses disproportionately on issues which are often far more divisive.

Adverse Economic Effects

While most of this paper is concerned with the adverse effects of secrecy on the political process, I should also note the adverse *economic* effects.

The most obvious concern the *economic* consequences of *political* decisions: A large fraction of the decisions taken in the political arena have economic consequences – not only for aggregate output, but also for its distribution. Openness affects the decisions that get made – including who bears the costs of the risks inevitably associated with the uncertainties of public policy making.

It is now generally recognized that better, and more timely, information results in better, more efficient, resource allocations. The increasingly large fraction of the workforce involved in gathering, processing and disseminating information bears testimony to its importance. Ironically, many of these are engaged in ferreting out information from the public sector – information which, one might argue, of right ought to be public. While businesses have legitimate reasons for maintaining secrecy in some of their activities (after all, the fact that information is valuable means that disclosing information is giving away something of value to their rivals), the same reason leads to the conclusion that information that is paid for by the public should be publicly disclosed. Does it make sense, if better information leads to better resource allocations, for the government to deliberately not disclose information – letting the market itself decide what is or is not relevant?[23]

But the most adverse economic consequences are associated with the corruption that so often follows from excessive secrecy. It is not an accident that the leading international non-government organization fighting corruption is called Transparency International. Research at the World Bank, reported in the *1997 World Development Report*, has shown that corruption has strong adverse effects on investment and economic growth.

Public officials do have strong incentives for secrecy. But if we are to avoid the myriad adverse political and economic consequences of secrecy, in the design of the architecture of public institutions, we need to take this into account: we need to force more openness than public officials might willingly offer.

THE IMPLEMENTATION OF SECRECY

Given the strong interests of public officials in secrecy, it is not surprising that so many governments have engaged in such extensive secrecy, going well beyond the requirements of national security. But while it may be in the interests of the government as a whole to maintain secrecy, it may not be in the interests of particular individuals. Indeed, that is what gives rise to the whole problem of leaks. As in the case of other forms of collusive behavior, there are incentives for individuals to deviate. If a secret is shared among a number of individuals, any one of the individuals can reap the scarcity rents for himself by disclosing the information to the press.

Here again reputation mechanisms become important: the press must be relied upon not to disclose the source of their leak. If they do, their source dries up. Indeed, if the source of the leak becomes public knowledge, others within the government are likely to "sanction" the individual, denying him access to the information or ostracizing him in some other way.

The press and the officials thus have an incentive to engage in symbiotic activity. But as in any reputation model, there is always a danger of unraveling in any finite game. From the point of view of the government official, what matters is the reputation of the reporter: can he be discreet in keeping his sources confidential? Since new government officials will quickly become apprised of each reporter's reputation, he has a strong incentive to maintain this confidentiality.

Still, the nature of the bilateral relationship is such as to give an advantage to some public officials over others: it pays to develop a good relationship with someone who leaks more regularly and more exclusively (excessive leaking diminishes the value of the information being leaked), and who is likely to be a source for a long time. (If a reporter has a limited supply of puff pieces to give out, it is better to use them on those for whom the present discounted value of the information disclosed is high.)

Secrecy serves another sociological function. Many clubs, not to mention secret societies,[24] have secret rituals. Secrets serve to set apart those with the secret from those that do not have the secret. It provides a form of bonding. I described earlier the "sanctions" which make each hostage to the bond, but the sanctions are only part of the story. Ethical values, subscribing to group norms, affect most members of the group. If the group norm is to keep a secret, they feel an individual responsibility to conform to that norm.

In recent years, however, there has been weakening of these norms. This is partly because of the increasing recognition of the undemocratic and corrosive effects of secrecy. While many directly involved with government condemned the leaking of the *Pentagon Papers*, many outside thought this an act of moral courage.[25] But there is another reason. As norms more generally have broken down, there are more instances of individuals who do not feel or at least react to the "peer pressure", who put their own interests above that of the group, who recognize the nature of the secrecy game, recognize that even if it comes to be widely believed that they are a source of leaks, it is sufficiently hard to prove that they may be immune from sanctions. Worse still, their special relationship with the press gives them a kind of immunity: they can use this special relationship to fend off any attacks. (Individuals who establish this special relationship may, in an almost hypocritical way, be the strongest advocates of secrecy; for their rents depend on *their* controlling the flow of information; their position is undermined if there are independent sources of information.) It would thus appear that the "complete" secrecy equilibrium may be somewhat fragile. But the partial secrecy equilibrium is just as distortive of democratic processes. Indeed, because not all government officials are equal players in the "leaking game" the information flow may be particularly distorted.

THE EXCEPTIONS

In their quest to maintain secrecy, public officials do not, of course, appeal to the effects that I have just described. They do not argue that secrecy is important because it gives incumbents an advantage over outsiders. They point to a number of problems that excessive openness gives rise to. (In today's world, no one argues against openness, only against excessive openness.) In this section, I try to provide taxonomy of the arguments against secrecy that I have heard. I conclude that while there are indeed limits to openness, governments today, even the most open governments in the West, are far too secretive. Many, if not most, of the arguments are simply self-serving rationalizations.

The privacy exception

The most important and convincing exception concerns privacy matters affecting individuals (and organizations). The government, in the exercise of its duties, gathers enormous amounts of information concerning individuals (such as income and health statistics). But few, if any, of the issues with which I am concerned here fall within the privacy exception.

The confidentiality exception

A closely related exception concerns certain information the receipt of which would be impaired by the knowledge that it would be subsequently disclosed. For instance, the World Bank is sometimes asked by a country to help it restructure its banking system. In the process of doing so, certain weaknesses in the banking system might be uncovered. If it were known that the World Bank would disclose those weaknesses – at least, before they are repaired – the countries would have a strong incentive not to come to us for advice. There has been a worry that more extensive disclosure of letters of recommendation may have resulted in less informative letters. The importance of confidentiality of doctor-patient and lawyer-client relationships has long been recognized; there are a limited number of interactions within the public sector that should fall within the confidentiality exception.

The national security exception

The importance of secrecy in times of war has long been recognized. When a nation's survival is at stake, it must do everything in its power to increase its chance of winning. The success of a military attack may well depend on surprise – on the enemy not being able to take the necessary precautions.

The problem is that the national security exception has been extended to issues where clearly national security is not what is at issue. What is often at issue is covering up mistakes. This was brought home forcefully by the *Pentagon Papers* that looked not at how the country was currently engaged in the Vietnam War, but how it got into the war in the first place.

There will remain hard choices; one of the hardest questions the US faced in the late 1960s and early 1970s was whether to continue the war in Vietnam. Critical to that decision was information about how the war was faring. Yet that information itself might have been of value to the perceived enemy.

The worry is that much of government secrecy extends well beyond issues of national defense.

Crying "fire" in a crowded theatre

Occasionally, the disclosure of information can have life-threatening effects. Typically, the issue is not *whether* to disclose the information, but *how*. Justice Holmes' famous exception to the right of free speech was based on causing a panic by crying "fire" in a crowded theatre.

In matters economic, this particular exception takes on a special form; open discussion of certain issues (such as monetary policy) might roil the market, leading to instability. Curiously, those who take this position are typically those who are strong advocates of markets: while they have a great deal of confidence in the market, they evidently believe that market allocations are affected by irrelevant "noise". If, of course, the information being discussed or disclosed is of relevance, that is, it affects economic fundamentals, then disclosing the information as soon as possible allows the more efficient allocation of resources.

A particular variant of this focuses on monetary policy. There has been extensive discussion of the extent to which central banks should act in secret; should they disclose their proceedings, and if so, with what lag and with what fullness of detail? Again, there is a certain irony in these discussions: while market advocates praise the price "discovery" function of markets, much of the price discovery function in the bond market is directed at figuring out what the central bankers believe and are likely to do. Rather than having this indirect "dance", would it not make far more sense to have the Central Bank directly disclose the information? If the market believes that that information is of value – as evidenced by the huge number of individuals who watch the actions of central banks throughout the world – then shouldn't government make that information available? And in a timely way? Evidently, central banks (and their governments) are less than committed to transparency when it comes to their own operations!

Neither theory nor evidence provides much support for the hypothesis that fuller and more timely disclosure and discussion would have adverse effects. Indeed, since information eventually comes out, the current procedures, which attempt to bottle up information, result in periodic disclosures of large amounts of information. Just as the economy is likely to be more stable with frequent small adjustments in exchange rates than with few large ones, so too is the economy more likely to be stable with a steady flow of information. With a flow of information, less attention would be paid to any single piece; and there would be smaller revisions in posterior distributions.

Similarly, there seems to be no evidence of increased instability following the UK decision to have greater transparency on the part of its central bank.

Secrecy in matters economic may not only contribute to overall instability, but in many countries can be a major source of corruption, undermining confidence in government more generally.

At best, however, the argument that fuller disclosure and discussion might roil markets is only an argument concerning the timing and manner of disclosure; it is not an argument for an indefinite postponement of public discussion. To return to the metaphor of "crying fire in a crowded theatre", no one would argue that, if one knew that there was a fire in the theatre, the patrons should not be informed in a way that allows an orderly evacuation. No one would argue, I think, that after the fire is over, there oughtn't be a thorough investigation of the fire, to determine what caused the fire, and, if there were deaths or severe injury, to see what might be done (both in the construction of the theatre and in the design of the response) to avoid similar disasters in the future. And no one would argue that, because it might "roil" theatre-goers, one shouldn't have lighted exit signs, to indicate how to evacuate the theatre in case of fire – since we know that no matter how well theatres are constructed, there is still a danger of fire.

In the case of information that, it is feared, might disturb markets, there is another point: shouldn't we have enough confidence in democratic processes and in the market to believe that the market can see through the cacophony of voices, assess the fundamental arguments and weigh the evidence?

I am not convinced that there is any real trade-off between the pursuit of democratic transparency on one hand and the stability and growth of the economy on the other. But in the event there is a conflict, I put my voice solidly behind the importance of democratic processes of openness.

To be sure, democratic societies must find and have found ways of engaging expertise in complicated and technical decision-making in a manner that reflects both shared values and expertise. But the decisions cannot reflect just the interests of the industry groups which are likely to have a disproportionate share of expertise and should be forged in ways that leave open both the decisions and the framework within which those decisions should be made to democratic processes. Indeed, to the extent that there has been greater delegation of responsibilities, e.g., to independent agencies, to engage greater expertise and to isolate the decision-making from the vicissitudes of the political process, there appears an even greater need for openness and transparency.

Open covenants not openly arrived at[26]

A part of the American credo that every school child learns is Woodrow Wilson's dictum in the aftermath of World War I: open covenants openly arrived at. Eighty years ago, transparency was at the top of the international public agenda. It was widely perceived that secret treaties secretly arrived at were a major problem prior to and during World War I. But both before and after, there has been little enthusiasm for *excessively* open deliberations. The worry is that open discussions will inhibit free expression of ideas, and special interests will take advantage of the situation to weigh in, before the delicate compromises and complex coalitions which are at the heart of successful democratic processes have a chance to work themselves out. Secrecy is needed for the successful completion of delicate negotiations.

There is, I think, some validity to this argument. The question is, how much weight should we give it? After all, the proposals will have to be put forward to public debate eventually. Special interests will still have time to undermine any coalitions that have been formed. And indeed, if there were more public disclosure of the debate as it proceeded, the news that a particular idea was being explored would carry far less weight than today, when the very fact that an idea becomes public leads to the belief that it is being very seriously considered, bringing down the full force of close scrutiny.

The thrust of this exception is again one of timing: there may be a period of secrecy, while deliberations proceed, but eventually positions – and the arguments that went into them – should be fully disclosed.

As a practical matter, I have observed two dangers however with this position. First, the time is never ripe for public discussion. One "delicate" moment is followed by another. And secondly, the public is all too often treated disparagingly: it is entitled to know the arguments for the proposal, but not the pros and cons that went into it – like a child who should not witness disagreements between the parents. But the public knows that few matters are black and white. Issues of public policy involve judgments, often about matters concerning which there is considerable complexity and uncertainty.

Positions are asserted with a confidence that the available evidence simply did not warrant. At the very least, public agencies should be honest and more transparent in describing the uncertainties. One of the arguments for not doing so is that confidence in these institutions would be undermined.

Undermining authority, or "don't air your dirty linen in public"

The argument that public discussions – including discussions of uncertainties and mistakes – will undermine the authority of public institutions is one of the most corrosive of democratic processes. It is akin to the kinds of arguments that authoritarian regimes conventionally use. I would argue, on the contrary, that were governments to deal honestly with their citizenry, confidence in government and public institutions would increase, not decrease. We all know, in the immortal words of Alexander Pope, that "to err is human". Human fallibility is at the cornerstone of the design of our political institutions. It is why we have systems of checks and balances. We all know that there is imperfect information and that these imperfections of information play out in some of the most important decisions we have to make.

Thus, to pretend that any institution is infallible, or that there is perfect confidence in the actions being undertaken, is to fly in the face of reality. Only those who want to be fooled will be. Admission of fallibility and demonstration that one can learn from one's mistakes should enhance public confidence in an institution, at least by demonstrating that the institution has enough confidence in itself and in democratic processes to engage in open discussions.

Yet organizations cannot function without a certain degree of loyalty and structure.[27] Democratic processes cannot work without well-functioning organizations within it. It is here that the most delicate issues arise. Making the democratic system work in its entirety may indeed necessitate working to increase the credibility of the institutions within it, (though, to repeat, this does not mean trying to persuade anyone either of an infallibility or a degree of certitude which is simply not there), and this may entail circumscribing full disclosure.

Again, what is most at stake is the question of timing. Once a decision has been made, any government must convince others of the correctness of its views. This may not be effectively accomplished if the disagreements that existed prior to a decision being made continue to be aired in public. More broadly, one can view any government as a *team*. Before decisions are made, there needs to be open discussions, at least within the team, though within any government, there will be a division of responsibility, with each agency taking ultimate responsibility for the decisions which fall within its purview – though often within the public sector there are several agencies with significant interests at stake. Without effective participation in the decision making over which they have some jurisdiction, there will, of course, not be "ownership" and "buy-in" of the decision, and it will be difficult for the team to work smoothly. After a decision is made, the team must work together in the agreed-upon strategy. Part of that strategy for public agencies is a strategy to convince others of the appropriateness of the actions.

But to repeat what I said a minute ago, the public might be more effectively convinced if there were more openness both in the process of decision-making and concerning the nature of the disagreements. Openness in process assures the public that the decision does not reflect the exercise of special interests. And a summary of the argument convinces the public that all of the important arguments were considered, all sides were looked at: a judgment was made that the weight of evidence came down in favor of the course of action being undertaken. After all, governments are elected in part to make these difficult judgment calls. What the public wants to know is that there has been real deliberation.

But government needs to be committed to openness *after the fact*: there must eventually be honest and open evaluations of the actions. Otherwise, there will be no basis for learning from experience.

Like the preceding argument, while worries about "undermining credibility" and "being a member of the team" have considerable validity, they are often exaggerated and taken too far. The incentives for secrecy of incumbents that I described earlier make leaders of these organizations particularly prone to invoke this argument.

Each of us in public life must weigh what we say in public and in private, mindful of the abuses to which excessive secrecy is prone. In the end, my confidence in the democratic processes leads me to the conviction that there is far more scope for open disclosure, far less risk of "undermining" the authority of institutions, than those who invoke this argument claim. My predecessor as chairman of the Council of Economic Advisers under Ronald Reagan, Martin Feldstein, engaged in an honest discussion of the consequences of the huge deficits that were then mounting. Though he did not succeed in changing the policies, he played an important role in the formation of the consensus that eventually led to the deficit reductions of the 1990s. The fact that there could be such an open discussion I think actually enhanced confidence in democratic processes and institutions.

THE IMPLEMENTATION OF OPENNESS

I have tried to make a case for greater openness in government. How can such greater openness be implemented? At the same time, I have tried to describe the strong incentives on the part of those in the government for secrecy. While the incentives for secrecy are great, so too are the opportunities for evading the intent of any disclosure regulations. If formal meetings have to be open, then all decisions can be made in informal meetings. If written material is subject to disclosure, there will be an incentive to insure that little is written down, and what is written down will be for the public record. Because of these limitations of legalistic approaches, emphasis must be place on creating a *culture* of openness, where the *presumption* is that the public should know about, and participate in, *all* collective decisions. We must create a mindset of openness, a belief that information that public officials possess is "owned" by the public, and to use it for private purposes – if only an exchange of favors with a reporter – is as much a theft of public property as stealing any other form of property.

There is a narrow set of exceptions that I have laid out in the preceding section. But these exceptions need to be highly circumscribed. The objective should be to make them as small and narrowly defined as possible. And there should be public discussion about the extent of those exceptions.

One basic framework for public access to information is contained in the Freedom of Information Act that the US Congress passed in 1966. In principle, this law enables any citizen to gain access to any information in the public domain, with narrow exceptions for privacy. But such legislation can only be partially successful unless there is a real commitment to openness. Government officials may be careful in what they write down and what remains a "mouth-to-ear" secret precisely because they do not want to disclose important information to the public.

One of the strong incentives for secrecy is to provide cover for special interests to do their work. Requirements on disclosure of campaign contributions have been valuable – they have at least sensitized the electorate to the role, for instance, of tobacco money in affecting legislative outcomes. But I must confess that, while the United States has strong disclosure requirements (including those affecting lobbyists), special interests still seem to have considerable scope. Presumably matters might have been even worse without these requirements.

The press plays an essential role in the battle for openness. But the press, as we have seen, is at the same time a central part of the "conspiracy of secrecy". The press must commit itself to working for openness. It is too much to expect them to disclose their secret sources inside the government, or to seek out exclusive sources of information. But there needs to be more reporting on the reporting process itself, exposing the nefarious system, if not the key players.

Non-government organizations, like Amnesty, also have an important role to play in helping create a culture of openness – and in checking the proclivity of government officials for secrecy.

CONCLUDING REMARKS

Amnesty International has long been devoted to ensuring that all governments protect basic human rights. It has been one of the most effective voices for human dignity in the world. Openness – transparency – is one of the most important instruments for achieving this goal. It is behind the cloak of secrecy that the rights of individuals are most frequently abrogated.

I have long been concerned with a special aspect of human rights and dignity: in the words of Franklin Delano Roosevelt, with the right to "freedom from hunger". There can be no human dignity, no basic rights, when an individual sees his child die of starvation or his/her daughter sold into a life of prostitution for mere survival. There is little doubt that decisions by governments do have profound implications for this basic human right. These decisions should be made openly, and with the active and open participation of those affected by them. I am convinced that *openness* and *participation* will affect the nature of the decisions being made.

Greater openness can be justified on *instrumental grounds*, as means to ends – ends like reducing the likelihood of the abuse of power. Greater openness is an essential part of good governance. A powerful case has been made that greater openness might have avoided the extremes of the Cold War. I believe that better decisions would have been made than emerged from the reliance on the secret wisdom of the cognoscenti. The end of the Cold War has both laid bare the failures of the culture of secrecy and undermined the necessity of continuing it further. Perhaps the greatest irony of the Cold War is that in the attempt to preserve democracy and democratic values, we adopted policies that undermined democratic processes. The culture of secrecy was like a virus, spreading from one part of the government to another, until it invaded areas where national security played no role at all.

But I also believe that greater openness has an intrinsic value. Citizens have a basic right to know. I have tried to express this basic right in a number of different ways: the public has paid for the information; for a government official to appropriate the information that comes to his or her disposal in his role as a public official for private gain (if only for the non-monetary return of good newspaper coverage) is as much a theft of public property as the stealing of any other public property. While we all recognize the necessity of collective action, and the consequences of collective actions for individual freedoms, we have a basic right to know how the powers that have been surrendered to the Collective are being used. This seems to me to be a basic part of the implicit compact between the governed and those that they have selected to temporarily govern them. To be sure, there are exceptions, and I have dealt at length with these exceptions; but I have tried to argue that they are, or at least should be, limited in scope.

It also seems to me that the less *directly* accountable a governmental agency is to the public, the more important is it that its actions be open and transparent. By the same token, the more independent and the less directly politically accountable a government agency, the greater the presumption for openness. Openness is one of the most important checks on the abuse of public fiduciary responsibilities.

We are at an exciting time. The end of the Cold War has provided us with the opportunity – I would say, has made it necessary for us – to re-examine the role of secrecy and openness. At the same time, new technologies have provided mechanisms through which information can be more effectively shared between government and those governed. We can now have a more informed electorate than in any time in history. Further, advances in education, of a kind unthinkable a century ago, have put more and more citizens in a position to evaluate and assess the information that can so readily be made available.

We need but one step more: a commitment by government to greater openness, to promote dialogue and open discussion, to eschew secrecy in all of its myriad of forms. While I have outlined concrete legislation to which all governments might subscribe, I have recognized the limitation of such legislation. The incentives of secrecy are simply too great, and the scope for discretionary actions is too wide. I have therefore stressed the importance of creating a culture of openness, a task where organizations like Amnesty International have an essential role to play. Such openness may not guarantee that wise decisions will always be made. But it would be a major step forward in the on-going evolution of democratic processes, a true empowerment of individuals to participate meaningfully in the decisions concerning the collective actions that have such profound effects on their lives and livelihoods.

NOTES

1. Sen (1981).
2. Moynihan (1998).
3. A minister to Louis XIV cunningly described taxation as follows: "The art of taxation consists in so plucking a goose as to obtain the largest amount of feathers with the least possible amount of hissing." See *Newsweek* (1984).

4. Atkinson and Stiglitz (1976)
5. See Chapter 2, "Well-Kept Secrets", in Greider (1992) for the role of secrecy in the savings and loan crisis.
6. Stiglitz (1992)
7. Banks have an incentive to sell assets that have increased in market value, thus increasing their "book" value, while retaining assets that have decreased in value so that they will not have to recognize losses.
8. See Bok (1982) for a comprehensive overview.
9. See Emerson (1967) and (1970) for a survey.
10. "And though all the winds of doctrine were let loose to play upon the earth, so Truth be in the field, we do injuriously, by licensing and prohibiting, to misdoubt her strength. Let her and Falsehood grapple; who ever knew Truth put to the worse, in a free and open encounter?" Milton's argument was later echoed by Jefferson in his 1779 Virginia "Bill for Establishing Religious Freedom" which argued in part that truth "is the proper and sufficient antagonist to error, and has nothing to fear from the conflict unless by human interposition disarmed of her natural weapons, free argument and debate; errors ceasing to be dangerous when it is permitted freely to contradict them".
11. Letter from James Madison to W.T. Barry, 4 August 1822, in Padover, 1953. Quoted in Carpenter, 1995, p. 1.
12. "Without publicity, all other checks are fruitless: in comparison of publicity, all other checks are of small account. It is to publicity, more than to everything else put together, that the English system of procedure owes its being the least bad system as yet extant, instead of being the worst." (Bentham, 1838–43, vol. iv. p. 317. Quoted in Halévy, 1972, p. 403.)
13. Mill argues, "(t)he peculiar evil of silencing the expression of an opinion is, that it is robbing the human race; posterity as well as the existing generation; those who dissent from the opinion, still more than those who hold it. If the opinion is right, they are deprived of the opportunity of exchanging error for truth: if wrong, they lose, what is almost as great a benefit, the clearer perception and livelier impression of truth, produced by its collision with error." See Mill, 1961 (1859).
14. "As between one form of popular government and another, the advantage in this respect lies with that which most widely diffuses the exercise of public functions...by opening to all classes of private citizens, so far as is consistent with other equally important objects, the widest participation in the details of judicial and administrative business; as by jury trial, admission to municipal offices, and above all by the utmost possible publicity and liberty of discussion, whereby not merely a few individuals in succession, but the whole public, are made, to a certain extent, participants in the government, and sharers in the instruction and mental exercise derivable from it." (Mill, 1972 (1861), p. 262.)
15. "Every bureaucracy seeks to increase the superiority of the professionally informed by keeping their knowledge and intentions secret." (Weber, 1958, p. 233.) Weber gave the authoritative treatment of the role of secrecy in a bureaucracy.
16. Hirschman (1970).
17. For a discussion of market incentives for disclosure and the need for government intervention, see e.g., Stiglitz (1975a, 1975b, and 1998a) and Grossman (1981).
18. A key issue, as society increasingly faces complicated and technical issues, is how to integrate expertise, democratic accountability, and representativeness. See e.g., Stiglitz (1998b).

19. See Mueller (1997).
20. In more technical terms, the practice of secrecy leads to an inefficient Nash equilibrium.
21. See Edlin and Stiglitz (1995). See also Shleifer and Vishny (1989).
22. In arguing against the Alien and Sedition Acts at the end of the 1700s, James Madison noted how the incumbents "will be covered by the 'sedition-act' from animadversions exposing them to disrepute among the people" while the challengers would have no such protection. So, he asked, "will not those in power derive an undue advantage for continuing themselves in it; which by impairing the right of election, endangers the blessings of the government founded on it?" (Madison, 1966 (1799), p. 225.)
23. To be sure, some of the value of information is associated with asymmetries – obtaining information *before* one's rivals; some of the returns to information are thus private returns, not social returns. Still, it is hard, especially in government bond markets, to argue for the value of the market's "discovery" function, and at the same time not argue for more public disclosure of the public information that the market is expending so many resources "discovering".
24. See Chapter IV "Secret Societies" in Bok, 1982.
25. In affirming the *New York Times'* right to publish the *Pentagon Papers*, Supreme Court Justice Hugo Black wrote, "In my view, far from deserving condemnation for their courageous reporting the *New York Times*, the *Washington Post* and other newspapers should be commended for serving the purpose that the Founding Fathers saw so clearly. In revealing the workings of the government that led to the Vietnam war, the newspapers nobly did precisely that which the founders hoped and trusted they would do." See *New York Times* (1971). Furthermore, a public opinion poll conducted in the weeks after the disclosure of the *Pentagon Papers* reflected that 58 per cent of the public felt the newspapers did the right thing (whereas 29 per cent felt they had been in the wrong) in publishing the top-secret papers. See Roper (1989).
26. I am indebted to Alan Blinder for this articulation.
27. On the delicate issues of whistle-blowing, see Peters and Branch (1972 or Bok, 1982.

REFERENCES

Aizenman , Nurith C. 1997. "National Security for Sale." *Washington Monthly.* December. 17–23.

Atkinson, A.B., and Stiglitz, J. E. 1976. "The Design of Tax Structure: Direct Versus Indirect Taxation" *Journal of Public Economics*, 6, July-August. (Subsequently published in *Modern Public Finance*, vol. 2, International Library of Critical Writings in Economics. 1991. A. Atkinson (ed.), Elgar.)

Bagehot, Walter. 1948 (1869). *Physics and Politics*. New York: Knopf.

Bentham, Jeremy. 1838–43. *The Works of Jeremy Bentham*. J. Bowring (ed). 11 vol. Edinburgh: Tait.

Bok, Sissela. 1982. *Secrets*. New York: Pantheon.

Carpenter, Ted G. 1995. *The Captive Press: Foreign Policy Crises and the First Amendment*. Washington: Cato Institute.

Edlin, A., and Stiglitz, J.E. 1995. "Discouraging Rivals: Managerial Rent-Seeking and Economic Inefficiencies." *American Economic Review*, 85 (5). December. (Also NBER Working Paper 4145, 1992.)

Emerson, Thomas. 1967. *Toward a General Theory of the First Amendment*. New York: Vintage Books.

Emerson, Thomas. 1970. *The System of Freedom of Expression*. New York: Vintage.

Greider, William. 1992. *Who Will Tell the People: The Betrayal of American Democracy*. New York: Simon & Schuster.

Grossman, S. 1981. "The Informational Role of Warranties and Private Disclosure about Product Quality." *Journal of Law and Economics* 24: 461–84.

Halévy, E. 1972. *The Growth of Philosophic Radicalism*. London: Faber.

Hirschman, Albert O. 1970. *Exit, Voice, and Loyalty: Responses to Decline in Firms, Organizations and States*. Cambridge, Mass.: Harvard University Press.

Madison, James. 1966 (1799). "The Virginia Report of 1799–1800, Touching the Alien and Sedition Laws." In *Freedom of the Press from Zenger to Jefferson*. L. Levy (ed.). Indianapolis: Bobbs-Merrill. 197–229.

Mill, J. S. 1961 (1859). *On Liberty*. In *The Philosophy of John Stuart Mill*. M. Cohen (ed.). New York: Modern Library. 185–319.

Mill, J. S. 1972 (1861). "Considerations of Representative Government." In *J.S. Mill: Utilitarianism, On Liberty and Considerations on Representative Government*. H.B. Acton (ed.). London: J.M. Dent and Sons.

Moynihan, D.P. 1998. *Secrecy: The American Experience*. Yale University Press.

Mueller, D. (ed.). 1997. *Perspectives on Public Choice: A Handbook*. Cambridge: Cambridge University Press.

New York Times. 1971. *Supreme Court, 6-3, Upholds Newspapers on Publication of Pentagon Report*. 1 July. *www.nytimes.com/ books/97/04/13/reviews/papers-final.html*.

——. 1997. *Mishandling Russian Uranium*. 11 June. A24.

——. 1998a. Selling Uranium Plant to Enrich the Private Sector? 2 July. D2.

———. 1998b. *Nuclear Security for Sale*. 20 July. A14.

Newsweek. 1984. 16 April. 69.

Orszag, P. 1997. "Privatization of the US Enrichment Corporation: An Economic Analysis." London School of Economics, Ph.D. dissertation.

Padover, Saul (ed.). 1953. *The Complete Madison*. New York: Harper.

Peters, C. and T. Branch. 1972. *Blowing the Whistle: Dissent in the Public Interest*. New York: Praeger.

Roper Center. 1989. *Public Opinion Online*. Poll originally conducted by Louis Harris and Associates, University of Connecticut.

Shleifer, A., and R.W. Vishny. 1989. "Management Entrenchment: The Case of Manager-Specific Investments." *Journal of Financial Economics* 25: 123–9.

Sen, A. 1981. "Ingredients of Famine Analysis: Availability and Entitlements." *Quarterly Journal of Economics*: 96 (3), August: 433–64.

Stiglitz, J.E. 1975a. "Incentives, Risk and Information: Notes Towards a Theory of Hierarchy" *Bell Journal of Economics*, 6 (2): 552–79.

———. 1975b. "Information and Economic Analysis" In *Current Economic Problems*, Parkin and Nobay (eds.) Cambridge University Press, 27–52.

———. 1992. "S&L Bailout" In *The Reform of Federal Deposit Insurance: Disciplining the Government and Protecting Taxpayers*, J. Barth and R. Brumbaugh, Jr. (eds.). Harper Collins Publishers.

———. 1998a. "The Private Uses of Public Interests: Incentives and Institutions." *Journal of Economic Perspectives*. 12: 3–22, Spring.

———. 1998b. "Central Banking in a Democratic Society" *De Economist* (Netherlands); 146, No. 2.

Weber, Max. 1958. "Bureaucracy." In *From Max Weber: Essays in Sociology*. H.H. Gerth and C.W. Mills (eds.). New York: Galaxy. 196–244.

Chapter 9

Democratic Development as the Fruits of Labor

Keynote Address at the Industrial Relations Research Association
Boston, January 2000

DEVELOPMENT STRATEGIES AND THE LABOR MOVEMENT

Objectives of Development

Today, there is growing recognition that the objectives of development go beyond simply an increase in GDP: we are concerned with promoting democratic, equitable, sustainable development.[1] If that is our objective, then it is natural that we should pay particular attention to the issue of how the plight of workers changes in the course of development; and we should look not only at their incomes, but broader measures – at their health and safety, and even at their democratic participation, both at the workplace and within the broader political arena. Workers' rights should be a central focus of a development institution such as the World Bank.

I am just completing serving three years as Chief Economist of the World Bank. During that time, labor market issues did arise, but all too frequently, mainly from a narrow economics focus, and even then, looked at even more narrowly through the lens of neoclassical economics. Wage rigidities – often the fruits of hard-fought bargaining – were thought to be part of the problem facing many countries, contributing to their high unemployment; a standard message was to increase labor market flexibility – the not so subtle subtext was to lower wages and lay off unneeded workers. Even when labor market problems are not the core of the problem facing the country, all too often workers are asked to bear the brunt of the costs of adjustment. In East Asia, it was reckless lending by international banks and other financial institutions combined with reckless borrowing by domestic financial institutions – along with fickle

279

investor expectations – which may have precipitated the crises, but the costs – in terms of soaring unemployment and plummeting wages – were borne by workers. Workers were asked to listen to sermons about "bearing pain" just a short while after hearing, from the same preachers, sermons about how globalization and opening up capital markets would bring them unprecedented growth. And nowhere, in all of these discussions, did issues of workers' rights, including the right to participate in the decisions which would affect their lives in so many ways, did get raised.

It was finance ministers and central bank governors – and outsiders who often seemed to be representing international financial interests – who had the seats at the table, not labor unions or labor ministers. Indeed, even as debate on reforming the international economic architecture proceeded, these people, who would inevitably face much of the costs of the mistaken policy, were not even invited to sit in on the discussions; and I often felt myself to be the lone voice in these discussions suggesting that basic democratic principles recommended that not only should their voices be heard, but they should actually have a seat at the table. To be sure, increasing attention did get focused on safety nets, but was it simply an attempt to assuage feelings of guilt, providing too little too late, or even worse, an attempt to moderate public criticism of "globalization without a human face"? The suspicion of the international institutions evidenced in Seattle was the perhaps the not surprising outcome of the attitudes and policies of recent decades.

As Chief Economist, I faced several problems. I simply could not ignore the standard arguments about the adverse effects of inflexible labor markets – and while I agreed with some of the arguments, there were others that left me unconvinced. I had to tackle those issues on terms that the economists themselves – viewing the world from their particular perspective – could understand. But there was a more positive agenda: improving labor relations, including promoting core labor standards.

More instruments

These concerns quickly led to the older and broader questions of labor and development. There is a strange "studied inattention" to the possible role of the labor movement in economic development. Organized labor has played a well-known role in the already developed countries of North America, Europe and East Asia/Pacific (e.g., Japan, Korea and Australia) to:

- stabilize industrial relations;

- contribute to preserving firm-specific knowledge and organizational capital;

- mitigate the income inequalities that might be aggravated by the unchecked power of employers.[2]

In addition, the labor movement in many countries has played highly constructive social and political roles; broadly construed, it has promoted

- the adult education movement;

- the mutualism movement in the form of credit unions, mutual banking, mutual insurance, cooperatives (consumer, marketing, worker), friendly societies and other self-help associations;

- the democratic movements to extend civil rights and the franchise to all adults;

- health and safety standards and improved working conditions;

- child labor standards.

These movements all made important contributions to the economic and social development of the broader population in the now-developed world.[3]

These perspectives bring me back to two themes that I have been stressing over the past three years. The first is that not only was the Washington consensus too narrow in its objectives – in its focus on GDP – but also in what it saw as the *instruments* of development, the improvement of resource allocation, through trade liberalization, privatization and stabilization. The second, related theme is that development needed to be seen as a transformation of society, a change in mindsets. If that is the case, then workers have to be at the center of the development transformation, and workers' organizations can be a key institution in the development process.

The objectives and organization of this lecture

This lecture thus has three objectives. First, I want to review the standard economic arguments; while there was much in that analysis with which I agreed, there were hidden assumptions that limited the domain of applicability, even given the limited objectives of economic efficiency on which the economics literature focused. Indeed, in recent years, there has developed a large literature that has stressed the efficiency benefits of worker involvement in the workplace. Today, the World Bank sees one of its roles as disseminating knowledge. If it were clear that increased worker involvement led to increased efficiency, then one could let the matter rest at that: simply informing firms of this new finding would lead them to change their behaviors. There would be no need for government intervention – the profit motive would drive firms towards a "high worker involvement" workplace. My second objective, then, is to ask why that may not be the case, why government action may be required.

Over the past three years, I have been particularly concerned about developing countries, and this brings me to the third objective: are there particular reasons, rationales, for government intervention in developing countries? Development entails not only creating market institutions, but also political institutions – and the two are intimately intertwined. I began this lecture by emphasizing both a broader conception of development – the transformation of society – and a broader set of objectives – democratic development. That, in turn, entails participation and involvement both within the workplace and at higher political levels.

NEOCLASSICAL PERSPECTIVES ON LABOR

If one didn't know better, it might seem as if the fundamental propositions of neoclassical economics were designed to undermine the rights and position of labor:

282

- In the standard formulations of general equilibrium, e.g., Arrow and Debreu (1954) and Debreu (1959), labor is just *another* factor, denoted by its own subscript, x_L, just like capital and land – or any intermediate good. There is nothing special about labor, nothing to suggest that labor should be treated differently from any other factor.

- Indeed, from John Bates Clark on, there has been the view that it does not matter whether labor hires capital, or capital hires labor.

- Coase (1937) went one step further: not only did these institutional arrangements not matter, but the distribution of wealth did not matter; so long as property rights were well defined, outcomes would be (Pareto) efficient, and indeed, in some circumstances at least certain aspects of the patterns of resource allocation would not even depend on distribution.

- Thus, the central tenet of the Fundamental Theorems of Welfare Economics was that issues of distribution could be separated from issues of efficiency; again, so long as property rights were well defined – and so long as none of a limited number of market failures, such as externalities, arose – then the economy would be efficient. Issues of distribution could be left to a separate "branch" of government (Musgrave, 1959), and need not concern most policymakers.

- And Coase went one step further: even when there were externalities, so long as there were well-defined property rights and transactions costs could be ignored, efficient outcomes would emerge as a result of bargaining.

- Even issues of workers' working conditions could be embraced within the standard neoclassical formulation. If workers value working conditions, then the optimal "contract" will entail firms spending on improved working conditions an amount such that the marginal value of improving working conditions still further is just equal to the marginal cost. More generally, competition among firms forces them to be "good" employers, paying full attention to all *efficiency* aspects of the workplace, from working conditions to organization design (e.g., the extent of involvement of workers in decision-making); and issues of *distribution* should be handled not through labor market legislation, but through general legislation directed at redistribution.

- Keynes (at least in Hicks's interpretation [1936, 1937]) traced the problem of unemployment back to rigid wages.[4] He thus provided a ready prescription for the doctors of modern capitalism approaching the developing countries confronted with chronic unemployment: what is needed is more flexible labor markets, which reads: abolish minimum wages, lower wages, eliminate job protection, and privatize social security. When possible, the doctors of the international financial community force the painful medicine on the country in its times of need, when it comes to the international financial institutions for help.

If establishing these propositions that served to eviscerate the rights and positions of workers can be viewed as one of the great achievements of economics during the century from 1850 to 1950, one of the great achievements of economics during the last half century has been to show the fragility of each of the propositions. Indeed, one might argue that the real achievement of neoclassical theorists was to find the singular set of assumptions – involving perfect markets, perfect information, etc. – under which the propositions were valid, and then to dress up this highly restrictive set of assumptions in the fancy clothes of mathematical generality. The fundamental weaknesses – the assumptions concerning *economics*, e.g., information and markets – were not even listed by Debreu as assumptions; what were listed as assumptions were *mathematical properties of the relevant functions*. General equilibrium theorists spent much energy during the subsequent decades showing that those mathematical assumptions could be weakened, paying scarce attention to the underlying economics. It was only with the development of information economics, and the broader focus on transactions costs (Williamson, 1975, 1979, 1981), that the lack of generality of general equilibrium became apparent.

- Labor is not like other factors. Workers have to be motivated to perform. While under some circumstances, it may be difficult to coach a machine to behave in the way desired (e.g., trying to get a computer not to crash), what is entailed in eliciting the desired behavior out of a person and out of a machine is, I would argue, fundamentally different.

- Indeed, some might go further and argue that the central (or at least one of the central) issues of labor economics is the design of the appropriate mix of incentives and monitoring arrangements, and that some of the most important (physical and social) innovations have been those that have altered monitoring costs and devised new incentive arrangements.

- But whenever information is imperfect – that is essentially always – the Fundamental Theorems of Welfare Economics do not hold. The economy is in general not (constrained[5]) Pareto efficient, and issues of efficiency cannot be separated from issues of distribution (Shapiro and Stiglitz, 1984). Whether or not the economy is Pareto efficient can depend on the distribution of income. An economy in which workers own their own land may be efficient; there are no agency costs. But an economy in which wealth is concentrated in a few hands may not only be less productive – as agency costs lead to an undermining of productivity – but there is actual scope for government intervention to make both workers and capitalists better off. There are pecuniary externalities that arise that have *real* consequences. The distortions associated with *static* resource allocation may be increased over time, through distorted incentives to innovate (the savings in private costs for labor-saving innovations need not coincide with social benefits).[6] More generally, firm incentives to provide improved working conditions may depart significantly from what would be required by efficiency.

- The fact that redistributions are not costless (there are no lump sum transfers) implies that issues of distribution cannot simply be left to the "distribution" branch of government. Distribution issues should – and do – come into every aspect of public policy, from the design of expenditure programs to labor legislation. The redistribution of bargaining power that results from collective bargaining may lead to redistributions that would not occur through the tax/welfare system, or which would be far more costly to effect in that way.

Indeed, by redressing the asymmetries in bargaining associated with costly search, it is even conceivable that the overall efficiency of the economy will be enhanced.

- These information costs undermine Coase's attempt to resolve market failures (See e.g., Farrell 1987)

- With incomplete contracting and imperfect risk markets, it *does* matter whether labor rents capital, or capital hires labor: it determines not only who bears the residual risk, but who has residual control rights – the rights to take actions not specified in the contract.

- Recent changes in macro-economic analyses have suggested that increased labor market flexibility could actually exacerbate economic fluctuations.[7]

Before turning to an elaboration of the unique features of labor markets that make it more likely that such markets not conform to the Arrow-Debreu idealization – and that such markets are more likely to be characterized by "market failure" – there is one attribute of the labor market to which I would like to call attention, which highlights the differences between labor and other goods.

TO MARKETS AND BEYOND

There is an old saying that a kid with a hammer sees everything as a nail. An economist with a neoclassical toolkit sees every social problem as a "market" waiting to be developed and perfected. With a little hammering here and there, the market will solve the social problem. While the neoclassical perspective sees a role for government action in addressing market failures, there is a deeper question of what should or should not be "on the market" in the first place.[8] Some "markets" *should* fail – and government has a role to see that they *stay* "failed". We do not believe that individuals should buy or sell votes – regardless of whether the resulting exchanges might or might not be Pareto improvements.

The point is even more important within the labor market, and understanding this helps us understand the limitations in the idea of a competitive labor market as we see it in general equilibrium theory, e.g., the Arrow-Debreu model.

For capital goods or land, there is the buy-or-rent decision. One can rent the durable entity for a period of time (e.g., buy the services of several car-days from a car-rental agency), or one can buy the entity itself (i.e. all the services the durable can provide plus the remaining salvage value). But this free market choice of rent-or-buy is not available for people! Alfred Marshall (1920, Chapter IV and V of Book. VI noted this as the first in a number of peculiarities of labor. Paul Samuelson also recognized the first peculiarity.

> Since slavery was abolished, human earning power is forbidden by law to be capitalized. A man is not even free to sell himself; he must *rent* himself at a wage. (1976, p. 52 [emphasis in the original].)

The voluntary self-enslavement contract would be a contract to sell all of one's present and future labor services. Although now outlawed, the idea of such a contract is not just of antiquarian interest. The corresponding contract for the citizens of a country would be the Hobbesian contract of subjugation wherein people alienate their rights of self-determination to an absolute sovereign. The contemporary Harvard philosopher Robert Nozick[9] would allow the Hobbesian contract between individuals and a "dominant protective association". Nozick goes further:

> The comparable question about an individual is whether a free system will allow him to sell himself into slavery. I believe that it would. (Nozick, 1974, p. 331.)

This 'sophisticated' form of madness does not stop at the Harvard Philosophy Department; it is hidden within the assumptions of the competitive general equilibrium model. As Gerald Debreu puts it: a consumer/ worker "is to choose (and carry out) a consumption plan made now for the whole future, i.e., a specification of the quantities of all his inputs and all his outputs" (Debreu, 1959, p. 50) Thus a worker could sell all of her future labor at once. If sold to one buyer, it would essentially be the slavery contract. If complete future markets in labor were not allowed, then there could not be "capitalist acts between consenting adults"

(Nozick's phrase) that would be a Pareto improvement, so one could not have the fundamental theorem that a competitive equilibrium is Pareto optimal. Therefore the fundamental efficiency theorem requires revising constitutional law to allow voluntary slavery contracts! Needless to say, this labor market peculiarity is not emphasized in the standard texts but it has been occasionally pointed out. The Johns Hopkins economist, Carl Christ, made the point in no less a forum than Congressional testimony.

> Now it is time to state the conditions under which private property and free contract will lead to an optimal allocation of resources... The institution of private property and free contract as we know it is modified to permit individuals to sell or mortgage their persons in return for present and/or future benefits. (Christ, 1975, p. 334; quoted in Philmore, 1982, p. 52).

Thus the fantasy world of the "idealized" competitive equilibrium model is not only unrealistic – a point I have emphasized throughout my career; it has even been illegal since the abolition of slavery (involuntary and voluntary). Thus those of us who were trained as neoclassical economists should not feel too guilty as we try to devise institutional solutions that do not fit well into the idealized competitive model of the textbooks.[10]

These results stand in stark contrast to the previously prevailing wisdom. In the limited time available, I want to elaborate on questions of market failures, labor's role in corporate governance and industrial relations systems.

MARKET FAILURES: SEARCH COSTS AND MACRO-ECONOMIC RIGIDITIES

Search costs and asymmetric bargaining power

In the standard model, no firm and no worker has any bargaining power. There are an infinite number of firms offering identical jobs, and any firm attempting to lower its wage below the market wage would immediately lose all of its workers; and any worker attempting to increase his or her wage above the market wage would immediately find no job opportunity. But in the real world, there are costs to search, to finding out what wages other firms are offering, and even greater costs associated with moving from one employer to another. Even small costs can have large effects.[11] For instance, with ε search costs, the equilibrium wage is the *monopsony* wage; even when there are many employers, each firm has considerable bargaining power – indeed the same that it would have had had it been the *only* employer. Assume that all firms paid a wage above the monopsony wage. Then if any single firm were to lower its wage by less than ε, it would lose no workers. It thus pays each to lower its wage. The process continues until the wage is lowered to the monopsony wage.[12]

Thus, whenever there are search and moving costs, there may be, in effect, a mini-bargaining problem; outcomes of such bilateral bargaining problems – even when the scope of bargaining is limited – may depart markedly from those associated with the perfect competition model, especially when there are sunk firm-specific costs and incomplete contracting. Whenever one firm raises its wage to attract more workers, it may induce a worker elsewhere to quit (indeed, that was the intent), imposing additional training costs on other firms.[13]

Macro-economic equilibrium

Traditional Keynesian analysis focused around a single market failure, wage rigidity, and ignored key aspects of the dynamics of adjustment. If wages and prices start to fall more rapidly, in an economy facing downward rigidities in interest rates (e.g., nominal interest rates cannot fall below zero – a problem confronting Japan), then greater wage and price flexibility leads to higher real interest rates and decreasing investment and overall aggregate demand, potentially exacerbating the economic downturn.

Moreover, with incomplete contracting, there are large redistributions associated with unanticipated decreases in wages (and prices). Bruce Greenwald and I have argued that such redistributions may have large aggregate demand effects, because of compounding imperfections in capital markets. The unanticipated fall in wages and prices implies that firms have to pay back in real terms more than they had anticipated – a redistribution from debtors to creditors. Debtors (firms) contract investment and consumption expenditures more than creditors expand in their response to the redistribution. The net effect is a large contraction in aggregate demand, and possibly even in aggregate supply, as firms' real working capital also deteriorates, and cannot be compensated for (especially in a recession) by additional borrowing or equity issues (Greenwald and Stiglitz, 1993).

On a priori grounds, it cannot be ascertained whether the standard "wage" rigidity effect predominates over the real interest rate/redistribution effects just discussed. It is certainly theoretically possible that greater wage and price flexibility actually leads to a lowering not just of welfare (as in the discussion above of efficiency wages) but of output. Recent cross-section estimates of output variability and the likelihood of recessions suggests that greater wage flexibility is either unassociated with greater output stability or may actually contribute to an enhanced likelihood of a recession. (See Easterly, Islam and Stiglitz, 1999.)

LABOR AS A STAKEHOLDER IN CORPORATE GOVERNANCE

Much has been written over the past 70 years, and especially over the past 15 years, about the consequences of the separation of ownership and control[14]; in modern parlance, we say there is a principal-agent problem. Shareholders have limited ability and incentives individually to monitor fully managers; and managers have an incentive to make it more difficult for themselves to be monitored (Edlin and Stiglitz, 1995)

A central theme of the literature on corporate governance is that there are differences in interests among the various stakeholders in the firm. One strand of literature has argued that there is a variety of mechanisms by which a greater congruence can be obtained, e.g., by making workers partial owners, as under ESOPs [Employee Stock Ownership Programs –*Ed.*], or by making banks also equity holders. Unfortunately, these same practices often lead to conflicts of interest; a bank which is also an equity holder may have an incentive to make an excessively risky loan, partially at the public expense (as a result of the government guarantee to depositors).

There are several advantages to bringing workers within the fold of corporate governance beyond enhancing this congruence of interests. First, the sharing of information may lead to less conflict; under some theories, strikes are a result of imperfections of information – strikes are a costly way of conveying information between the parties. If firms have to disclose the same information to workers as they do to other board members, then the credibility of that information is enhanced; workers are more willing to accept a firm's claim that it cannot pay higher wages without threatening the viability of the firm.

There are also arguments that worker participation in decision-making, even if only through representatives, may increase the sense of "fairness" of any decisions made, and fairness in turn can affect worker morale and productivity. (See Akerlof and Yellen, 1988.)

Second, workers are often in a better position to monitor the firm than are creditors, since they are continuously on the spot. They can verify – or challenge – management claims about what is actually happening within the firm. It is for this very reason that management may resist having worker participation. It may limit the power that management exerts (and its rents) by reducing the asymmetries in information.

ON THE IMPORTANCE OF RESIDUAL CONTROL RIGHTS: LESSONS FROM THE EAST ASIA CRISIS

The issues with which I have been concerned here are not just theoretical niceties, but can take on first order importance, not only in affecting the prospects of particular individuals in particular firms, but in determining the nature of the market equilibrium. This was brought home forcefully in the context of the recent East Asia crisis. Standard contracts in place gave all (or at least a predominant proportion) of residual control rights to shareholders. Consider first the situation prior to the crisis. When workers came to work at a firm, they typically did not know the full risk profile of the firm, in particular its uncovered foreign exchange exposure. Though this risk represented a potential real cost to the worker, he would benefit little if at all from any returns. Had workers had a significant voice in management, they would have strongly argued against the firm taking on such a position, unless the firm provided adequate job security (severance benefits) to the workers. As it was, the workers had no say.

Next, consider how firms responded to the unanticipated macroeconomic events (the soaring interest rates, the falling exchange rates and declining demand). Workers' interests would probably have been maximized if the firms had gone into a speedy chapter 11 reorganization;

but this would hurt creditors, and it would have hurt equity owners (the presumed decision makers) even more. In this case, there was a natural alliance between international creditors and equity owners (supported by one of the international financial institutions, whose officials, in trying to ward off such a default, spoke repeatedly of the sanctity of contracts, paying little heed to bankruptcy being a core part of capitalism, and to the at least *implicit* contracts between workers and their firms that were being torn up, all in the name of protecting creditor rights). The point is that because workers were not represented – either at the firm decision-making counsels or within the international institutions that were attempting to address the crisis – the outcomes were clearly not in workers' interests, and were probably not even efficient. The costs to workers were not adequately weighed against the benefits to creditors or equity holders.

PRINCIPAL-AGENT PROBLEMS AND WORKER INVOLVEMENT

The problem of corporate governance is, of course, nothing more than a manifestation of the general principal-agent problem. I want to spend a few moments focusing on agency problems in industrial relations systems. The competitive model has some rough plausibility in a market populated by small firms. In our Jeffersonian tradition, we celebrate the family farm, the owner-operated shop, and the small independent craftsmen. In terms of the principal-agent relation, all these cases are characterized by the unity of principal and agent, i.e., the people are self-employed (no agency costs). Here the assumption that the principal and the agent have the same knowledge and incentives is obviously true, but how should that assumption be generalized to larger firms? For larger firms, the assumption that the principals (e.g., far-flung shareholders) are able to enforce their incentives on the agents (managers and workers in the firm) and monitor the behavior of the agents becomes a rather heroic assumption. Yet without that assumption, the basic theorem fails. (Greenwald and Stiglitz, 1986.) How in the actual world can the virtues of the limit case of self-employed individuals be best generalized to multi-person firms?

Let us consider some of the informational and incentive problems inherent in the employment relation and in other agency relationships.

The shareholders are principals relative to the managers as their agents, and the managers can be seen as principals relative to the workers as agents. In such pyramided principal-agent relationships, there may be many gaps in monitoring and incentives between the shareholders and workers: managers have imperfect incentives to ensure that the two are well aligned.[15]

One approach to the effort question was developed in the efficiency-wage theory as an explanation for involuntary unemployment in otherwise flexible labor markets.[16] Employers are assumed to fire workers who are caught shirking (working at chronically low effort levels) but if labor markets clear at the prevailing wage, then workers will be able to readily find new employment at the prevailing wage. Assuming effort is costly and the probability of being detected shirking is low, workers would tend to operate at low effort levels. Employers may pay more than the market-clearing wage, i.e., an efficiency wage, in order to give workers something extra to lose if they are fired for working at low effort levels. At that efficiency wage, there would be more job-seekers than vacancies resulting in involuntary unemployment. A higher level of unemployment would make dismissal more costly. Since fired workers would join the unemployment queues, there would be an incentive for work at a high effort level so as not to risk being detected shirking and fired.

For purposes of this paper, three observations concerning efficiency wage theories are relevant:

A. The extent of the agency problem depends on the distribution of wealth. Agency problems are less important in societies in which wealth is more equally distributed.
B. When there are agency problems, the market is, in general, not even constrained Pareto efficient. Costly supervision implies that workers are imperfectly monitored; when bad performance is discovered, a worker is fired, but if firing is to have a cost, there must be surplus associated with holding the job; there may be unemployment in equilibrium. In this case, firms have no incentive to provide job benefits (severance pay, grievance settlement mechanisms) which reduce the cost of leaving – even if such benefits are welfare enhancing. Indeed, the firm has an incentive to look for ways that increase the costs of separation, because in doing so it can lower wages.

    C.   This use of an efficiency wage to elicit high effort is best suited to what is typically called the low involvement or "low road" workplace[17] since it assumes a credible threat to fire shirking workers and it assumes no other motivation for high effort levels.

A high involvement or "high road" workplace (as in what we might call the "Japanese-style" workplace) uses quite different methods to elicit high effort from the workers. A high involvement labor participation program deals not just with economic variables such as pay (perhaps performance-related) and benefits but with a range of other factors such as worker-team involvement in decision-making and control on the shop floor or in the office. At the risk of oversimplifying the psychology, the idea is to increase each worker's involvement in and identification with the firm so that there will be some unification of agent and principal and a resulting tendency for higher effort. The high-involvement workplace, by approaching principal-agent unification (however in quite a partial manner), provides a different method of eliciting high effort than the "risk of unemployment" motivation emphasized in the "low road" approach.

In 1990, Laura Tyson and David Levine surveyed 43 empirical studies on the connection between participation and productivity. They found that the effect of worker participation on productivity was usually positive though sometimes small or statistically insignificant – but almost never negative. The effect improves the more the participation was close to the shopfloor or office.

Several dozen new studies have been conducted since then, several of which have particularly strong research designs and data quality. Their conclusions reinforce the earlier findings: a small-scale employee involvement plan, just as a small amount of training or a modest change in pay systems, may have some beneficial effects, particularly in the short run. Furthermore, a system of high involvement, strong rewards and high levels of skill and information, integrated with a corporate strategy that relies on front-line employees' ideas and creativity, is capable of impressive improvements in organizational performance. (Levine, 1995, p. 81.)

The literature on ESOPs and other forms of employee-ownership has generally, but not always, found a positive relationship between ownership and performance. But when the ownership is coupled with genuine participation, the positive relationship is quite clear.[18]

TWO INDUSTRIAL RELATIONS SYSTEMS:
THE LOW ROAD AND THE HIGH ROAD

The contrasts between the low and high involvement workplaces are part of a larger story about the interlocking attributes of different types of systems (see Aoki, 1994). Indeed, one way to look at the East Asian crisis is as the turmoil that occurs at the interface between two systems just as an earthquake is produced by the collision and rubbing of tectonic plates. In a system of information-rich and stable but highly leveraged relationships between firms and financiers, distress is handled with understanding and lenience on the part of the lenders. The high trust in the firm-financier relationship pairs together with the high leverage as part of a workable system.

But when the same firms start to become indebted with arm's-length short-term borrowing, there will be little slack in the face of distress and the high leverage may lead to crisis. Low trust and arm's-length finance relationships need to be paired with lower debt-equity ratios to provide more flexibility under distress. The point is not that one system or the other is "better" but that an unwise mixture of the two systems may be quite prone to crisis.

Yet the world changes; new circumstances arise. Each system must find ways to adjust their set of interlocking attributes to address the new realities and yet avoid unstable mixtures prone to crisis. Just to be even-handed, let me mention the opposite sort of problem when a low trust system adopts a sub-system from a high trust system. Many firms in the US and Europe have wanted to cut inventory costs and to foster the problem-solving induced by the just-in-time inventory system. But the JIT inventory system interlocks with rather cooperative labor relationships both in the firm and in the suppliers and truckers who supply the parts "just in time." In a more confrontational labor environment, the JIT system is rather unworkable.

I will proceed by outlining the two systems introduced as two ways of addressing the effort problem in the agency relationship and the more general problem of opportunistic behavior in contractual relationships. The two stylized industrial relations systems will be characterized with generic characteristics (e.g., low trust and low involvement of the low road versus high trust and high involvement of the high road) rather than geography – even though one system is commonly thought to be Anglo-American and the other is identified with Japanese and German systems.

In terms of Hirschman's exit-voice distinction (1970), dissatisfaction in a relationship leads in a low trust/involvement system to exit and the search for a better partner. In a high trust/involvement system, contractual relationships are more stable and long-term. Each partner is expected to have higher commitment to the relationship and more trust that the partner will not act opportunistically.[19] In the high road workplace, dissatisfaction would be addressed through various voice mechanisms (e.g., collective bargaining, grievance procedures and labor-management committees) rather than termination and exit. To paraphrase an old advertising slogan, the partners would "rather fight [to resolve the differences] than switch".

High trust is developed between workers and managers by managers exercising the self-restraint not to use their power to enrich themselves and to take advantage of the workers. On their side, the workers choose to be cooperative without feeling that they are exposing themselves to being opportunistically exploited by self-aggrandizing managers. That mutual cooperativeness in the high trust management-labor relationship is the basis for high "X-efficiency".[20] In a high trust and involvement environment, the genuine participation of the workers leads to their increased buy-in to the goals of the immediate work group, if not to some goals of the broader enterprise. As a result of this socialization into the enterprise, the worker tends to identify with and to affect the goals of the whole effort. Instead of better threats and monitoring to reduce opportunistic behavior in the agency relation, the high trust/involvement system strives towards identification of principals and agents.[21] In a 1991 symposium on "Organizations and Economics", Herbert Simon emphasized the importance of identification.

> Although economic rewards play an important part in securing adherence to organizational goals and management authority, they are limited in their effectiveness. Organizations would be far less effective systems than they actually are if such rewards were the only means, or even the principal means, of motivation available. In fact, observation of behavior in organizations reveals other powerful motivations that induce employees to accept organizational goals and authority as bases for their actions. [The]

most important of these mechanisms... [is] organizational identification. (Simon, 1991, p. 34.)

Moreover the greater congruence between the goals of the agents and the goals of the firm can be achieved by adjusting both instead of only the former.[22]

The body of employees is, together with the body of shareholders, explicitly or implicitly recognized as a constituent of the firm, and its interests are considered in the formation of managerial policy. (Aoki, 1987, pp. 283–4.)

We have thus seen how the system tries to generalize to larger enterprises the virtues of the family farmer, small producer, or shopkeeper who is self-employed. In doing so, we have seen several different levels of analysis:

a) Implicit contracts – reputational relationships, with incomplete contracts, with adjustments in response to changing circumstances based on voice and trust – may be more effective than explicit contracts with, say, one side having all "residual" rights to control and all residual income.

b) Adaptations in workers' preferences, identification, may be more effective in eliciting desired behavior of workers than incentive-based contracts; how to achieve such identification is one of the major challenges facing management. Profit sharing, which in terms of standard incentive theories, may be fairly ineffective, may still be effective because of its effects in facilitating identification.

Identification can also be facilitated by

c) Firms convincingly changing their stated objectives as going beyond simply profit maximizing, to include the welfare of their workers, not only as means to an end, but as ends themselves.

The following table (see p. 298) tries to concisely give the flavor of the two systems and how their internal interlocks might be played out in different markets.[23]

Enterprise Characteristic	Low Road	High Road
LABOR MARKET		
Inducement to high effort	High unemployment and efficiency wage	High involvement induces effort even with low unemployment
Compensation	Contractual wages	Wages plus profit sharing
Wage differentials	High differentials as incentive for individual advancement	Low differentials for increased group solidarity and cohesiveness
Employment security	Low: dismissal is credible threat for discipline	High security to promote identification with enterprise
Training costs	Paid by individual to increase marketability	Paid by firm as long-term human capital investment
Macro-environment	Can adjust to and contribute to larger recessions with layoffs	Works better with and contributes to fewer and smaller recessions by avoiding layoffs

PRODUCT & FACTOR MARKETS		
Relationship	Arm's-length, market-oriented and competitive	Long-term relation based on commitment, trust and loyalty
Product	Standardized (to foster competition)	Customized to buyer or seller
Curb to opportunism	Exit and competition	Voice, commitment and trust

CAPITAL MARKET		
Relationship	Arm's-length and market-oriented finance	Long-term relational finance
Time perspective	Short-term since hard to monitor; human capital investments downplayed	Long-term and patient to reap return to human capital investments
Debt/equity ratios	Need low D/E ratio to provide flexibility in face of unforgiving market	Can have higher D/E ratios with patient relationship to financial sources and with involved, more flexible workers
Low costs of equity	Low costs since no sharing of income or control rights with workers	Lower costs for internal equity since workers already share some income and control rights

DEVELOPMENT STRATEGY FOR LABOR:
FROM THE LOW ROAD TO THE HIGH ROAD

In the developing world, the picture of a market economy is often based on images of the "dark satanic mills" of eighteenth and nineteenth century England. Market-based development was conceptualized using what we have called the "low road" system of industrial relations. The modern experience in Japan and other East Asian countries shows that there is another model that more closely approximates the "high road" system. Until the East Asia crisis struck, there was, at least among some circles, the view that the high road had distinct advantages over the low road: macro-stability would be greater, productivity growth higher, worker morale stronger. I worry that one of the more adverse consequences of the East Asian crisis may be the abandonment of the high road, as firms are being encouraged to break long standing implicit contracts with workers, to "downsize" in response to the new economic realities – even if downsizing implies forcing long-term workers into unemployment. Such long-standing relationships are viewed as contributing to market rigidities, impeding the quick adjustments needed in the nimble world of modern globalization.

To be sure, *excessive labor market rigidities* (almost tautologically) can have adverse effects. But long-term social contracts between firms and their workers may make them more accepting of – and more promoting of – change and progress. Indeed, the breaking of the social contract and the undermining of social capital is increasingly being given "credit" for the huge decreases in productivity in the former Soviet Union.[24] But given imperfections of information (e.g., between workers and firms), arm's length market-based relationships will lead to an underinvestment in firm-specific human capital (relative to the first best optimum) and higher labor turnover. (See Arnott and Stiglitz, 1985.)[25]

The need for – and limitations of – collective action

I have stressed these market failures, often implicit in the discussions of labor relations, for an important reason. In the absence of the kinds of imperfections noted earlier, firms would have an incentive to have the "optimal" amount of worker participation in decision making – there would be no need for government intervention in governance. If the evidence for the "high road" is as compelling as many seem to believe, firms will move in that direction.

But the market failures depicted earlier explain why they may not move as much or as fast as is socially desirable, and provide a clear rationale for collective action. There is at least the possibility that government interventions in the labor market – through regulations affecting working conditions, collective bargaining and more broadly workers' rights – will bring about redistributions that might not otherwise be achieved. Such interventions may, under certain circumstances, actually be Pareto improvements.

But I hasten to add that there is a delicate balance: excessively strong unions can through collective action "hold up" the rest of the economy, reduce product market competition and interfere in other ways with the efficiency of the economy. This is particularly problematic in areas in which there is a natural monopoly, or a government-created monopoly or near monopoly. Wage increases can be passed on to consumers, and workers in these industries have in country after country been able to use their market power to extract wages far in excess of their opportunity cost. When the service is publicly provided – such as education – market discipline may too be limited. Though eventually voters may raise concerns about public employees being paid wages considerably in excess of market wages, the process is a slow one, and before the political process responds, considerable rents may be extracted from the public. Of particular concern are those instances in which, in order to maintain their rents, unions attempt to suppress competition, as many would argue has been happening in the United States, with unions' vehement opposition to vouchers.

Is there a role for collective action within the public sector?

I was going to ask, more broadly, what is the justification for unions in the public sector? The arguments presented earlier suggested that profit-maximizing private firms would act to exploit their monopsony power over workers, or otherwise engage in wage-setting policies that ignored the externalities that those policies exerted on others. Clearly, the government need not do so; with good economic advisers, they would be tamed against abusing any monopsony power and act in a way that is acutely sensitive to externalities. Indeed, correcting externalities is one of the major rationales for collective action. This reasoning would suggest that while there is a need for government-enforced collective bargaining rights in the private sector, such rights should not extend to the public.

But there is a strong qualification to this argument. Principal-agent problems arise in the public sector just as they do in the private. The manager of a public school may not act in a way that fully reflects the public interest. He is likely to see his job as producing high quality education at a minimum cost – just as the manager of a private school would – and as such he would have every incentive (absent collective bargaining) to keep wages as low as possible. More broadly, political control mechanism are far from perfect – far less effective than market control mechanisms. In such cases, the exercise of voice – through unions – may be particularly important. (See Hirschman, 1970.)

Systemic problems

The case for redressing the imbalance in bargaining power seems clear, but it provides only part of the rationale for the role for government in regulating corporate governance, especially given the magnitude of managerial discretion and the role that management plays in deciding on corporate governance. The fact that there exist quite different systems of corporate governance (those with and without a large role for workers) suggests[26] that there may be multiple equilibria, in which case government can play a role in moving the economy from one equilibrium to another.[27] Norms are established that govern "appropriate" behavior – not only the extent of consultation, but appropriate compensation differentials between management and workers. (Does one really believe that the ratio of managerial productivity to worker productivity differs so markedly across countries?) In a society in which workers participate on a regular basis in decision-making, any firm that took away that right would be castigated. But in a society in which workers do not regularly participate in decision-making, granting that right might not serve to make the firm that much more attractive; indeed, a self-selection process may be set in motion, whereby workers who feel most strongly about participation – and who in other ways are the most militant – may be attracted to the firm. Similarly, in societies that value long-term relations, the signal sent by a worker leaving his firm is markedly different from that sent in an economy like the United States.[28]

DEVELOPMENT AS DEMOCRATIC TRANSFORMATION

Finally, I would like to view this developmental strategy for labor within a broader framework for development. In my Prebisch Lecture [1998b; ch. 2, this volume – *Ed*.], I emphasized the concept of development as transformation.

> Development represents a transformation of society, a movement from traditional relations, traditional ways of thinking, traditional ways of dealing with health and education, traditional methods of production, to more "modern" ways. For instance, a characteristic of traditional societies is the acceptance of the world as it is; the modern perspective recognizes change, it recognizes that we, as individuals and societies, can take actions that, for instance, reduce infant mortality, increase lifespans and increase productivity.

If a change in mindset is at the center of development, then it is clear that attention needs to be shifted to how to effect such changes in mindset.[29] Such changes cannot be "ordered" or forced from the outside, however well-intentioned the outsiders may be. Change has to come from within. The kinds of open and extensive discussions that are central to democratic processes are, I suspect, the most effective way of ensuring that the change in mindset occurs not only within a small élite, but reaches deep down in society.

Change is also often threatening – and sufficiently risk-averse individuals are willing to pass up opportunities for expected gain to avoid the downside risks. Democratic and participatory processes involving labor unions and other social organizations ensure that these concerns are not only heard, but addressed; as a result, these processes dissipate much of the resistance to change. Consider an example that is particularly relevant in a time of globalization. As one who supports lowering trade barriers, I am nonetheless dismayed to note that all too often ardent free-trade advocates cavalierly dismiss the opponents, including those who stand to lose by free trade, and refer to them as "special interests" trying to protect their existing "rents". But among those hurt by trade reforms will be many who will lose their jobs. And if the society lacks an adequate safety net, the unemployed worker therefore risks true impoverishment, with disastrous effects on the lives of all family members. What is of concern is not just the loss of "rents", but the loss of a family's livelihood. Inclusive democratic processes involving unions and other popular organizations make it more likely that these legitimate concerns will be addressed.

We should be clear: workers in much of the world have grounds for suspicion. Capital market liberalization in East Asia did not bring the benefits that were promised, except to a few wealthy individuals. It did impoverish many – both through lower wages and increased unemployment. Worse still, workers have seen decisions that affect their lives and livelihoods being seemingly forced upon their countries, with hardly a nod towards the concerns of the workers, apart from sermons about the virtues of bearing pain. I believe, for instance, that there is some chance that some of the disastrous economic decisions that were made in responding to the East Asian economic crisis would not have occurred had workers had a voice (let alone a voice commensurate with their stake in the outcome) in the decision making.[30] And even if similar decisions had been made, at least workers would have felt that they had had their say.

Thus, I would argue that economic democracy is essential to effect the systemic change in mindset associated with the democratic transformation, and to engender policies that make change – which is at the center of development – more acceptable. And because labor and other affected social groups have had a voice in shaping the changes, in making them more acceptable, change is likely to be accepted or even embraced, rather than reversed at the first opportunity.

The economic benefits of workplace democracy are, however, as I have already suggested, more pervasive than just the acceptance of change: there is a growing literature arguing that participation in decision making increases efficiency.[31] Changes in technology would be expected to be associated with changes in the degree and nature of worker participation, as the efficiency benefits and economic costs of participation change. New information technologies and production modes hold open the promise of greater worker participation – just as they hold open the promise of more effective citizen participation in public governance.[32]

TOWARD ECONOMIC DEMOCRACY

So far, I have largely cast the analysis in traditional economic terms. I have argued that, given traditional objectives (Pareto efficiency) and traditional modeling of individual behavior, simply taking into account imperfections and costs of information, and the imperfections of mobility and asymmetries in bargaining to which they give rise, there is a rationale for government intervention in labor relations.

But I want to put forward a stronger hypothesis. We care about the kind of society we live in. We believe in democracy, regardless of whether it increases economic efficiency or not.[33]

I would argue that democracy entails far more than majority voting.[34] Indeed, there is a whole tradition that identifies "government by discussion" as the key to democracy.[35] Democratic processes must entail open dialogue and broadly active civic engagement, and it requires that individuals have a voice in the decisions that affect them, including economic decisions. Thus, we can speak of industrial or economic democracy in the workplace – where unions play a key role – and local democracy at the community level, as well as democracy at the national level.

A society in which there is a widespread view of class conflict between workers and capitalists is fundamentally different – and functions fundamentally differently – from a society in which there is perceived to be a wider congruence of interests. A society in which large portions of the labor force are marginalized, are treated as if their voice does not count, and see their opportunities for advancement highly restricted, will function in ways that are fundamentally different from a society in which there is perceived to be greater respect for every individual and greater attempts at comprehensive inclusion.

Economic democracy is thus an essential part of a democratic society. The limits and bounds of economic democracy are evolving, just as democracy itself is changing. Though democracy has a long tradition – in the West, it dates back at least to the Greek city-states – even political democracy has been slow to evolve. It was only in the century just ended that universal political suffrage became the norm. Many countries have been slow to grant those basic rights – of a free press, free speech, the right to organize to pursue common objectives (both in general, and for workers in particular) – that are so necessary for an effective democracy. Many governments continue not to recognize the people's fundamental "right to know" pursuing secrecy well beyond the domain where it is needed for national security.

There have been comparably great strides in economic democracy. Today, management is more willing to listen to the concerns of workers – they do not view this as an intrusion into managerial prerogatives. Even language is changing, as one speaks of partnerships, teams, community. One need not be Pollyannaish – believing that there is complete congruence of interests – to believe that such a change in language represents a fundamental shift in mindset, a move towards greater openness, to delineating more clearly the sources of conflict, clarifying the asymmetries of bargaining power that arise from costs of labor mobility, limited worker resources and asymmetries of information.

Democracy is also fragile. Repeatedly, we have seen high levels of social disorder lead to calls for strong (read "anti-democratic") government to restore the basic foundations of law and order without which individuals cannot live and work together. We have seen how economic policies, and the manner in which they are adopted, can contribute either to social cohesion or to social disorder. The world has experienced economic crises of increasing frequency and severity. There is a growing consensus on the causes of the crises, and on the policies that must be adopted to reduce their frequency and severity and to mitigate the consequences, e.g., by developing stronger safety nets. But there is no safety net that can fully replace the security provided by an economy running at full employment. No welfare system will ever restore the dignity that comes from work. It is imperative that countries not only work to put into place policies that prevent crises and minimize their magnitude and adverse consequences, but respond to these crises in ways that maintain as high a level of employment as possible. Too often, in advising countries on policies that they should pursue, the focus has been too narrow. While potential efficiency benefits were stressed, the downside risks were given short shrift; worse still, little attention was put on sequencing – ensuring that the country had in place the institutions that would enable the country (and especially the most vulnerable workers within it) – to bear the risks.[36] And in exposing the country, and its workers, to these risks, we not only put at risk the lives and livelihoods of the workers, but more fundamentally the systems of economic and political democracy.

CONCLUDING REMARKS

As we end the millennium and begin another, it is time to view the issues of labor relations through new lenses – and begin a shift in the prevailing paradigm. Few writing a history of capitalism in the United States would venture that organized labor did not play an important role not only in restructuring the relationships between workers and firms, partially redressing an imbalance of power, but also in improving living standards. Critics who say that these changes would have come on their own, simply as a result of higher GNP, are simply not credible.

But the world today is markedly different from the world 75 or 50 years ago. The statistics suggest that unions are playing a far less important role within the private sector than they did in the years immediately following World War II. Yet that does not mean that issues of labor relations have disappeared. Rather, the grounds have shifted – for instance, to issues concerning the role of workers in ownership and governance. There may be a need for government to facilitate this shift in economic organization, just as it did earlier in the century, in facilitating the growth of unions. Many of the developing countries – some of which are just emerging from a history of feudal relations – face more traditional problems of redressing fundamental imbalances of power. Those of us in the business of dispensing development advice must be aware of the social, political, economic and historical context in which that advice is given: advising countries to have more flexible labor markets may be tantamount to telling them to give up hard-won advances in labor standards. And even the welfare gains may be problematic, once the social costs of the risks imposed and the adverse macro-economic effects described earlier are taken into account. The streets of Seattle bear testimony to the sense of frustration that many within the developing world feel about how the international community has addressed their concerns.

But even more fundamental than the issues of economic efficiency are those concerning economic democracy: the kind of society we are attempting to create. There is more that we can do than just following the dictum of "do no harm" – though some might argue that that would, by itself, be going a long way. While globalization provides new challenges for sustainable democratic development, it also offers new opportunities to loosen the fetters of the past and to promote the democratic processes essential for long-run success. By becoming advocates of stronger workers' rights and representation at every level – from the workplace, to the local, regional and national level, to the international level – I believe that we can achieve much more than improvements in efficiency. Labor unions and other genuine forms of popular self-organization are key to democratic economic development. That is why today, the World Bank supports the Labor Standards of the ILO, including the rights to organize and collectively bargain.

NOTES

1. See e.g., Stiglitz (1998).
2. See Freeman and Medoff (1984) and Kochan and Osterman (1994).
3. "Industrialism has, wherever it has appeared, produced some form of trade unionism and some kind of exclusive organization of the working class. In all industrialized countries in Europe, trade unions and the working class movement connected with them have formed the most lively defenders of democracy. Even in Eastern countries like Japan and India industrialism has produced the need for trade unions and trade unions are the beginning of democracy." (Lindsay, 1943, p. 192).
4. But operating not just through the labor market, as in classical economics, but through the product market as well.
5. That is, taking into account the costs of obtaining information or creating markets. See Greenwald and Stiglitz (1986).
6. See Braverman and Stiglitz (1986).
7. See Easterly, Islam, and Stiglitz (1999).
8. See Kuttner [1999) for more discussion.
9. See Philmore (1982) for elaboration.
10. Robert Solow in his own way seeks to provide succor to the neoclassical faithful: "I want to emphasize to economists that it is not a betrayal of the structure of economic theory generally to admit the likelihood that labor is a peculiar sort of commodity and the labor market correspondingly a peculiar sort of market." (1990, p. 30.)
11. One of the important insights to emerge from the economics of information is that the economy is rife with convexities, so that small costs (or more generally small perturbations) can have large effects. See e.g., Stiglitz (2000).
12. See Diamond (1971). Under some circumstances, the wage may be somewhat higher

than the monopsony wage, or the equilibrium may be characterized by a wage distribution. See Stiglitz (1985a, 1987).

13. For an early discussion of the inefficiencies associated with labor turnover, see Stiglitz (1972). The problem is that imperfections of information and incomplete contracting make it impossible to distinguish between efficient quits, e.g., when the worker is badly matched with the firm, as a result of basic differences in preferences, and inefficient quits. See Arnott and Stiglitz (1985).
14. See Berle and Means (1932) and Stiglitz (1985b).
15. These agency relationships are a major topic in information economics, since many aspects of the agents' behavior are unobservable. Many of the unobservable factors that affect labor productivity are grouped under the label "effort". Managers cannot directly observe the workers' effort level, and yet effort can have a considerable effect on productivity and profits.
16. See Shapiro and Stiglitz (1984) and the other papers in Akerlof and Yellen (1986).
17. In Shapiro and Stiglitz (1984), this was described as the "lower-paid, lower-skilled, blue-collar occupations".
18. See Blinder (1990), Gates (1998), and the updated reports on www.nceo.org/library posted by the National Center for Employee Ownership in Oakland, California.
19. See Goldberg (1980) for a treatment of the contrast between relational contracting and arm's-length contracting.
20. Where we might take X = effort. See Leibenstein (1984, 1987).
21. These considerations raise a host of important questions that cannot be pursued here. See McGregor's classic treatment of "Theory Y" (1960) and the more recent literature on intrinsic motivation such as Lane (1991), Frey (1997), and Kreps (1997).
22. This formulation does not make clear whether the firm is supposed to abandon the goal of profit maximizing, or only that, it has to recognize that to achieve that goal, it must act *as if* it incorporated the concerns of workers within its own objectives. See Akerlof and Kranton (1999).
23. See Levine and Tyson (1990) and Levine (1995) for many of the same points and see Clark (1979) or Dore (1987) for similar tables comparing Anglo-American-type and Japanese-type firms.
24. See Stiglitz (1999a, 1999b) and Hussain, Stern, and Stiglitz (1999).
25. Similar arguments have been put forward to suggest arm's length financial relationships associated with securitization may be less efficient than "relationships" associated with banking. See e.g., Stiglitz (1992) and the references cited there.
26. It is only suggestive, since the legal environment differs in other respects as well.
27. The role of government in moving an economy from one equilibrium (that is Pareto inferior) to another is illustrated well by Basu's discussion of child labor. He argues that there may be a "low level equilibrium trap" in which wages are low; because wages are low, families send out their children to work; and because they send their children out to work, the equilibrium wage is low. There is another high wage equilibrium, in which at the high wage, families chose not to send out their children to work. Prohibiting child labor ensures that the economy avoids the low level equilibrium trap. (See Basu [1998].) Similarly, Basu, Genicot, and Stiglitz (1999) show that there may be a high unemployment equilibrium, with families sending many members into the labor market because of the risk that some will not be hired. A guaranteed family income may eliminate this "bad" equilibrium.
28. A similar argument has been used to show that while it may be more efficient for

firms to have more extensive risk sharing arrangements with their workers (Weitzman [1984, 1985, 1995]), it will not pay any firm to introduce such an arrangement. The firms that are most likely to do so are those whose profit expectations are most bleak. In effect, profit sharing arrangements are analogous to the firm issuing shares to its workers, and so the adverse selection arguments for why equity markets work poorly apply here. (See Greenwald, Stiglitz, and Weiss [1984]) By forcing all firms to have risk sharing arrangements with their workers, one dilutes, if one does not eliminate, the adverse signaling effect.

29. "All [vicious development) circles result from the two-way dependence between development and some other factor, be it capital or entrepreneurship, education, public administration, etc. But the circle to which our analysis has led us may perhaps lay claim to a privileged place in the hierarchy of these circles inasmuch as it alone places the difficulties of development back where all difficulties of human action begin and belong: in the mind." (Hirschman 1958, 11)

30. See Stiglitz (1998c).

31. See Blinder (1990) and Levine (1995).

32. See Stiglitz (1999c).

33. Within the development literature, there is a large and controversial literature addressing the issue of the two-way relationship between growth and democracy. See e.g., Knack and Keefer (1997), World Bank (1997), Stiglitz (1999d).

34. "In theory, the democratic method is persuasion through public discussion carried on not only in legislative halls but in the press, private conversations and public assemblies. The substitution of ballots for bullets, of the right to vote for the lash, is an expression of the will to substitute the method of discussion for the method of coercion." (Dewey 1939, p. 128)

35. See, for example, John Stuart Mill (1972 [1859]), Walter Bagehot (1948 [1869]), James Bryce (1959 [1888]), John Dewey (1927, 1939), Ernest Barker (1967 [1942]), Frank Knight (1947), and Charles Lindblom (1990).

36. Thus, a large literature now bears testimony to capital and financial market liberalization, whatever the efficiency benefits that might be derived from them (and some recent literature has even questioned that—see Stiglitz (1999e) and Rodrik [1998]), unambiguously contributing to economic volatility and an increased probability of financial and currency crises and recessions. See Demirgüç-Kunt and Detragiache (1997) and Easterly, Islam and Stiglitz (1999).

REFERENCES

Akerlof, George. 1984. *An Economic Theorist's Book of Tales*. New York: Cambridge University Press.

Akerlof, George, and Rachel Kranton. 1999. "Economics and Identity." Draft, presented at World Bank Summer Research Workshop, July.

Akerlof, George, and Janet Yellen (eds.). 1986. *Efficiency Wage Models of the Labor Market*. Cambridge: Cambridge University Press.

——. 1988. "Fairness and Unemployment." *American Economic Review*. 78 (2), May: 44–9.

Aoki, Masahiko. 1987. "The Japanese Firm in Transition." In *The Political Economy of Japan*. Kozo Yamamura and Yasukichi Yasuba (eds.). Stanford: Stanford University Press.

——. 1994. "The Japanese Firm as a System of Attributes: A Survey and Research Agenda." In *The Japanese Firm: Sources of Competitive Strength*. Masahiko Aoki and Ronald Dore (eds.). Oxford: Oxford University Press. 11–40.

Arnott, R., and J.E. Stiglitz. 1985. "Labor Turnover, Wage Structure and Moral Hazard: The Inefficiency of Competitive Markets." *Journal of Labor Economics*. 3 (4), October: 434–62.

Arrow, K.J., and G. Debreu. 1954. "Existence of an Equilibrium for a Competitive Economy." *Econometrica*. 22: 265–90.

Arrow, K.J., and F.H. Hahn. 1971. *General Competitive Analysis*. San Francisco: Holden-Day.

Bagehot, Walter. 1948 (1869). *Physics and Politics*. New York: Knopf.

Barker, Ernest. 1967 (1942). *Reflections on Government*. Oxford: Oxford University Press.

Basu, Kaushik. 1998. *Child Labor: Cause, Consequence and Cure, with Remarks on International Labor Standards*. Policy Research Working Paper No. 2027. Washington, DC: World Bank.

——, Garance Genicot and Joseph E. Stiglitz. 1999. *Household Labor Supply, Unemployment and Minimum Wage Legislation*. Policy Research Working Paper No. 2049. Washington, DC: World Bank.

Berle, A., and G. Means. 1932. *The Modern Corporation and Private Property*. New York: Macmillan.

Blinder, Alan S. (ed.). 1990. *Paying for Productivity*. Washington, DC: The Brookings Institution.

Bowles, Samuel. 1985. "The Production Process in a Competitive Economy: Walrasian, Neo-Hobbesian and Marxian Models." *American Economic Review*. 75 (March): 16–36.

Braverman, A., and J. Stiglitz. 1986. "Landlords, Tenants and Technological Innovations." *Journal of Development Economics*. 23 (2 October): 313–32.

Bryce, James. 1959 (1888). *The American Commonwealth*. New York: G.P. Putnam & Sons.

Christ, Carl F. 1975. "The Competitive Market and Optimal Allocative Efficiency." In *Competing Philosophies in American Political*

Economics. John Elliott and John Cownie (ed.). Pacific Palisades, CA: Goodyear: 332–8.

Clark, R. 1979. *The Japanese Company.* New Haven: Yale University Press.

Coase, R. 1937. "The Nature of the Firm." *Economica*, 4: 386–405.

Debreu, G. 1959. *Theory of Value.* New York: John Wiley & Sons.

Demirgüç-Kunt, Asli, and Enrica Detragiache. 1997. *The Determinants of Banking Crises: Evidence from Industrial and Developing Countries.* Policy Research Working Paper 1828. Washington, DC: World Bank and International Monetary Fund.

Dewey, John. 1927. *The Public and Its Problems.* Chicago: Swallow Press.

——. 1939. *Freedom and Culture.* New York: Capricorn.

Diamond, P. 1971. "A Model of Price Adjustment." *Journal of Economic Theory*, 3 (2), June: 156–68.

Dore, R. 1987. *Taking Japan Seriously.* Stanford: Stanford University Press.

Easterly, W., R. Islam, and J.E. Stiglitz. 1999. "Shaken and Stirred: Volatility and Macroeconomic Paradigms for Rich and Poor Countries." *Michael Bruno Memorial Lecture*, given at the XII World Congress of the IEA, Buenos Aires, 27 August.

Edlin, A., and J.E. Stiglitz. 1995. "Discouraging Rivals: Managerial Rent-Seeking and Economic Inefficiencies." *American Economic Review*. 85 (5): 1301–12.

Farrell, J. 1987. "Information and the Coase Theorem." *Journal of Economic Perspectives*. 1(2), Fall: 113–29.

Freeman, Richard, and James Medoff 1984. *What Do Unions Do?* New York: Basic Books.

Frey, Bruno. 1997. *Not Just for the Money: An Economic Theory of Personal Motivation.* Cheltenham: Elgar.

Gates, Jeff. 1998. *The Ownership Solution.* Reading: Addison-Wesley.

Goldberg, V. 1980. "Relational Exchange: Economics and Complex Contracts." *American Behavioral Scientist* 23 (3, January/ February): 337–52.

Greenwald, Bruce, and Joseph Stiglitz. 1986. "Externalities in Economics with Imperfect Information and Incomplete Markets." *Quarterly Journal of Economics.* 101(2), May: 229–64.

——. 1988. "Pareto Inefficiency of Market Economies: Search and

Efficiency Wage Models." *American Economic Review*. 78 (2 May): 351–5.

——. 1993. "Financial Market Imperfections and Business Cycles." *Quarterly Journal of Economics*, 108(1), February: 77–114.

Greenwald, Bruce, Joseph E. Stiglitz and Andrew Weiss. 1984. "Informational Imperfections in the Capital Markets and Macroeconomic Fluctuations." *American Economic Review*, 74(2), May: 194-199.

Hicks, J. 1936. "Mr Keynes' Theory of Employment." *Economic Journal*, 46 (182), June: 238–53.

——. 1937. "Mr Keynes and the 'Classics': A Suggested Interpretation." *Econometrica*, 5(2), April: 147–59.

Hirschman, Albert O. 1958. *The Strategy of Economic Development*. New Haven: Yale University Press.

——. 1970. *Exit, Voice, and Loyalty: Responses to Decline in Firms, Organizations, and States*. Cambridge: Harvard University Press.

Hussain, A., N. Stern and J.E. Stiglitz. 1999. "Chinese Reforms from a Comparative Perspective." Unpublished paper, the World Bank.

Knack, S., and P. Keefer. 1997. "Does Social Capital Have an Economic Payoff?: A Cross-Country Investigation." *Quarterly Journal of Economics* 112 (4): 1251–88.

Knight, Frank. 1947. *Freedom and Reform*. New York: Harper & Row.

Kochan, Thomas, and Paul Osterman. 1994. *The Mutual Gains Enterprise: Forging a Winning Partnership among Labor, Management and Government*. Boston: Harvard Business School Press.

Kreps, David. 1997. "Intrinsic Motivation and Extrinsic Incentives." *American Economic Review*. 87: 359–65.

Kuttner, Robert. 1997. *Everything for Sale: The Virtues and Limits of Market*. New York: Knopf.

Lane, Robert E. 1991. *The Market Experience*. New York: Cambridge University Press.

Leibenstein, H. 1984. "The Japanese Management System: An X-Efficiency Game Theory Analysis." In *The Economic Analysis of the Japanese Firm*. M. Aoki (ed.). Amsterdam, Elsevier: 331–57.

—— 1987. *Inside the Firm: The Inefficiencies of Hierarchy*. Cambridge: Harvard University Press.

Levine, David I. 1995. *Reinventing the Workplace*. Washington: the Brookings Institution.

—— and Laura D'Andrea Tyson. 1990. "Participation, Productivity and the Firm's Environment." In *Paying for Productivity: A Look at the Evidence*. Alan Blinder (ed.). Washington: Brookings Institution. 183–237.

Lindblom, Charles. 1990. *Inquiry and Change*. New Haven: Yale University Press.

Lindsay, A.D. 1943. *The Modern Democratic State*. Oxford: Oxford University Press.

Marshall, Alfred. 1920. *Principles of Economics*. New York: Macmillan.

McGregor, Douglas. 1960. *The Human Side of Enterprise*. New York: McGraw-Hill.

Mill, John Stuart. 1972 (1859). *On Liberty*. In *J.S. Mill: Utilitarianism, On Liberty and Considerations on Representative Government*. H.B. Acton (ed.). London: J.M. Dent & Sons.

Musgrave, R.A. 1959. *The Theory of Public Finance*. New York: McGraw-Hill.

Nozick, Robert. 1974. *Anarchy, State and Utopia*. New York: Basic Books.

O'Toole, James. 1995. *Leading Change: Overcoming the Ideology of Comfort and the Tyranny of Custom*. San Francisco: Jossey-Bass.

Philmore, J. 1982. "The Libertarian Case for Slavery: A Note on Nozick." *Philosophical Forum*. XIV (Fall 1982): 43–58.

Samuelson, P. 1976. *Economics*. New York: McGraw-Hill.

Shapiro, Carl, and Joseph Stiglitz 1984. "Equilibrium Unemployment as a Worker Discipline Device." *American Economic Review*. 74 (June): 433-44.

Simon, Herbert. 1991. "Organizations and Markets." *Journal of Economic Perspectives*. 5 (Spring): 25–44.

Solow, Robert 1990. *The Labor Market as a Social Institution*. Cambridge, Mass.: Basil Blackwell.

Standing, Guy. 1999. *Global Labour Flexibility: Seeking Distributive Justice*. London: Macmillan.

Stiglitz, Joseph E. 1985a. "Equilibrium Wage Distribution." *Economic Journal*. 95, (September): 595–618.

——. 1985b. "Credit Markets and the Control of Capital." *Journal of Money, Banking, and Credit*. 17 (2): 133–52.

——. 1987. "Competition and the Number of Firms in a Market: Are Duopolies More Competitive Than Atomistic Markets?" *Journal of Political Economy*. 95 (5): 1041–61.

——. 1992. "Banks versus Markets as Mechanisms for Allocating and Coordinating Investment." In *The Economics of Cooperation: East Asian Development and the Case for Pro-Market Intervention.* J.A. Roumasset and S. Barr (eds.) Boulder: Westview Press. 15–38.

——. 1998a. *More Instruments and Broader Goals: Moving toward the Post-Washington Consensus.* Helsinki, Finland: World Institute for Development Economics Research, United Nations University [ch. 1, this volume – *Ed.*].

——. 1998b. *Towards a New Paradigm for Development: Strategies, Policies. and Processes.* Raul Prebisch Lecture at United Nations Conference on Trade and Development (UNCTAD). Geneva, 19 October. [ch. 2, this volume – *Ed.*].

——. 1998c. "Responding to Economic Crises: Policy Alternatives for Equitable Recovery and Development." Paper presented to North-South Institute Seminar, Ottawa, Canada, 29 September.

——. 1999a. "Whither Reform? Ten Years of the Transition." Keynote address to the 1999 Annual Bank Conference on Development Economics, Washington, DC, 28–30 April 28-30 [ch. 4, this volume – *Ed.*].

——. 1999b. "Quis Custodiet Ipsos Custodes?" *Challenge*, 42 (6), November–December: 26–67.

——. 1999c. "Public Policy for a Knowledge Economy." Paper presented to the Department for Trade and Industry and Center for Economic Policy Research, London, UK, 27 January.

——. 1999d. "Participation and Development: Perspectives from the Comprehensive Development Paradigm." Paper presented in Seoul, Korea, 27 February [ch. 7, this volume – *Ed.*].

——. 1999e. "Capital Market Liberalization, Economic Growth, and Instability." *World Development*, 28 (6): 1075–86.

——. 2000. "The Contributions of the Economics of Information to Twentiety Centuryr Economics." *Quarterly Journal of Economics*, 115 (4): 1441–78.

Weitzman, Martin. 1984. *The Share Economy: Conquering Stagflation.* Cambridge: Harvard University Press.

——. 1985. "The Simple Macroeconomics of Profit Sharing." *American Economic Review* (December): 937–53.

——. 1995. "Incentive Effects of Profit Sharing." In Horst Siebert (ed.). *Trends in Business Organization: Do Participation and*

Cooperation Increase Competitiveness? Tubingen: Mohr (Siebeck): 51–78.

Williamson, Oliver E. 1975. *Markets and Hierarchies: Analysis and Antitrust Implications.* New York: The Free Press.

——. 1979. "Transaction-Cost Economics: The Governance of Contractual Relations," *Journal of Law and Economics*, 22 (2): 233–61.

——. 1981. "The Modern Corporation: Origins, Evolution, Attributes." *Journal of Economic Literature*, 19 (4), December: 1537–68.

World Bank. 1997. *Crime and Violence as Development Issues in Latin America and the Caribbean.* Mimeographed. Office of the Chief Economist, Latin America and the Caribbean. Washington, DC: World Bank.

Index